Crime and Violence in Latin America

Crime and Violence in Latin America
Citizen Security, Democracy, and the State

Edited by

Hugo Frühling

and

Joseph S. Tulchin

with

Heather A. Golding

Woodrow Wilson Center Press
Washington, D.C.

The Johns Hopkins University Press
Baltimore and London

EDITORIAL OFFICES

Woodrow Wilson Center Press
Woodrow Wilson International Center for Scholars
One Woodrow Wilson Plaza
1300 Pennsylvania Avenue, N.W.
Washington, D.C. 20004-3027
Telephone 202-691-4010
www.wilsoncenter.org

ORDER FROM

The Johns Hopkins University Press
Hampden Station
P.O. Box 50370
Baltimore, Maryland 21211
Telephone 1-800-537-5487
www.jhupbooks.com

2 4 6 8 9 7 5 3 1

Library of Congress Cataloging-in-Publication Data

Crime and violence in Latin America : citizen security, democracy, and
the state / edited by Hugo Frühling and Joseph S. Tulchin with
Heather A. Golding.
    p. cm.
Includes index.
    ISBN 0-8018-7383-5 (hardcover : alk. paper) — ISBN 0-8018-7384-3
(pbk. : alk. paper)
1. Crime—Latin America. 2. Violence—Latin America. 3. Criminal
justice, Administration of—Latin America. 4. Crime—Latin
America—Case studies. 5. Violence—Latin America—Case studies. 6.
Crime—Latin America—Prevention. 7. Violence—Latin
America—Prevention. 8. Crime—Government policy—Latin America. 9.
Violence—Government policy—Latin America. I. Frühling, Hugo. II.
Tulchin, Joseph S., 1939- III. Golding, Heather A.
    HV6810.5.C747 2003
    364.98—dc21

                                                        2003002438

ABOUT THE CENTER

The Center is the living memorial of the United States of America to the nation's twenty-eighth president, Woodrow Wilson. Congress established the Woodrow Wilson Center in 1968 as an international institute for advanced study, "symbolizing and strengthening the fruitful relationship between the world of learning and the world of public affairs." The Center opened in 1970 under its own board of trustees.

In all its activities the Woodrow Wilson Center is a nonprofit, nonpartisan organization, supported financially by annual appropriations from the Congress, and by the contributions of foundations, corporations, and individuals. Conclusions or opinions expressed in Center publications and programs are those of the authors and speakers and do not necessarily reflect the views of the Center staff, fellows, trustees, advisory groups, or any individuals or organizations that provide financial support to the Center.

Contents

Figures and Tables

Preface

We in the Woodrow Wilson Center's Latin American Program initially became interested in the issue of citizen security out of a concern for judicial reform and corruption in Latin America. We addressed these questions in two earlier publications: *Combating Corruption in Latin America* (2000), edited by Joseph S. Tulchin and Ralph H. Espach, and *Modernización de la Administración de Justicia en la Argentina* (1998), edited by Joseph S. Tulchin and Allison M. Garland. These twin interests led us to focus on the larger issue of citizen security, on which topic we, along with Hugo Frühling, organized a seminar. The research gathered in this volume represents the first phase of our inquiry into this topic.

The second phase of our citizen security work examines police and judicial reform and the relationship between citizens and police. The Woodrow Wilson Center organized groundbreaking forums throughout Latin America to communicate the knowledge we had gained as a result of the first project to the police, the judiciary, and other state officials using the Wilson Center's position as a "safe" nonpartisan forum to bring together all the stakeholders in the reform process. A volume compiling the results of this policy work will be in press shortly.

These first two projects on citizen security convinced us that the increase in the rates of crime and violence is not the only danger facing Latin American countries. The citizens' often inflated perception of insecurity represents a real threat to democratic governance as well. Consequently, we determined that citizen participation in reform efforts is invaluable in abating the feeling of insecurity and, therefore, diminishing its harmful impact on democratic governance. Our latest project on citizen security was formulated with this in mind; it consists of an action research project aimed at reducing the distance between citizens and the forces of law and order to foster better communication between the two groups and help reduce the perception of insecurity.

The Latin American Program's activities on citizen security would not have been possible without the generous support of the Tinker Foundation, which funded the project on judicial reform, and the William and Flora Hewlett Foundation, which supported the publication of this volume.

The editors would also like to extend our special appreciation to Meg Ruthenburg, program associate with the Latin American Program, who saw this volume through the final stages of publication. In addition, thanks are due to Latin American Program interns Kristin Berger, Carolina Dallal, Craig Fagan, Jacqueline Lee, and Audrey Yao for their meticulous work in preparing the manuscript for publication.

1

Introduction: Citizen Security in Regional Perspective

Joseph S. Tulchin and Heather A. Golding

One of the more striking features of the global community today is that large numbers of people around the world feel increasingly "insecure." In survey after survey and in local, regional, and national elections, people give voice to their sense of insecurity. In political terms, it has become imperative to respond to this malaise. Failure to respond has immediate and clear electoral consequences.

But the appropriate response to citizen insecurity is not always clear. At the local level, it may simply be a matter of increasing the number of police on the street to combat crime—a question of political will and resources. In some cases, however, the underlying institutions of law and order—the police and the judiciary—may be inadequate to the task or may themselves have become a major source of the insecurity. Whatever the cause of citizen insecurity, nearly every country in Latin America has embarked upon some form of police and/or judicial reform.

1

Financing Reform Efforts

One of the reasons for the widespread incidence of reform efforts in the region is the fact that such programs can be supported by the international financial institutions. Where police reform is a national priority, the World Bank and the Inter-American Development Bank offer loans whose objectives are to make these institutions more efficient and more productive.

The first question we should ask is "what kind of resources would be required to professionalize the police in a particular country?" Specifically, how much training and what level of salary would be necessary? This is a major problem for most governments throughout the region. This would allow a common approach to problems that assume national variations. Some nations are better organized than others; some have more resources than others. By using these indicators, the international financial institutions could clarify their approach to the problem on a regional basis and adapt their loan programs to national requirements.

One approach has been to use federal or international funds to study local crime conditions. Techniques that have been successful in the United States and Europe to map the occurrence of crimes against property, to take one example, have been applied to urban areas in Latin America to allow the more efficient allocation of limited resources to combat crime. Resource constraints also come into play when considering the links between the victims of violence and those who feel most insecure as a result of rising rates of crime. The overwhelming majority of crimes against persons and property occur among and are inflicted on poor people. But poor people are least likely to report crimes to the authorities and are most likely to perceive the police or judiciary as distant, alien, or worse, hostile. In line with these concerns is the observation that Hugo Frühling makes (chapter 2) that the absence of adequate public funding for police forces has led to increased private financing, which has caused the police to direct more attention to the sector supplying the funds: the upper class. Furthermore, given the fact that the poorest people are least likely to be mobilized politically, their attitude or opinions concerning the various solutions available to society or the state are not likely to be taken into account.

Efforts to Reform the Systems of Law and Order

Although virtually everyone admits that some reform is necessary, there is not yet a broad consensus as to how best to accomplish this common goal. At the national level, several countries have attempted to clarify their penal codes, while others have begun formal training programs for the police, including such topics as the penal code, citizen rights, human rights and due process. As Frühling explains, reform efforts throughout Latin America and the Caribbean have concentrated mainly on the development of new strategies to reduce crime and violence, the professionalization of police forces, the improvement of relations between the police and community, and an emphasis on resource management to improve police efficiency. Although many of the authors in this volume analyze the experiences of a particular country or region, nearly every chapter examines broader efforts to reform the systems of law and order.

In several countries, although not all, efforts are being made to educate the public and the police on how to get along with one another to mutual advantage. The first round of loans to support community policing and other changes in local culture are under way in several countries, generally in the form of one or more test cases paid for by soft loans from the Inter-American Development Bank. There is a broad consensus that reform efforts should aim to reduce the distance between social groups and between the society and the state. Catalina Smulovitz (chapter 6), Paulo de Mesquita Neto and Adriana Loche (chapter 9), and Laura Chichilla (chapter 9), in particular, outline one of the most popular methods that governments and police forces throughout Latin America have adopted to achieve this goal: community policing programs. Such programs have as their goal bringing the "protectors" and the "protected" closer to increase trust, decrease actual crime rates, and improve citizens' perceptions of personal safety.

In countries that have long, powerful traditions of citizen participation and local initiatives, community policing is easy to sell to the population. In Latin America, where such traditions do not exist or are very weak, there are at least three major difficulties in even discussing the concept. First, in countries that have suffered military dictatorships in the recent past, bringing the forces of law and order closer to the community is the last thing some people would wish. Second, the absence of a bond of trust between citizens and the forces of law and order makes communication between the two, which is indispensable to the success of community policing, difficult and halting. Third, as the state is reduced in size and capacity, and as the police appear to the citizens to be incapable of providing the security they want or need, groups of citizens have been using the cloak of community policing to establish private security forces and to engage in what amounts to vigilantism. Privatizing security is not the answer; it actually worsens people's sense of insecurity and excludes large segments of the population from any participation in seeking their own security.

Devising Public Policies to Increase Citizen Security

Having said that, however, we are still a long way from achieving confidence in a specific "model" of reform or identifying a "best practice" to alleviate citizen insecurity. As policymakers approach the challenge of formulating public reform proposals, several factors must be taken into account. First and foremost is the gap between subjective "feelings of insecurity" and the objective conditions of crime and violence in any particular society.

Without dismissing these feelings of insecurity, it is important to pierce through them to identify their causes. The sense of insecurity is real and should not be dismissed. The rise in rates of crime is also real. However, as Smulovitz (chapter 6) and Carlos Basombrío (chapter 7) stress, public opinion data also indicate that the public grossly exaggerates the rates of crime and exaggerates the consequences of crime in their neighborhood and their society. As a consequence, it is important to adjust the public response to the concrete reality, not to the wildest of perceptions. In political terms, this is the danger. Seeking votes, candidates promise to be "tough on crime," to allow "zero tolerance" to criminals. The tendency in Latin America is for such promises only to further weaken the foundations of law and order and of due process.

Furthermore, as Paul Chevigny argues in chapter 3, few data suggest that the use of force increases order. In fact, Chevigny refers to a series of studies indicating that there is no relation between the use of deadly force and the rates of arrest or crime, and it goes on to hypothesize that although reliable evidence to prove it is scarce, the same is likely true of nondeadly force.

Another obstacle to reform is the tension between short-term solutions to immediate problems and the need to attack the underlying causes of the problem, an approach that may only produce results in the long term. For example, politically sensitive mayors are much more likely to put more police on the street to lower the incidence of crime in certain neighborhoods than they are to formulate comprehensive policies to reduce unemployment, inequality, or poverty. Federal governments have a powerful sense of their mortality, which impels them to seek quick solutions. Andrew Morrison, Mayra Burinic, and Michael Shifter (chapter 5) argue that the tendency to combat violence with punitive action rather than through social policies is further encouraged by the lack of data on program costs, even from a simple accounting perspective, to evaluate the benefits of programs targeted to address underlying social problems. There is a great need for more countries to invest in prevention programs, to allow for a comparative analysis of their costs and benefits.

Insecurity and Democratic Governance

All these sources of insecurity impinge on the quality of citizenship in democratic governance. In democratic societies, improving citizen security—like other major issues, such as equity and social welfare—is really a question of enhancing accountability and citizen participation. Mauricio Duce and Rogelio Pérez Perdomo discuss the importance of police oversight, by both domestic and international actors, and it emphasizes that citizens who sense that their leaders pay attention and that police are held accountable are likely to feel more secure.

"Feeling insecure" has the effect of alienating the individual from his or her society, and this alienation is detrimental to creating a sense of community. A fragmented community is one in which policy solutions to the problems of violence and insecurity are less likely to be effective; they are likely to drive wedges between social groups and create distance between them. This is one of the key concepts in defining the policy options that are available and in evaluating the relative success of any given policy.

Formulating public policies in response to rising crime rates or to a growing sense of insecurity is further complicated by the fact that, in some cases, the cause of insecurity may be transnational crime groups, the response to which may require multilateral action. Chinchilla (chapter 9) and Anthony P. Maingot (chapter 10) illustrate how the problem is especially sensitive in smaller countries, such as those in Central America and the Caribbean, where institutions of law and order have been subjected to so much pressure from international organized crime that they can no longer protect the public. The governments of these countries, faced with the limited capability of local police forces, frequently turn for assistance and protection to their military forces, to multilateral agencies, and to the United States.

However, because efforts to separate the police from the military are a priority throughout the region—particularly in countries that have recently emerged from periods of military authoritarian rule and whose institutions of law and order are still being consolidated—mobilizing the armed forces to fight crime causes trepidation. Because of the international nature of crime, citizen insecurity in these cases blurs into a debate that once was the exclusive domain of national security policy. In the sensitive case of dealing with the narcotics trade, the use of U.S. military aid or pressure from the United States to use the armed forces to fight a "war on drugs" often makes citizens feel less, not more, secure.

An Overview of Findings

The public policy challenge, again, is to disaggregate our understanding of the problem, our definition of the constituencies, and to devise solutions appropriate to each case. The link among solutions—what all solutions should have in common—is the strengthening of democratic institutions and the strengthening of the connections between those institutions and the citizens for whom they were designed.

In studying the problem of citizen security, the comparative perspective has important advantages. First, it provides a sense of scale to the problem. Second, it suggests how one facet of the problem, such as delinquency, is linked to others and, more important, in devising solutions, how policies can be formulated that focus on a single facet of the problem to good effect. The third advantage is that comparative study points us to examples of success and failure. All are important in understanding what makes specific policies effective or ineffective. This is the fashionable "best practices" approach to problem solving.

But, there are dangers in the comparative method to which we must be alert. What works in New York may not work at all in Santiago. For instance, though former mayor Rudolph Giuliani's draconian campaign for zero tolerance in New York might seem attractive to the officials of any metropolitan region, the harsh tones in which the campaign was conducted in New York and the yawning chasm it opened between the city's ethnic and socioeconomic groups might become corrosively destructive in a different cultural and political environment.

History and culture play crucial roles in determining whether a specific measure or reform is appropriate in a given case. For example, the recent history of military dictatorship in countries such as Argentina and Chile suggests that militarizing the struggle against crime, even organized international crime as in drug trafficking, will create more problems than it might solve. The feelings of antimilitarism in these societies are more powerful than most decision makers in the United States understand.

In Latin America, the objective of any effort to address citizen security must be to strengthen both civilian institutions of law and order and also the sense of citizenship among the populace. In those cases where criminality and citizen security impinge on the more traditional agenda of national security and cross international boundaries, mechanisms will have to be created or strengthened to allow for more effective and fluid cooperation among national agencies of law and order. This may require international agreements and treaties. It does not require remilitarization of citizen security.

An Overview of the Book

The chapters of this volume cover a wide geographic range and focus on the issue of citizen security from a variety of perspectives. The volume is divided into three parts. The chapters in the first part examine the issues and themes that dominate discussions of citizen security in the Americas: police reform and democratization; efforts to control police misconduct; reform of the criminal justice system; and the policy implications of social and domestic violence. The second part offers case studies that deal with the experiences of the countries in Latin America and the Caribbean. In the third part, the editors offer a series of policy recommendations aimed at reducing violence and crime in the Americas.

In chapter 2, Frühling examines the steps that many nations in the region have taken to reform their police forces. He notes that current reforms in Latin America indicate a shift toward police management models that are more and more democratic and emphasize a respect for individual rights. He argues that, though police reform is considered necessary to economic development and the quality of democracy in many Latin American nations, various challenges to reform—such as a legacy of military control over police forces and skyrocketing crime rates throughout the region—have caused many police forces to revert back to repressive measures.

Frühling defines the roles and responsibilities of a police force in a modern democratic state. He then considers some of the challenges and deficiencies faced by Latin American police forces, such as a lack of specialization, professionalism, and public-mindedness. Drawing on three current police reform efforts in the province of Buenos Aires, Colombia, and São Paulo, he concludes that the sociopolitical context in which the reforms were introduced greatly influenced the origin, development, and success of the efforts. Finally, he considers the complexity of applying theoretical models derived from industrial countries to the urban, social, and cultural realities of Latin America.

In chapter 3, Chevigny begins with a general discussion of corruption in Latin American systems of law and order. He argues that corruption essentially stems from citizens' own hypocrisies; we want to abuse certain laws as we deem it justifiable, but we are not willing to abolish the laws that prohibit such actions. Corruption, however, constitutes a grave threat to citizen security because it leads to the arrogance of office on the part of those wielding power.

Chevigny surveys the available options for combating corruption, and he outlines steps that can be taken by the central government, the legislature, and the courts to curb the problem. He argues that it is imperative to establish a system in which police understand that they will be held accountable for their improper actions. In this sense, police discipline and external oversight are critical to rid the institutions of corrupt practices. Equally important, in Chevigny's eyes, is the need to establish minimal international standards of impropriety. If a police force then fails to meet these basic standards, the issue can be addressed by the international community. He concludes that regulations and training to minimize police misconduct will remain unsuccessful as long as the police perceive that these regulations will not be enforced.

In chapter 4, Duce and Pérez Perdomo trace the evolution of criminal justice systems from the Middle Ages to present-day Latin America from a sociopolitical viewpoint. They argue that even after the European reform in the second half of the nineteenth century, the Latin American criminal justice system remained more linked to the medieval inquisitorial system.

The chapter examines the principal components and current status of criminal justice system reform in Latin America and analyzes potential reform models. Duce and Pérez Perdomo describe recent modifications in the criminal trial system across the region, focusing on the extent to which criminal reform has an impact on citizen security. They argue that reform cannot be expected to satisfy all the social demands created by problems of objective and subjective insecurity, and that excessive expectations constitute one of the most serious short-term obstacles to achieving reform. They conclude that the reform process will fulfill its objectives only if a more moderate police force, a more efficient judicial system, and a better understanding on the part of the public are achieved.

In chapter 5, Morrison, Buvinic, and Shifter examine patterns of crime and violence in Latin American societies and offer considerations for the formulation of policy responses aimed at their reduction. Although the authors note that perceptions of security are heavily influenced by the media's portrayal of violence, they choose to investigate the causes of violence rather than the perceptions that surround it.

Morrison, Buvinic, and Shifter present data on homicides, the health effects of violence, and the prevalence of domestic violence. They then discuss the various types of violence plaguing the region and categorize them according to several variables: the victims of violence, the agents of violence, motives for committing violence, and the relationship between the perpetrator and the victim. They then address the principal risk factors for violence at the community, household, and individual levels.

The authors attempt to estimate the socioeconomic costs of violence, and they conclude by offering policy options for reducing violence: integrated versus targeted programs, national versus local initiatives, and—perhaps most contentious—prevention versus remedial or treatment measures. The authors argue that preventive policies are generally more cost-effective than treatment options.

The second part of the book, which consists of case studies, begins with a discussion of citizen insecurity in Argentina by Smulovitz in chapter 6. Consistent with the trend in Latin America, the crime rate in Argentina has increased, yet data show that it remains low relative to that in other countries and urban areas. Argentine citizens perceive that there is more crime and violence in their society than official statistics indicate. This inaccurate perception of insecurity is very important, for it generates more policy demands and calls for a need, in formulating these responses, to distinguish between the actual and perceived reality of crime rates.

Smulovitz examines a variety of data in an effort to assess the actual dimension of the crime problem in Argentine society. She analyzes the nature of fear, examining exactly what people fear and how these fears vary among socioeconomic and age groups. In conclusion, she highlights three contradictory assessments of the perceived causes of insecurity in Argentina: an actual increase in crime, an increased perception of crime, and deficiencies in the structure and functioning of the police.

The lack of consensus regarding the root causes of the problem, concludes Smulovitz, hinders the development of a comprehensive plan to combat the problem. In addition, she emphasizes that it is imperative for officials drafting policy responses to be sensitive to the historical legacies left by years of military rule. The expansion of police rights is an area where policymakers must exercise particular discretion.

In chapter 7, Basombrío examines the militarization of public security in Peru. Peru's unique history, including a transition from military to democratic rule in the 1980s and the consequent return to an authoritarian regime, has left the police subordinate to the military. In a country such as Peru, it is difficult to convince a weary population of the benefits of analyzing the root causes of violence in a society plagued by crime, especially in the wake of periods of extended violence. It is precisely this fear of insecurity and the modern democratic state's inability to address the problems of crime and violence that give legitimacy to authoritarian regimes, argues Basombrío.

In the mid-1980s, the police pulled out of rural areas that were particularly subject to political violence and drug trafficking by guerrilla groups such as the Shining Path. Death tolls grew to frightening numbers in rural areas, and in the absence of an organized state response to the violence, the Peruvian rural population took direct control of public order. Although this community response is said to have aided in the defeat of the Shining Path, Basombrío explains that its continued presence today represents an obstacle to the rise of democratic institutions.

In chapter 8, de Mesquita Neto and Loche examine police–community relations since Brazil's transition to democracy. They argue that the efforts of the government and the police to combat crime and violence have been undermined by the persistence of police brutality and the low level of respect that the community has for these institutions. In an effort to control crime and to encourage police officers to develop a greater respect for human rights and democratic institutions, the Brazilian state adopted a strategy of community policing.

The authors explore numerous cases of community policing efforts in Brazil. In conclusion, they point to three main differences in the characteristics of the case experiences: community policing projects directed primarily by the state; projects directed mainly at the municipal or local level; and, less common, those conducted by nongovernmental community groups. According to the authors, it is still too early to provide a general evaluation of these experiences.

In many Central American nations, explains Chinchilla in chapter 9, the death rates from criminal activity are higher than those registered during periods of armed conflict. She describes the principal factors associated with crime in the region: deteriorating socioeconomic conditions, the aftereffects of armed conflict, the growing presence of organized crime, and the inchoate development of institutions for social control.

Chinchilla then critically examines efforts to reform criminal justice and public security institutions in Central America. With regard to public security, she argues that the region has seen a shift toward a new security doctrine that embraces security as a condition for development; the concept of human development; the relationship between the government and the governed, rather than focusing on the control of the government over the governed; and the drawing of a sharp distinction between national security and citizen security, thus somewhat demilitarizing the latter.

A main feature of this doctrinal shift are community policing projects. Chinchilla describes, in detail, the features of three projects in Costa Rica, El Salvador, and Honduras. The cases she presents all address the need for preventive action, greater reliance on citizen participation, and the reform of democratic institutions. She argues that additional studies are necessary to enrich the analysis of these types of initiatives and that parameters must be established to judge the success of such experiences.

Internationalized crime and the vulnerability of small states in the Caribbean is Maingot's subject in chapter 10. He describes the economic, ecological, and political vulnerability of the small Caribbean island nations. He suggests that the islands' small size alone is not the fundamental factor in determining state weakness, pointing instead to the importance of internal social cohesion and the strength of institutions. The most challenging threat to these states, he argues, is that posed by international crime, precisely because it undermines these two factors.

It is now calculated that close to 40 percent of the cocaine destined for U.S. and European markets moves through the Caribbean. Maingot describes the factors that make the islands so attractive to international cartels: geography, widespread corruption, lax banking laws, an extensive network of nonbanking financial institutions, and the open nature of their economies. He then describes the region's reaction to the current crime pandemic, and its eagerness to strike back rather than to debate causes. Caribbean nations, according to Maingot, instead of reforming the relevant institutions of law and order, seek to solve their problems through even harsher enforcement by these same flawed institutions.

In conclusion, Maingot explores whether a process of militarization will eventually transform these countries into a "garrison state." The unwillingness of the government to cede any authority to the military and a clear resistance to constitutional change, he argues, are two reasons why they will not.

The third part of the book offers seven policy recommendations, which propose the implementation of reforms to close the gap between public security forces and the citizens and to create tools to define objectives and measure police effectiveness in addition to providing better oversight of police activity. It is recommended that crime be addressed through preventive action and through the strengthening of democratic institutions. Approaches to the issue of crime and violence in Latin America must also include professionalizing the forces of law and order, designing policies that are sensitive to the wounds caused by past military rule, and creating partnerships between international organizations, the state, and civil society.

These recommendations are imperative for achieving public security in the context of democratic governance. The danger of not appropriately addressing the issue of citizen insecurity could be that citizens would resort to demanding more repressive forms of control and protection and thus weaken the prospects for democratic governance in the region.

Part I

Issues and Themes

2

Police Reform and the Process of Democratization

Hugo Frühling

In recent years, coinciding with the consolidation of civil institutions in a significant number of Latin American countries, there has been a widespread increase in criminal violence. As chapters 5 and 9 in this volume show, during the first half of the 1990s, at least, there was a sharp increase in violent crime, making it necessary to implement a range of policy measures. Notable among these are efforts by a number of Latin American countries to reform the criminal justice system, including their police forces.

These reform efforts include the creation of new civilian police in El Salvador, Guatemala, and Haiti; ending military control over the police in Honduras; efforts to purge the National Police of corrupt elements and create a new institutional structure in Colombia; changes in the security system in the province of Buenos Aires; and the implementation of a community policing strategy by the Military Police of São Paulo. There are also less comprehensive reforms in progress, such as the creation by the

Chilean police of management indicators to assess their performance, and efforts to professionalize the Nicaraguan National Police.

These changes are still in their initial stages. At times, they contain contradictory elements, and in some cases they have even been reversed after a period of time. However, they must be viewed as a response to the serious problems these police forces face in dealing with today's realities. In general terms, especially in Central America, they have sought to separate the police from the armed forces and give them autonomy; to strengthen monitoring of police violence; to professionalize the police by making changes in recruitment and training; and to establish a dialogue, at least, on the importance of community involvement.

For some years now, analysts have demonstrated that a substantial number of the region's police forces were inefficient and were structured according to models inconsistent with the democratic system. Bayley (1993) stated that many Latin American police forces were military in nature, indicating that there was not a strict separation between the police and the armed forces.

On the basis of this proposition, he set forth five hypotheses concerning police–community relations. First, a significant percentage of public complaints against the police involved allegations of serious crimes. Unlike what was typical in developed democracies, the public resorted to the police only when absolutely necessary. Second, the police responded much more to the needs of the government than to the demands of citizens. Third, Latin American police used force more frequently than the police of developed democracies in comparable situations. Fourth, there was less supervision of the police than in democratic countries. Fifth, there was likely to be a low degree of public support for the police and, as a result of internal functioning and structure, subordinate personnel obeyed orders but lacked the autonomy to respond creatively to problems they faced.

In fact, though there are differences from country to country (Rico 1998), the police forces in a number of countries in the region have been subject to serious questioning and criticism, as a result of many factors: excessive violence in carrying out their duties (Mingardi 1996, 283; Zaffaroni 1993), corruption (Schmid 1996, 301; Oliveira and Tiscornia 1998), lack of autonomy from the armed forces (Costa 1998), institutional corporatism (Frühling 1998), and serious problems of professionalism (Pinheiro 1998, 183–87). There is a great amount of distrust of the police, except in Chile,[1] and even there, people trust the police less than in the United States.[2]

It is precisely this dissatisfaction with current police systems that has led to contradictory efforts to reform or restructure them. In some Latin American countries, these efforts have occurred in conjunction with the end of armed conflict and have been achieved with international participation and support (El Salvador, Guatemala, Haiti). In these cases, new civilian police forces have generally been created, and organizational structures and training have been designed with the assistance of the international community.[3] In other countries of the region, police forces that have undergone reform have maintained greater continuity with their past. Such has been the case in Brazil, Colombia, and the province of Buenos Aires, where the police's lack of credibility has had an unacceptably severe impact on public security and on the legitimacy of political authorities.

The solutions undertaken in these cases do not involve establishing new civilian police forces. Rather, they attempt to decentralize the police command structure, create closer relations between police and the community, and strengthen oversight mechanisms to monitor police behavior. The evaluation and documentation of these reforms remain incomplete, though reports on the situation have contributed valuable information.[4] Systematic recommendations have proposed specific steps to implement police reform (Costa 1994, 106–8), and suggestions have been made regarding ways to further the process of reform now in progress (Mesquita Neto 1998).

This chapter attempts to contribute to the discussion of the reform process by examining four important areas. The first section examines the basic defining concepts of a police force in a modern democratic state and considers some of the challenges and deficiencies faced by Latin American police forces. The second section deals with new features of modern police forces, emphasizing democratic controls and doctrinal changes in today's policing, the importance of recruiting duly trained personnel, and the role of planning and research in determining police action. These changes constitute a frame of reference influencing the process of police reform in Latin America. The third section provides a schematic description of three of the processes of change currently in progress, attempting to identify their common features, as well as their differences. Finally, certain conclusions are drawn from experiences to date, including a consideration of the problems involved in applying theoretical models derived from industrial countries to the urban, social, and cultural realities of Latin America.

Police reform is viewed as a necessity in many of the region's countries. Without it, neither economic development nor the quality of democracy can be assured. It is not, however, an easy process, in view of the fact that, for years, the police were part of the military and the military resisted relinquishing its control over the police. Furthermore, the call for reform is occurring at a time when the countries involved are experiencing a severe crime wave. Thus, it is inevitable that there will be frequent demands to curb the reform process and allow the use of whatever force is viewed as necessary to deal with crime.

The Nature and Structure of the Police

The police are the primary instrument for law enforcement. Institutions and individuals responsible for maintaining public order have existed since ancient times, but it is only in the modern era that the police have come into being as a specialized, professional, public organization authorized to use coercion to enforce the law (Bayley 1985, 7–14).

The police are a public entity, inasmuch as they are directed and financed primarily by the community or the state, are subject to management by public entities, and are designed to serve the public in a nondiscriminatory manner.[5] Originally, the police were closely linked to the process of state building, because they arose out of the need to have a body capable of maintaining order at a time when social groups had effectively lost their own capacity to do so. The public nature of police services, however, is being redefined and tested. The increasing flow of private financing for Latin American police forces has meant that their attention and resources have been targeted more and more to the sectors providing these funds. Preliminary analyses of police activity in different municipalities within Santiago show that the police are more active in areas suffering the greatest losses from crimes against property—that is, in wealthier neighborhoods. A lack of regulatory constraints on this type of funding, as well as the limited availability of public funding for police, contributes to this negative effect and has led to a deterioration in the public's confidence in the work carried out by the police (Frühling 1999, 84–85).

A second feature of modern police forces is that they are institutions that specialize in the use of force to reestablish social order. The emergence of the police accompanies the disappearance of the military role in maintaining public security. In Europe, this occurred definitively in the nineteenth century due to two simultaneous developments: the rise of social revolutionary movements and the growing capacity of the military to wreak destruction on their opponents. Under these conditions, it seemed more prudent to put the preservation of domestic order in the hands of specialized forces whose normal forms of operation were not centered on destroying an enemy.

The specialization of police forces did not occur quickly. In English-speaking countries, police have always been clearly distinguishable from the armed forces. The London police were created in 1829 to garner popular consent and support. Thus, they generally do not use firearms and maintain a close relationship with their local community. In continental Europe, this specialization or differentiation from the armed forces is less clear; some police forces still use military discipline, military ranks, and are considered a military reserve in case of war. This is the case of the French *gendarmerie*, the Italian *carabinieri*, and the Spanish *guardia civil*. The military character of the functional structure of these forces may have advantages or disadvantages, but it is not inherently incompatible with democracy, unless these forces are subordinated to the armed forces or carry out functions based on military criteria (Beato 2001).

The lack of specialization in Latin American police forces and their lack of differentiation from the military go far beyond hierarchies and military customs, which also exist in European democracies. Due to the lack of democracy, the region's armed forces have performed police functions in maintaining social order, and they have relegated police forces to that primary objective, as well as to a militaristic repression of political opposition (Mingardi 1998, 144). In Honduras, up until 1995, the public security force was a militarized body under the command of the armed forces (Rico 1998, 177). In El Salvador, at the time of the 1992 peace agreements, there were three police forces and all were under the control of the Ministry of Defense, were directed by military personnel, were trained almost exclusively for dealing with insurgency, and lacked training in basic police functions (Palmieri 1998, 315).

This militarization has unquestionably had an impact on the excessive use of force by the police, which in the case of Latin America means a high number of citizen deaths, along with other human rights violations. One result of militarization is that police doctrine places little importance on the rights of individuals. Another is that it contributes to creating hostile relationships and expectations on the part of the police vis-à-vis certain citizens, because the police use social profiling in dealing with crime—leading, in some situations, to the use of violence to resolve conflicts quickly.

A third feature of the modern police force is that it is a professional body, in that it attempts to maintain a proper and assessable level of efficiency. This is reflected in the criteria used for recruiting and training personnel, in rules governing promotion and retirement, and in a substantive interest in, and emphasis on, familiarity with and use of technology (Bayley 1985, 47–50). This process of professionalization is similar to what occurs in businesses and other institutions; thus, it is not particularly surprising that it should also be the mark of a modern police organization. For long periods of time, however, this process has been compromised in Latin America.

Though it is difficult to generalize, the history of a large number of Latin American police forces reflects the dominance of individualistic criteria in the process of selecting, promoting, and removing police officers, who often depend on the support or loyalty of parties, groups, and officials. Such a situation doubtless affects the Venezuelan police, which are part of the executive branch and which, furthermore, consists of agencies whose priority is to provide service primarily to the executive and only secondarily to the population (Santos Alvins 1998, 211–12).

This situation is found in other countries as well. When then Argentine minister of justice León Arslanián began a thorough reorganization of the police of the province of Buenos Aires in 1997, he stated that despite previous efforts, the police had consistently managed to preserve a system in which the choice of personnel was driven by the imperative of maintaining a staff that would keep the existing corruption and inefficiency in place (Arslanián 1998, 63). In the case of Brazil, one author recounts a series of criticisms of the way the police system functions—criticisms that, no doubt, apply to other countries in the region: the inefficiency and poor quality of police services, a lack of external controls by ministries of security, conflict and a lack of cooperation with civilian and military police in the individual states, and the questionable quality of police investigations (Pinheiro 1998, 184–87).

The creation of new civilian police forces in Guatemala, El Salvador, and Haiti illustrates some of the same problems. In Guatemala, for example, the pressure to add more police to patrol the streets has led to a relaxing of the criteria used to select new recruits. Similarly, the number of applicants has been lower than that needed to guarantee the quality of new personnel (Byrne, William, and Garst 2000, 22–23). The process itself also appears not to be as rigorous as it should be (Glebbeek 2000). There are reported to have been serious problems also in training former members of the police or armed forces to become part of the new national police (Garst 1997, 6–8).

Thus, a majority of Latin American police forces have severe problems in terms of a lack of specialization, professionalism, and public-mindedness—three areas central to modern police organizations. These problems are particularly noticeable in the current environment, where two basic features are in play: the consolidation of civil society and democratic institutions, and an increase in crime. These issues call for police service that provides equal treatment to the entire population, that achieves the necessary separation of police and military functions, and that meets the need to ensure greater professionalism to reduce levels of violence.

New Features of Modern Police Institutions

Increases in crime in both Western Europe and the United States, which began in the 1950s, have provoked considerable discussion on and substantial changes in police activity. Three particularly important aspects of this are the consideration of new strategies needed to reduce crime and violence, the implementation of programs to strengthen relations between police and society, and an emphasis on modern resource management strategies to ensure police efficiency. This process of debate, thought, and change points to the need for reform and suggests particular approaches (Goldstein 1977; Bayley 1994; Bayley and Shearing 1996).

Three elements define this process of change (Frühling 2000). The first is changes in police doctrine aimed at incorporating democratic values into police activity, with police relating to citizens as equals. The second is the use of sophisticated methodologies to evaluate the impact of policing strategies on crime, with an emphasis on recruiting and training police officers to develop a more highly trained force. The third is the effort to implement police research and planning to respond more precisely to public demand.

Democratic Control of Police Activity and New Police Doctrine

Traditionally, police have emphasized the need to carry out their duties in accordance with the law. Professionalism is generally viewed as inimical to such observance of the law, arguing that the purpose of police work is to enforce the law, without, however, considering social or political values that go beyond this. This interpretation of professionalism derives from the fact that police training is essentially legalistic. The authority that police officials have over subordinates, their authority over the public, and their immunity from undue interference from the political realm are based on current law. Respect for the law leads to the argument that the police are a totally professional institution that maintains order in any circumstance and supports the stability of any government. Legalistic professionalism, however, is not conducive to respect for concepts such as democracy and human rights. To the extent that these concepts are supported by current law, they are accepted, but the incorporation of these concepts into police activity is slow to show itself. The lack of respect for these concepts as a guiding force leaves the police distrustful of the citizenry. As a result, police strategies for combating crime pay scant attention to the concerns of the people.

Today's democratic conception of police doctrine simply means that the police follow a code of conduct that is acceptable in terms of human rights. Thus, they carry out their duties in the public interest and with a public service orientation; they are fully responsible for violations of the law; and there are mechanisms to ensure that they are also responsible to the public for the strategies they use to protect the public, for the efficiency and seriousness which with they carry out their duties, and for respecting the perceptions, interests, and values of the people.

As Stone and Ward (2000) point out, this definition of accountability goes well beyond complying with legal obligations, and it requires numerous monitoring and oversight mechanisms involving more than merely judicial measures. In this view, the police as an organization, and its members personally, are responsible both for reducing insecurity and fear, and for any corrupt or improper conduct in the organization. In the former case, the line of accountability points upward to the governmental officials responsible for public order and peace, to the judges and prosecutors in charge of investigations. However, the police are also responsible to society—to citizen security committees that may be formed at the neighborhood level, neighborhood associations, and the media.

In the matter of police abuse, the police must be accountable under systems of internal control, through their chain of command and through the courts, in cases where they have committed crimes (Stone and Ward 2000). According to this approach, the police are not only subject to control in regard to illegal activity but also with respect to the efficiency and timeliness of their performance. In addition, control is exercised by institutions whose only objective is police oversight (e.g., citizens' committees processing complaints against the police in the United States), as well as by other entities not exclusively dedicated to this objective.

As a result of this new way of thinking, a variety of mechanisms to provide for police discipline have been implemented. Although they are essentially internal in Europe and in Latin America, the systems for discipline and management of police conduct in Canada and the United States have a strong outside component, involving citizens' committees that process complaints from the public regarding the police and recommend sanctions, which are carried out by the chief of police. These committees came into being because of a lack of transparency in internal investigations carried out by the police themselves (Kravetz 1998; Lapkin 1998). The only study of which the present author is aware regarding the functioning of an internal review system in Latin America indicates negative results. In the case of the police of the province of Santa Fe, Argentina, it was ascertained that serious police misconduct—generally involving the possible commission of a crime—was treated with impunity. Administrative investigations are normally suspended in these cases until criminal proceedings have been carried out (Sozzo 1999), which can take years.

In response to the profound mistrust provoked by the lack of objectivity of internal disciplinary procedures, institutions have been created in Latin America during the past several years to provide for outside controls on police conduct, as a complement to criminal justice procedures. Thus, São Paulo has created the Monitoring Office for the Police of the State of São Paulo, which acts as an ombudsman for the police and publishes public reports on complaints made against the police. In El Salvador, the prosecutor for the defense of human rights not only receives complaints against the police but also publishes annual reports and refers complaints regarding police conduct to a number of public entities (Palmieri 1998, 329–32). In 1998, the province of Santa Fe created a Provincial Office of Internal Affairs under the deputy secretary of public security, one of whose principal functions was to investigate crimes, offenses, and serious administrative mishandling on the part of police personnel.[6]

An essential tool in the efforts to evaluate the quality of policing is the establishment of parameters against which results for a given period are measured and compared. Each indicator corresponds to a particular variable or aspect of organizational performance, such as efficiency, efficacy, or quality. Although the use of indicators is unquestionably important, it is also important to bear in mind the limitations of such procedures (Bayley 1996, 46–49). The difficulty of using indicators to evaluate police work derives from the fact that increased crime is caused by a multiplicity of factors, involving elements other than police performance.

Thus, the impact of police activity is not easy to determine. It should also be noted that in recent years the monitoring of police work has shifted from government to citizens themselves. Thus, in Sweden and Denmark, citizen advisory panels are in constant communication with the police, providing them with the citizens' point of view on their work. In Santiago, a similar experiment was carried out—resulting, according to some accounts, in failure. Very preliminary instances of democratic supervision of the police are beginning to emerge in Latin America. One such example is the community policing project in the state of São Paulo, described below, which is designed and implemented with the participation of committees composed of a broad range of representatives from society.

Emphasis on Recruiting and Training Police Personnel

Given that the ability of the police to reduce crime is clearly limited, more emphasis is being placed on improving the quality of personnel. Before determining the desirable qualities to be sought in prospective recruits, it is important to define the essential doctrine and strategy to be adopted by the police in carrying out their functions to protect the citizenry. Such a process will dictate whether to emphasize characteristics of discipline, obedience, strong character, and personality or to meet a need for individuals with interpersonal skills and imagination.

Recruits must, of course, indicate emotional stability, through a process of psychological testing and interviews, as well as a minimum educational level, because their work requires comprehension of the laws they are called upon to enforce. It would also be wise to determine whether applicants have criminal records or other elements in their background that may be contraindications to professional police work. The industrial democracies have increased educational requirements for police employees, especially in the case of officials in positions of command—a logical step, for the police not only have great power but are also generally charged with overseeing considerable human and material resources. In addition, the increasing complexity of police work makes a higher degree of academic training desirable.

In El Salvador, following the peace accords, new legislation governing police employment defines three levels for the National Civilian Police: basic, executive, and senior. The basic level includes officers, corporals, and sergeants; the executive level includes deputy inspector, inspector, and chief inspector; and the senior level includes deputy commissioner, commissioner, and commissioner-general. Requirements for basic level entry cover an age range of 18 to 28, with applicants required to have graduated from secondary school. For executive positions, applicants must be under 30 years of age with a bachelor's degree or the equivalent. Legislation stipulates that senior positions may only be filled from among those already occupying executive positions on the force (CEPES-FESPAD 2000).

In the United Kingdom, at least half of the police in command positions have college degrees. In the United States, the average education of police officers rose considerably between 1969 and 1990; in 1969, the average educational level was a secondary school diploma, whereas by 1990 it was 2 years of college (Bayley 1994, 85). Chilean police officials undergo a 4-year training period, and those with the rank of colonel must take an additional 2-year course at the Advanced Police Academy. The required educational level of police personnel will also depend on the availability of candidates, which in turn depends on the employment conditions the police are able to offer. Thus, at times, the police will have to settle for the best they can find, rather than what is actually needed. When possible, police recruitment should also draw on a large number of candidates from different cultural and social backgrounds. If the objective is to introduce new and innovative policing strategies, it is desirable to hire individuals without prejudices or preconceptions regarding the work they are intended to perform.

One final consideration is the quality and content of training that recruits are to receive. Although this is a subject that reaches beyond what can be covered here, three general points can be given. First, the less prior schooling recruits have had, the longer or more intense their police academy training must be. Second, training should combine theory (especially legal knowledge) with application to concrete cases, along with practical exercises. Special emphasis should be put on basic analysis of dangerous situations in which the police must exercise judgment: arrests, response to attack, and so forth (Goldstein 1977, 274). Many potential human rights abuses and police dismissals can be prevented by proper training in the use of firearms and control of situations involving the arrest of dangerous suspects. Third, it is important that training approximate, as closely as possible, the real experiences that police officers will in fact confront. This means preparing them to respect the rights of individuals who may be violent and to act rapidly in high-stress situations. Without such preparation, new police officers will face an inevitable gap between what they were taught and the realities they face in the course of their actual work.[7]

Police Planning and Research

A third feature of police work is the recognition that successful perform-ance in the modern social context requires intensive efforts to anticipate problems, to plan strategies for responding to them, to carry out daily as-sessments of results, and to make organizational modifications, as neces-sary. The police must change from being a force accustomed to carrying out preestablished routine procedures to being a flexible organization able to mobilize in response to goals—combining traditional law enforcement duties, such as the arrest and interrogation of suspects, with other social service functions, including the provision of crime prevention information, organizing youth clubs, and so on.

The importance of research and planning in dealing with crime is clear. Police officers must be intimately familiar with the spatial and temporal distribution of criminal activity, must have a realistic view of changing patterns of crime, and must be aware of relevant geographic changes. William Bratton, former police chief of New York City, summarized the necessary strategic structure (Bratton and Knobler 1998, 224): Determine, on a daily basis, where crimes are occurring and at what times they are oc-curring. Once these data are mapped, different police units must be coordi-nated effectively to provide quick response. Before police arrive at a site, it is essential to know what tactics will be necessary to confront the criminal activity: the investigation of crimes already committed, large-scale de-ployment to reduce criminal activity in an area, or a community policing program. The final element of this structure involves a number of ques-tions to assist in the process of evaluation: Do the tactics used produce re-sults? Did the local police commander coordinate efforts with other offi-cials? And finally, how do statistics on known crimes change with the application of given strategies?

Planning must be a multilevel process, not solely a central one, and it must include all police stations. It is clear that in today's world, decentral-ization is essential to police work. Local commanders, however, inevitably face crucial limitations. They lack authority to select their own personnel, and they are compelled to operate within a budget over which they have no control. Decentralization of the planning process should produce a more targeted approach to responding effectively to local as well as central needs. One of the negative effects of having a police strategy limited to re-sponding to criminal acts after the fact is that human and material re-sources are distributed only in reaction to the number of criminal incidents that have occurred in each area of a city (Beato 2001). But with a more sophisticated information system, it becomes possible to identify patterns linking the individual criminal incidents.[8]

In summary, police reform in industrialized countries combines a concern for modern organizational management techniques, aimed at addressing new societal challenges, with an emphasis on the rights of individuals who may be affected by police action. This theoretical frame of reference has influenced some police reforms in Latin America, leading to greater attempts to deal with the public security crisis that has characterized the region in recent years. As will be noted, the depth and stability of these reforms, over time, are not always clear.

Police Reform in Latin America

Though there are undoubtedly certain similarities in recent reform efforts among Latin American police forces, the contexts in which they have occurred vary. Generally speaking, in line with the scheme suggested here, they have attempted to create specialized police forces—that is, free of military control and guided by principles of public service and professionalism. Efforts include attempts to strengthen monitoring mechanisms and to introduce changes in recruiting practices and in the curricula used in police academies. Despite such similarities, however, such reforms have significant differences.

One distinction relates to the civilian nature of the police forces created as a result of the process of change. In countries where a peace process has brought an end to civil war, as in Central America, demilitarization has taken place, leading to the creation of new civilian police forces. In South America, conversely, the military nature of police forces has remained unchanged. This is, in part, a consequence of the fact that these forces were more than mere arms of the military, but rather, had significant influence within the governmental structure—more than was true of their counterparts in Central America. The Colombian police continued to report to the Ministry of Defense, as mandated by Law 62 of 1993, whereas Brazil's state military police retained its vertical hierarchical character, pursuant to the military structure set forth in the 1988 Constitution.

Efforts at demilitarization in South America have been limited to a recognition of the community's role in preventing crime, involving a degree of community monitoring of police activity. Studies, however, indicate that such programs have failed to successfully address an intrinsic conceptual contradiction: the autonomy of the police in determining how to deploy their personnel, on the one hand, and the interest of community organizations to monitor or provide guidance for police activity, on the other.

Another difference among reform processes is the extent to which the international community plays a role. Some reforms now under way have been made possible because of a strong international assistance component. The National Civilian Police in El Salvador has received bilateral resource and training support from a number of European and Latin American countries. In addition, the United Nations office for El Salvador has monitored and verified the implementation (Costa 1999).

In other instances of reform, the international role has been less visible. In Colombia, reform was overseen by police officials, who instituted a thorough purging of the institution. These efforts were supported by the U.S. government, with its interest in combating drug trafficking—efforts that turned the head of the Colombian police into a national figure, while providing material and technical support to the institution (Camacho Guizado 2000, 18). The role of international cooperation has been considerably less pronounced in the case of the São Paulo military police and the police of the province of Buenos Aires, though in both, the influence of internationally inspired police management models can be seen—for example, in the use of community policing.

Finally, this brief overview of differences among current police reforms should include mention of the leadership encouraging such reform. The Colombian case illustrates a reform process designed and implemented by the police leadership itself. Though the Colombian government, as well as the United States, has certainly supported the process—initiated pursuant to a law passed by the Congress—the primary responsibility for implementation has fallen on the police leadership itself and, specifically, on General Rosso José Serrano. The consensus seems to be that changes that have occurred within the police have been brought about by the police force itself and through decisions on the part of the leadership (Camacho Guizado 2000, 18). Partly due to the hierarchical nature of the institution, actions taken by the leadership have encountered little internal resistance. It has therefore been possible to purge the force of many officers accused of corruption or other criminal activity.

The case of the police of the province of Buenos Aires represents the other extreme. After an initial process of change implemented in 1996 began to lose momentum, Governor Eduardo Duhalde intervened in 1997 to reorganize the force. The plan, implemented by León Arslanián, who later became minister of justice and security, was formulated entirely by civilians. Despite the fact that there was minimal participation by the police in bringing about these changes, the greatest resistance seemed to come not from the police but from legislators and politicians belonging to Governor Duhalde's own party, undermining the support that the minister of justice and security relied on to implement the reform (Saín 1999, 36, 37).

Transformation of the Security System of the Province of Buenos Aires

In 1996 and 1997, two factors contributed to the decision to intervene in the operation of the police force in the province of Buenos Aires. First, there was a marked increase in citizens' concerns about crime; second, it was proven that members of the Buenos Aires police had participated in the attack against the Jewish Community headquarters, AMIA, as well as in the crime involving José Luis Cabezas, a reporter from the print media (Saín 1998, 70).

The executive branch launched an active intervention in the Buenos Aires police, creating a Ministry of Justice and Security that would be responsible for dismantling the force as it existed. The entire upper command was dismissed, and more than 300 police superintendents and senior officers were removed. The existing police force was replaced by eighteen departmental security police forces, an investigatory police force, a service overseeing custody and transport of arrestees, along with a proposed municipal street police unit. The departmental security police forces were to function autonomously and maintain active mutual relations, with their principal function being that of preventing crime (Government of the Province of Buenos Aires 1998). The project sought, in addition to a decentralization of command, to dismantle the existing networks of corruption through a process of functional differentiation, creating a number of police organizations that would carry out the functions previously carried out by a single entity.

To ensure external oversight of efficiency and monitor the manner in which the police functioned, departmental security councils were created, made up of a representative of the municipalities' Municipal Security Advocacy; one provincial assembly deputy and one provincial senator; two executive department heads from the municipalities making up the judicial district; the judicial district's prosecuting attorney; a representative of the bar association; and representatives of unions, business, and religious institutions. The function of the councils, established by provincial law, is to monitor and assess the performance and activity of the province's police forces, obtain reports from the heads of the various newly established police forces, and engage, as needed, in finding peaceful solutions to social conflicts.

In addition, it was proposed that neighborhood security forums be formed composed of nongovernmental community organizations or entities recognized for their social participation. These would be involved in evaluating the performance and activity of the province's police forces, and they could participate in planning to prevent activities or events that are of a criminal nature or that would be harmful to public security. Finally, the Municipal Security Advocacy was created to protect inhabitants' individual and collective rights vis-à-vis action, or failure to act, on the part of government, police forces, or private policing firms.[9] In regard to the internal oversight of police conduct, an Office for the Control of Corruption and Abuse of Official Duties was created, including an internal affairs auditor, reporting to the minister of security, and an Ethics Court—with the auditor responsible for investigating all complaints of ethics violations or abuses committed by police personnel and bringing charges before the Ethics Court.

This process of change was a gradual one. Not until January 1999 were rules implemented to govern the mechanisms by which the neighborhood and municipal security forums were to be created. According to official information, as of April 1999, only 22 of the 134 municipalities of the province of Buenos Aires had selected municipal security defenders, with security forums installed in 75 municipalities. The reform also involved ending the authority of the police in the investigative phase of the criminal justice process. However, despite the entry into force of a new code of criminal procedure, government prosecutors did not, in fact, take over this task, because they suffered from lack of material resources and personnel (Saín 1999, 27).

In reality, the major obstacle to the reform effort was that it failed to have any visible effect on citizen insecurity. It was probably unreasonable to expect immediate success; nevertheless, as the electoral campaign approached, Carlos Ruckauf, the Peronist candidate for governor, criticized the management of Minister Arslanián and expressed his opposition to the police reform initiated in 1997, claiming that it was too protective of human rights.[10] Arslanián was forced to resign.

In 1999, Duhalde was replaced as governor by Ruckauf, who pursued a completely different approach to the reform process, given that crime was still on the rise. Ruckauf appointed as his first minister of security Aldo Rico, a former military colonel who had participated in a coup attempt against the democratic government. A study by the San Isidro courts showed that during the first months of Ruckauf's administration, the number of complaints involving police mistreatment of youths doubled (*Clarin* of Buenos Aires, September 28, 2000; cited by Ward 2000, 15). The Centro de Estudios Legales y Sociales reported (2000) that 273 civilians were killed by the police during 1999, compared with 172 in 1998.

The lack of a systematic assessment of the experiences of public participation makes it difficult to draw solid conclusions regarding the impact of the reform process in the province of Buenos Aires. However, it seems certain that, because the government has not followed a coherent policy of controlling police abuses and corruption, the creation of participatory schemes in the province has not resulted in increased police accountability. Thus, police violence has increased even since police reform was initiated. Why was the reform program in the province of Buenos Aires reversed? There might have been a number of reasons for this decision, but the deciding factors were most likely the continued increase of crime and Governor Ruckauf's belief that citizens of the province were more tolerant of police violence and corruption than of common crime against them.

Colombian Police Reform

In February 1993, the rape and murder of a young girl in a Bogotá police station was made public. This crime marked a low point in police credibility, and it triggered the reform of an institution that was considered corrupt, ineffective, and fraught with drug dealing. The process began as a result of a resolution by then–minister of defense Rafael Pardo, who created two commissions to assess the situation and a set of proposals to transform the police. In 1993, the work of these two commissions became codified in Law 62.

Unlike the situation in the province of Buenos Aires, however, the reform of this police force was driven primarily by the institution's own leadership, rather than through political intervention. Today, the results are generally regarded as highly positive; both international observers and national public opinion reflect a considerable increase in confidence in the police force (LaFranchi 1998). Nevertheless, doubts remain as to whether the police have in fact become more efficient in combating crime; there is a perception that there is a lack of human and material resources being devoted to criminal investigations, with such resources going instead toward antidrug efforts, which receive greater media coverage and international attention (Llorente 1999, 454–57).

The reform process began with the appointment of Major General Rosso José Serrano as head of the National Police in 1994. He obtained authorization from Congress to remove officers who, on the basis of sound evidence, were suspected of having engaged in corrupt activity. Approximately 7,000 police officers were dismissed. Unlike other operations to purge corruption, the effort was perceived as credible, and it affected not only subordinates but also upper-level officials. The second step involved changing the structure and culture of the force, introducing management concepts from the modern business culture. The School of Administration of the Universidad de los Andes collaborated with the police in this phase of the project.

The 1998 Institutional Strategy Plan recommended six institutional policies: community participation, a new work culture, strengthened operational capacity, development of management, an emphasis on knowledge, and effective management of the administrative system. Flowing from these policies were strategic goals and tasks for each police division. To encourage creativity, a less hierarchical, less concentrated structure was created, composed of three levels: governing entities; consultative and support entities, including the Office of the Inspector General, which carries out the important task of developing indicators to determine whether the strategic plan is being met; and executive entities, which develop and carry out the tasks necessary to implement this entire process (Policia Nacional n.d., 40–41).

The predominant discourse with regard to this reorganization process is oriented toward enhancing the management ability of officials and substantially improving the administration of resources. In addition, it includes a component of community collaboration, which is reflected in a number of elements, including "consultation with the citizenry to provide the basis for new police service; creating new, expedited channels of communication for complaints and claims, including the provision of customer-service lines; and lastly, creating so-called citizens' consortiums for change, which are interdisciplinary work teams led by the National Police, involving the development of formulas for fostering conditions in which everyone can live together peacefully" (Policia Nacional n.d., 16–17). Examples of the latter include the "Plan Dorado," which brings together public and private service providers who work at the El Dorado International Airport.

The transformation of the Colombian police has had a distinctly positive effect on public confidence in the police, though there is a need for a more detailed assessment of how it has affected the community, as well as of the effect on crime rates. The community monitoring of police policy is weak (Llorente 1999, 459–65) and there is a lack of available information in this regard. In the case of Colombia, the presence of internal armed conflict presents special difficulties not faced by police forces in other countries of the region. In many towns and small cities where guerrillas present a potential threat, the police function as a military force; this demands an attitude on the part of police officers that is diametrically opposed to the sense of mutual cooperation with the citizenry that should prevail in police work (Camacho Guizado 2000, 22).

The Community Policing Plan in São Paulo

In Brazil, increasing crime and violence, as well the killing of civilians by the police in several states, have pressed the federal and state governments to implement new security policies that are less punitive. New experiences with community policing projects have emerged in states such as Espiritu Santo, Minas Gerais, Pará, and Rio Grande do Sul. Probably the longest lasting and most studied effort is the project implemented in the state of São Paulo.

As in all of Brazil's states, the military police in São Paulo is an auxiliary force of the army that performs preventive police functions and is regulated, organizationally and functionally, through the Ministry of the Army. Between the 1980s and 1990s, the state of São Paulo, like the rest of Brazil, experienced a huge rise in crime. According to Health Ministry data, the number of deaths due to homicide or intentionally inflicted injuries rose from 3,452 in 1980 to 12,350 in 1996, with the homicide rate reaching 36.20 per 100,000 inhabitants. These increases were also accompanied by a dramatic rise in theft. The failure of the police in the face of this situation was reflected in a number of areas. There were frequent incidents of police violence, which received wide coverage in the media. During 1995, 618 citizens were killed by the military police in São Paulo state. Surveys indicated that because people viewed the police as inefficient and feared involvement with the police forces, only 33 percent of crimes were actually reported (Mesquita Neto 1998, 22–23).

On December 10, 1997, the top commander of the military police officially adopted the concept of community policing as both an institutional

philosophy and operational strategy. In São Paulo, the main body responsible for implementing the community policing program is the Advisory
Commission for the Implementation of Community Policing. This commission has no fixed number of members; in August 1998, it had representatives from human rights organizations, community councils, the Federation of Industry, and business councils, among others. Within the
commission, there were discussions of public security problems and an attempt to set priorities and identify solutions. This led to a defined set of
goals and objectives for the police, including an emphasis on democratic
values and respect for human rights that had never been part of military police doctrine. The commission's goals were to implement the community
policing model as an organizing strategy for the military police, to improve
the quality of police instruction and training, to improve the recruitment
and promotion system, to integrate the police with other public entities, and
to improve the status and rights of the police (Mesquite Neto 1998, 48).

Forty-one military police companies were chosen for the program, including patrols, women police officers, traffic police, railroad police,
forestry police, and firefighters. Company commanders chose the neighborhoods in which the program was to be implemented. The number of
companies involved gradually grew, and as of August 1998, 7,269 police
officers were involved in community-based work. Within the police, the
project's implementation was undertaken by the São Paulo Military Police's Department of Community Policing (Smulovitz 2000, 21).

The new plan of action led to more patrolling in selected areas and to
the establishment of permanent 24-hour police posts. In addition, efforts
aimed at school security and drug abuse programs were undertaken. To
provide officers with training in community policing, courses on the subject were offered; 16,963 police officers attended during the first semester
in 1998 (Mesquita Neto 1998, 66).

The initiative is seen as positive; however, the success of community
policing projects depends on changing the organizational and command
structure of the police. There is a need for greater decentralization, with
less distance between the various hierarchical positions, thus creating a
more horizontal relationship among personnel, who also need to incorporate more democratic cultural and professional values (Mesquita Neto
1998, 89). Another source of resistance to implementing the model comes
from the conviction of many police officers that this program could very
well be discontinued when a different administration takes power, as has
happened in other states in Brazil (Smulovitz 2000, 25).

Data regarding the impact of the program on police violence are not entirely conclusive. Just prior to the implementation of community policing, the number of civilians killed by the police in confrontations in the street had begun to decrease as a result of a program that monitored, retrained, and provided psychological assistance to police officers involved in high-risk confrontations (Cano 2001). However, this form of violence has increased recently. In 1997, 466 civilians were killed by the police, rising to 546 in 1998 and 647 in 1999 (Mesquita Neto 2000; cited in Smulovitz 2000, 24). Nonetheless, researchers in the field believe that the level of police violence is lower than at the beginning of the 1990s (Smulovitz 2000, 24).

The program's impact on crime also is not very conclusive. According to the Department of Community Policing, crime rates have gone down in those areas where the program has been successfully implemented, as in the Jardim Angela neighborhood. However, data compiled by the Public Security Secretariat of the São Paulo government showed that the homicide rate went up 23 percent in that neighborhood between 1996 and 1999 (Smulovitz 2000, 24).

In the case of the community policing project in the state of São Paulo, both the design and the implementation involved the participation of a number of committees with a socially diverse membership. There was an Advisory Committee for the Creation of the Community Police that engaged in a dialogue with police to assess the problems arising during implementation. Although the establishment of such a committee was certainly an achievement, relations between its civilian members and the police were difficult (Mesquita Neto 2000, 69–71). At their meetings, the police took note of problems, but rarely was there any rigorous follow-up on the measures taken to resolve these concerns.

Community Security Councils—established by state government decree—are autonomous in their objectives and operations. They convene monthly, and forward the minutes of their meetings to the Office of the Public Security Councils Coordinator, which is an agency of the State Security Secretariat. The dialogue between police and citizens that takes place in these councils does not appear to be highly productive, though it represents a first step toward citizen monitoring. These councils have functioned more as venues for individual complaints about and demands of the police than as a means of solving collective problems. Use of the councils for political purposes and a lack of interest and training on the part of both the police and the civilian participants have also hindered their success (Mesquita Neto 2000, 71–74).

Community participation in the process of bringing about change in the police force was somewhat lacking. Attendance of citizen participants at meetings of the Advisory Commission for the Implementation of Community Policing declined with time, whereas the proportion of participating police officers increased. The United Nations Latin American Institute for the Prevention of Crime, based in São Paulo, recently conducted a survey in 46 neighborhoods to evaluate the community policing program. Twenty-three of these neighborhoods were covered by the community policing program, and the results for these 23 neighborhoods were compared with those for the other 23 not covered by the survey. Apparently the program has brought about an increased perception of safety among those surveyed who knew it was being implemented in their neighborhood.

São Paulo's experience reveals a commitment to change on the part of the police command and the state government. One of its clear objectives is to reduce the levels of police violence, not only by increasing accountability of police officers in the street but also through special retraining programs for officers who participate in violent confrontations. It is not known why the number of civilians killed by the police has been increasing in recent years. One possible explanation is that community policing is still an expanding pilot project that does not include the whole police force; more important, it is not being implemented in the most dangerous areas of the state, given the *favelados'* distrust of the police. Another explanation is that the idea of community policing is not supported by some members of the police who believe more forceful measures are required to deal with crime.

Athough the impact of this program on crime is not entirely clear, it is apparent that community policing alone will not achieve the objective of reducing crime, because police forces also must improve their managerial systems and the use of crime analysis to deploy their forces (Beato 2001). In São Paulo, as in other states of Brazil, experiences with public participation have been promising, but the difficulties involved in engaging the community still persist. Above all, it is not clear whether this program has had a progressive or a regressive impact, given that members of the business community were more eager to participate than were residents of poor neighborhoods.

The Plan Cuadrante in Chile

The case of Chile is of interest, given that conditions there are quite different from those in Argentina, Brazil, and Colombia. The militarized police force, the Carabineros, enjoys popular support because it is seen as being largely free of corruption and well disciplined. Nonetheless, it has been criticized for being closed, corporatist, autonomous, and not accountable to civilian authorities. The Carabineros recently announced and is implementing a series of institutional changes aimed at putting more police on the streets, redeploying them in patrol sectors in accordance with certain quantifiable variables, establishing performance indicators to evaluate each member of the force, and strengthening relations with the community. This plan is still in its early stages and has not yet been evaluated, but it constitutes a radical departure from the lack of interest in social participation that the force had shown in the past (Frühling 1998).

The basis for the reform is the so-called Plan Cuadrante, which attempts to respond to two dilemmas that the institution has been facing in recent years: increased calls for service in urban areas and a regressive imbalance between the officers and resources assigned to rich municipalities and poor ones (Ward 2000, 20). The plan creates patrol sectors based on the composition of the population, crime rates, and demand for police services. Each *cuadrante*, or sector, is assigned a patrol level in accordance to a rating of its respective risk level. Although the plan is not, in fact, a community policing program, it has been complemented by other announcements that signal a commitment to engaging the community in crime prevention initiatives. For example, an Office of Community Relations and Crime Analysis was created to coordinate operations in response to demands, complaints, and suggestions coming from the public.[11] The plan is seen by experts as an important first step toward recognizing the role of the community in the prevention of crime. However, it still does not signal a shift from the police as a law enforcement institution to a service provider; moreover, aspects such as internal disciplinary controls, internal organization and doctrine remain largely untouched.

Changes in the Carabineros coincide with efforts implemented by the central government. In recent years, the government has been promoting the organization of Citizen Security Neighborhood Committees in Santiago. Since 1997, these committees have received assistance and training from the Division of Social Organizations of the Ministry General Secretariat of the Government. The number of committees formed is unclear. By the end of 1998, 261 committees existed, although the level of intensity of their work differed greatly (Sandoval 2001). More recent data fix their number at 70 in Santiago (Smulovitz 2000, 34). The information that exists shows that participants in these committees are mostly women (57.1 percent) who do not work outside the home and generally already participate in other neighborhood, religious, or political groups (Jordan and Sotomayor 2000). Their activities include street patrolling, organizing sports workshops for the youth, and lobbying the municipality to get better street lighting and garbage removal.

The success of most of these organizations depends on developing close relations with the municipality and the Carabineros. However, the reality is different in each community and depends very much on the people in charge of these two structures. Some groups have excellent relations with their municipalities; others do not. The relationship with the Carabineros also varies widely. The committees in certain municipalities distrust the lower ranks of the Carabineros, fearing they might be involved in protecting street drug trafficking. Participants in these committees are not necessarily peace-loving citizens. Many of those interviewed expressed the view that the only way to deal with criminals was to unite with other citizens to punish them (Jordan and Sotomayor 2000, 52). However, very few incidents of vigilantism have been reported.

In August 2000, the government launched a new initiative aimed at institutionalizing social participation in the prevention of crime. The new "Safe Municipality: Commitment 100" Program aims to create security councils in every municipality whose members include the mayor, representatives of both the Carabineros and the investigative police, and delegates from other community organizations. Established by law, these councils would determine security policies at the local level and fund security projects presented by the Citizen Security Neighborhood Committees. Funding will be provided by the central government to those municipalities that lack monetary resources and are most affected by crime.

The Santiago experience is still too recent to have been subject to serious evaluation. The number of people involved in the neighborhood committees is still too small to expect major changes. The police reform has been decided by the Carabineros itself, and so far, there is no evidence that patterns of accountability have changed significantly with increasing social participation in the prevention of crime. Both the Plan Cuadrante and the development of social participation in crime prevention might eventually increase democratic control over the police. However, at this juncture this does not seem to have happened.

Conclusions

At the beginning of the 1990s, Latin American police forces were seriously deficient in fulfilling their functions as public, specialized, professional bodies. The advent of democratic regimes, faced with increased citizen insecurity, has highlighted these problems.

Most recent reforms discussed here emphasize new decentralized police management models, incorporating comprehensive quality criteria, which have resulted in efforts to provide incentives for greater flexibility in the police force as well to promote personal initiative rather than compliance with a rigid set of rules. Police forces—influenced by experience at the international level—are emphasizing planning and are establishing indicators to measure their effectiveness. An interesting example, in this regard, is the announcement by the Chilean police that officers' performance will be evaluated on a daily basis, according to indicators established for that purpose.[12]

Part of the reform process described here involves an ongoing dialogue with the community, including the need to involve the community in managing security policy. However, though such community participation is an integral part of the process of change in some instances, such as in São Paulo, it has a more secondary role in other situations, such as Buenos Aires, where the central emphasis has been on dismantling criminal networks within the provincial police. Finally, another element in the reforms described, particularly in the case of Buenos Aires province, is the incorporation of new institutions to ensure better internal and external oversight of police activity. When reform also involves implementing a community policing program, grassroots organizations are usually formed to monitor and evaluate police work.

There are few studies that provide a serious, objective analysis and evaluation of the degree to which the official goals of police reform have been met, and they are based on limited information. In the case of most of the reform programs referred to, goals are set internally and neither these, nor the methodology used to conduct internal evaluations, nor the results of such evaluations, are made public. This makes it impossible to determine either the extent to which changes have been implemented or the impact of such changes.

The implementation of new policing strategies that bring the police closer to the people could result in positive changes in the organization and in a reduction of violence. The case of São Paulo shows that these strategies do improve the image of the police. Once the reform process begins, two primary sources of resistance can be seen. The first comes directly from the police and its officers. The new policing strategy could be seen as "soft" on crime by many, and others could feel that this approach will change once a new government takes office. This internal resistance seems to have put an end to the initial efforts at police reform in 1996 in the province of Buenos Aires (Saín 1999, 8).

The second source of resistance to reform comes from conservative politicians, who are always ready to bring in tougher law-and-order policies to control violence. For example, some of the community policing programs in Brazil have ceased to function due to political changes that have ushered in governors with a hard-core, law-and-order stance and little concern for democratic issues. This occurred in 1995 in Rio de Janeiro and resulted in an increased number of civilians killed by the police (Cano 2001). It is very important, then, that the changes have an impact upon crime rates and citizens' fear of crime. However, this will also require a better use of crime analysis and an extensive use of problem-solving techniques, which has not happened so far.

The crisis facing Latin American police forces is indeed serious. Current reforms hold forth the prospect of police management models that are more democratic and more respectful of the rights of individuals. They constitute a new dynamic and represent the gradual abandonment of the traditional paradigm of police organization and activity in the region. This potential may, indeed, come to fruition; or it may fail if it does not succeed in producing solid results. Proper monitoring of the process and careful documentation of the strategies followed can make a major contribution to future experiments. It is also vital that organizations outside police forces be involved in discussing and evaluating programs, to ensure that the results of evaluations are disseminated and contribute to the formulation of public security policy in the region.

Notes

1. The Pan American Health Organization's ACTIVA project found that 15.6 percent of the population in Santiago, 18.1 percent in San Salvador, 25.1 percent in Cali, 27.6 percent in Caracas, and 28.7 percent in Rio de Janeiro considered police efficiency poor or very poor. A 1996 survey by ADIMARK, in Chile, showed a high degree of support (70 percent) for the director general of the police and the director general of the investigatory police in their fight against crime. See also, United Nations (1999), which compares results of victimization surveys done in different regions of the world. Results show lower reporting rates of crimes to the police in Latin America than in other regions of the world.

2. A survey by *El Mercurio* and sixteen other newspapers in the United States and Latin America found that 81 percent of respondents in the United States had great confidence or some confidence in the police, whereas in Chile this was only 38 percent. In general, in the fifteen Latin American countries involved, average confidence in the po-

lice did not exceed 28 percent. See "Espejo de las Américas" in *El Mercurio*, Economía y Negocios section, April 16, 1998, pp. 8 and 9.

3. An exception is Honduras, where the Public Security Force was separated from the armed forces through a reform process that was essentially internal, though it drew on advice from the governments of Spain and the United States (Foro Ciudadano 2000).

4. Costa 1999; Garst 1997; National Coalition for Haitian Rights 1998; Neild 1995; Serrano 1997; Riedmann 1996; Byrne, Stanley, and Garst 2000; Camacho Guizado 2000; Saín, 1999; Llorente 1999; Glebbeek 2000; Ward 2000; Smulovitz 2000; Kahn 2000.

5. The concept of majority public financing is used because of the increase in sources and resources from the private sector flowing to police forces. Examples are contributions from large companies for the construction of police stations, hiring of police officers as private guards by municipalities within the city of Lima (Rivera Paz 1998, 6–7), and payment for police guards at concerts and sporting events.

6. In recent years, external monitoring of police effectiveness has become increasingly frequent. In English-speaking countries, outside assessment of the effectiveness of specific police programs, as well as of police effectiveness in general, occurs regularly and frequently. The first type of assessment gauges a project's cost–benefit relationship, while the general type of assessment examines process and impact (Barrientos 2000).

7. The British model, in which the student police officer is trained for a number of months, followed by 3 months at a police station under the tutelage of an experienced officer, appears to be an excellent model. At the conclusion of this period of practical experience, the student returns to and graduates from the academy. During this final stage, he or she can discuss his field experience with his teachers, including the discrepancies between theoretical training received and the actual reality of the work.

8. Crime is not distributed randomly or diffusely throughout a city. The concentration of crime in central areas of a city occurs on a different "timetable" from that in residential areas. Some types of property crimes, such as residential or business burglaries, occur at fairly predictable hours of the day. Concentrations of workers and visitors within an area also tend to follow a given schedule, offering corresponding opportunities for robbery.

9. Of particular interest in terms of gaining a deeper understanding of the role of the public security advocacy is "El Defensor de Seguridad," *Milenio*, summer 1998, pp. 99–122.

10. See "Renuncia del Ministro de Seguridad y Justicia de Buenos Aires: Cambio de rumbo en la reforma policial," *Policía y Sociedad Democrática*, no. 5, 1999, pp. 6–7.

11. "Nueva estrategia: Carabineros crea oficina que prioriza denuncias vecinales," *El Mercurio* (Santiago), February 21, 2001, p. C1.

12. "Por primera vez los carabineros serán evaluados a diario por su desempeño." *La Segunda*, March 24, 2000, p. 19.

References

Arslanián, C. León. 1998. El Informe Arslanián. *Milenio* 2: 62–75.
Barrientos Ramírez, Franklin. 2000. *La gestión policial y sus métodos de evaluación.* Cuadernos del CED 34. Santaigo: CED.

Bayley, David H. 1985. *Patterns of Policing. A Comparative International Analysis.* New Brunswick, N.J.: Rutgers University Press.

―――. 1993. What's in a Uniform? A Comparative View of Police–Military Relations in Latin America. Paper presented at a conference on police and civil–military relations in Latin America, Washington, D.C., October.

―――. 1994. *Police for the Future.* New York: Oxford University Press.

―――. 1996. Measuring Overall Effectiveness. In *Quantifying Quality in Policing,* ed. Larry T. Hoover. Washington, D.C.: Bill Blackwood Law Enforcement Management Institute of Texas at Police Research Center of Sam Houston University and Police Executive Research Forum.

Bayley, David H., and Clifford D. Shearing. 1996. The Future of Policing. *Law and Society Review* 30: 585–606.

Beato F., Claudio. 2001. Acción y estrategia de las organizaciones policiales. In *Policía, sociedad y estado: Modernización y reforma policial en América del Sur,* ed. Azun Candina and Hugo Frühling. Santiago: Centro de Estudios del Desarrollo.

Bratton, William, with Peter Knobler. 1998. *Turnaround: How America's Top Cop Reversed the Crime Epidemic.* New York: Random House.

Byrne, Hugh, Stanley William, and Rachel Garst. 2000. Rescatar la reforma policial: Un reto para el nuevo gobierno guatemalteco. Washington, D.C.: Washington Office on Latin America.

Camacho Guizado, Alvaro. 2000. La Policía colombiana: Los recorridos de una reforma. Unpublished.

Cano, Ignacio. 2001. El control de la actividad policial: El uso de la fuerza letal en Rio de Janeiro. In *Policía, sociedad y estado: Modernización y reforma policial en América del Sur,* ed. Azun Candina and Hugo Frühling. Santiago: Centro de Estudios del Desarrollo.

Centro de Estudios Legales y Sociales. 2000. *Derechos humanos en Argentina: Informe anual 2000.* Buenos Aires: Centro de Estudios Legales y Sociales.

CEPES-FESPAD (Centro de Estudios Penales de El Salvador–Fundación Estudios para la Aplicación del Derecho). 2000. La Policía Nacional Civil de El Salvador, Evolución y estado actual. CEPES-FESPAD, San Salvador.

Costa, Gino. 1994. Cómo encarar la reforma policial. *Ideele* 71–72: 106–8.

―――. 1998. La propuesta de nueva ley orgánica de policía del Perú: Novedades y limitaciones. In *Control democrático del mantenimiento de la seguridad interior,* ed. Hugo Frühling. Santiago: Centro de Estudios del Desarrollo.

―――. 1999. *La Policía Nacional Civil de El Salvador.* San Salvador: UCA Editores.

Foro Ciudadano. 2000. La reforma policial en Honduras. Foro Ciudadano, Tegucigalpa.

Frühling, Hugo. 1998. Policía y consolidación democrática en Chile. *Pena y Estado* 3: 81–116.

―――. 1999. La policía en Chile: Los nuevos desafíos de una coyuntura compleja. *Perspectivas* 3(1): 63–90.

―――. 2000. La modernización de la policía en América Latina. In *Convivencia y Seguridad: Un reto a la gobernabilidad,* ed. Jorge Sapoznikow, Juana Salazar, and Fernando Carrillo. Alcalá de Henares: Inter-American Development Bank and University of Alcalá.

Garst, Rachel. 1997. *The New Guatemalan Nacional Civilian Police: A Problematic Beginning.* Washington, D.C.: Washington Office on Latin America.

Glebbeek, Marie-Louise. 2000. Police Reform and the Peace Process in Guatemala: The Fifth Promotion of the New National Civilian Police into Action. Paper presented at the Latin American Studies Association Conference, Miami, March 16–18.

Government of the Province of Buenos Aires. 1998. La transformación del sistema de seguridad. Internal document.

Goldstein, Herman. 1977. *Policing a Free Society.* Cambridge, Mass.: Ballinger Publishing Company.

Jordan, Mariana, and Cecilia Sotomayor. 2000. Seguridad ciudadana y comunidad local organizada. Estudio de los comités vecinales de seguridad ciudadana en tres comunas de Santiago. Paper prepared for the Course on Social Policy, Sociology Institute, Catholic University of Chile, Santiago.

Kahn, Túlio. 2000. Policia comunitária: Avaliando a experiencia. United Nations Latin American Institute for the Prevention of Crime, São Paulo.

Kravetz, Katharine. 1998. El control a la policía en Estados Unidos. In *Control democrático del mantenimiento de la seguridad interior,* ed. Hugo Frühling. Santiago: Centro de Estudios del Desarrollo.

LaFranchi, Howard. 1998. Latin Police Can Be Reformed. *Christian Science Monitor,* September 28.

Lapkin, Gerald S. 1998. A Globalized Approach to Public Accountability: How Citizens Can Watch the Watchmen. Paper presented at the conference Democracy and the Rule of Law: Institutionalizing Citizenship Rights in New Democracies, McGill University, Montreal, March 19–20.

Llorente, María Victoria. 1999. Perfil de la Policía Colombiana. In *Reconocer la guerra para construir la paz,* ed. Malcom Deas and María Victoria Llorente. Santa Fé de Bogotá: Ediciones Uniandes.

Mesquita Neto, Paulo. 1998. Policiamiento comunitario: A experiencia en São Paulo. Unpublished.

———. 2000. Violência e segurança pública nas grandes cidades: A experiência de policia comunitaria em São Paulo. Paper presented at a seminar of violence and security in big cities, comparative experiences of São Paulo, Rio de Janeiro, and Buenos Aires, Buenos Aires, June 20–21.

Mingardi, Guaracy. 1996. Corrupcão e violencia na policia de São Paulo. In *Justicia en la calle. Ensayos sobre la policía en América Latina,* ed. Peter Waldmann. Medellín: Biblioteca Jurídica Diké.

———. 1998. Problemas da policia brasileira. O caso paulista. *Pena y Estado* 3: 143–53.

National Coalition for Haitian Rights. 1998. Can Haiti's Police Reforms Be Sustained? Washington, D.C.: Washington Office on Latin America.

Neild, Rachel. 1995. Policing Haiti. Preliminary Assessment of the New Civilian Security Force. Washington, D.C.: Washington Office on Latin America.

Oliveira, Alicia, and Sofía Tiscornia. 1998. Estructuras y prácticas de las policías en la Argentina. Las redes de la ilegalidad. In *Control democrático del mantenimiento de la seguridad interior,* ed. Hugo Frühling. Santiago: Centro de Estudios del Desarrollo.

Palmieri, Federico Gustavo. 1998. Reflexiones y perspectivas a partir de la reforma policial en El Salvador. *Pena y Estado* 3 :313–40.

Pinheiro, Paulo Sergio. 1998. Policia e consolidacao democratica: O caso brasileiro. In *São Paulo. Sem medo*, ed. Paulo Sergio Pinheiro et al. Rio de Janeiro: Garamond.

Policía Nacional. No date. Transformación cultural. La fuerza del cambio. Policía Nacional, Bogotá.

Rico, José María. 1998. La policía en América Latina: Del modelo militarizado al comunitario. *Pena y Estado* 3 :173–87.

Riedmann, Arnold. 1996. La reforma policial en Colombia. In *Justicia en la calle. Ensayos sobre la policía en América Latina*, ed. Peter Waldmann. Medellín: Biblioteca Jurídica Diké.

Rivera Paz, Carlos. 1998. Los municipios y la seguridad ciudadana. La institución del Serenazgo en Lima. *Policía y Sociedad Democrática Boletín* 2 : 6–7.

Saín, Marcelo. 1998. Democracia, seguridad pública y policía. Centro de Estudios Legales y Sociales Working Documents of the seminar Las Reformas Policales en Argentina, part of the regional project Policía y Sociedad Democrática, Buenos Aires.

———. 1999. Sin pena y sin gloria. Colapso y reformulación del sistema de seguridad bonaerense. Unpublished.

Sandoval, Luis. 2001. Prevención Local de la Delincuencia en Santiago de Chile. In *Policía, Sociedad y estado: Modernización y reforma policial en América del Sur*, ed. Azun Candina and Hugo Frühling. Santiago: Centro de Estudios del Desarrollo.

Santos Alvins, Thamara. 1998. Policía y democracia en Venezuela. *Pena y Estado* 3: 199–218.

Schmid, Robert. 1996. La corrupción en la policía preventiva del Distrito Federal de México. In *Justicia en la calle. Ensayos sobre la policía en América Latina*, ed. Peter Waldmann. Medellín: Biblioteca Jurídica Diké.

Serrano, Rosso José. 1997. La transformación cultural en la policía. Paper presented at International Forum on Public Administration, Bogotá.

Smulovitz, Catalina. 2000. Policiamiento comunitario en Argentina, Brasil y Chile. Lecciones de una experiencia incipiente. Paper prepared for Woodrow Wilson International Center for Scholars, Washington, D.C.

Sozzo, Máximo. 1999. Informe de avance sobre el Funcionamiento de los mecanismos de control interno del servicio policial en la Provincia de Santa Fé. Paper presented at the symposium Mechanisms for Internal Monitoring of the Police, organized by Centro de Estudios Legales y Sociales and the Extension Office of the Universidad del Litoral, part of the project Policía y Sociedad Democrática, Santa Fe.

Stone, Christopher, and Heather H. Ward. 2000. Democratic Policing: A Framework for Action. *Policing & Society*, 1 : 11–45.

United Nations Office for Drug Control and Crime Prevention. 1999. *Global Report on Crime and Justice*. New York: Oxford University Press.

Ward, Heather H. 2000. Police Reform in Latin America: Current Efforts in Argentina, Brazil, and Chile. Paper prepared for Woodrow Wilson International Center for Scholars, Washington, D.C.

Zaffaroni, E. Raúl. 1993. *Muertes anunciadas*. Bogotá: Editorial Temis.

3

The Control of Police Misconduct in the Americas

Paul Chevigny

A woman is arrested by two members of the vice squad. She was charged with the offense of offering to commit prostitution with an unknown man for the sum of fifteen dollars. Her social and financial status is such as to render the charge utterly incredible. After effecting an entrance into her apartment, the police officers question her about her finances and assets for about forty-five minutes before taking her to the police station. . . . She is taken to the . . . Police Station and is there prevented from using the telephone until after she makes an arrangement with one John Steiner, a professional bondsman, for her release on bail. Before he consents to go on her bond, Steiner relieves her of her jewelry and takes it out to have it appraised. After the necessary arrangements for releasing the woman on bail have been completed, Steiner . . . states: "We fix these cases up all the time. No matter how innocent you are, you are going to get yourself in a jam and they might jail you because they all work hand in hand and they (the magistrates) will take their word."

. . .

On the day of the trial she is again called for by [the bondsman], who takes her to court, informing her on the way "It is going to be fixed and don't worry. Everything will be fixed. . . . Now don't you get excited and say anything."

. . .

At no time was she informed that she would be represented by an attorney, but when she arrived at the Court House and her case was called for trial, there was a man present who asked the policeman questions after the District Attorney had finished his direct examination. . . . All she knows is that all persons concerned were very insistent upon her maintaining silence and that at the conclusion of the officer's testimony she was told that she could go home. . . . The Deputy Assistant District Attorney . . . testified that after the conclusion of the case, he received a sum of money from the defense attorney. (From Samuel Seabury, *In the Matter of the Investigation of the Departments of the Government of the City of New York* [Seabury Report, 1932] in Chin 1997, vol. 3, 21–23)

Introduction: Police Abuse and the System of Justice

The case quoted above occurred in Manhattan some 70 years ago. The then-governor of New York, Franklin Roosevelt, together with the judges of the appeals courts, had appointed Judge Samuel Seabury in 1930 to investigate corruption in the lowest criminal courts in New York. Judge Seabury discovered a conspiracy to pervert justice among judges, lawyers, bail bondsmen, politicians, and police as well as underworld figures; he exposed it, using this case as one example of many, in his report of 1932, one of six such reports about police scandals that occurred in New York City about every 20 years in the century from 1894 to 1994.

Judge Seabury's investigation and report was the most successful of the six, even though he made few recommendations specifically about the police. He recommended instead that the lower courts be completely reorganized, with new judges appointed, that the bail system be reformed, and that indigent defendants be defended in an organized way rather than by "hangers-on" at the courts. The political situation was such that the existing lower courts were completely discredited, and the governor and superior judges were actually able to push through these reforms. The result was that the system of fixing cases in the courts largely passed away, and the practice of beating and coercing suspects to extract confessions entered a long process, over the next 30 years, toward near-extinction.

The experience of the Seabury investigation shows that police abuses of suspects may take the form of false charges or of brutality, or both, and these may be connected to acts of corruption by the police. The most important point to take from Judge Seabury's report, however, is that police abuses are virtually impossible to control if the criminal justice system as a whole tolerates or encourages them. If the prosecutor and the judge expect to take bribes and to overlook police brutality, then they rely on the police to participate, and it is sheer hypocrisy to focus criticism on the police. Conversely, if the criminal justice system sets its face against police abuses—if, for example, the courts try consistently to exclude coerced confessions—then the incidence of such abuses is going to drop.

Although the reforms after the Seabury investigation enormously improved the criminal justice system in New York City, the police misconduct that was part of the pattern has not passed away. Police brutality and corruption persist in New York and other cities in the United States, just as they do elsewhere in the Americas. One reason for the persistence is that city dwellers, as well as politicians, are not altogether sure that the abuses are a bad thing. It is important to come to grips with this political ambivalence about police abuses. We must see clearly the problems that police abuses create, for citizen security as well as for the consolidation of democracy, if we are to talk of control.

This chapter will briefly consider, in the next section, the connection between corruption and violence and the citizens' sense of security. Following that, the chapter will survey the options available in the Americas for the control of police violence, considering in turn the functions and duties of the central government as a whole, then focusing on the legislature, the courts, and, most extensively, systems of oversight and discipline. In this last connection, the chapter will take up criminal and civil liability of police personnel and/or the state for police abuses, as well as problems of administrative regulation, either within the police institution itself or from government institutions outside the police. Finally, the chapter will briefly discuss controls through international institutions.

Police Abuse and Citizen Security

Even though corruption is the most generally condemned of police abuses, it is nevertheless clear that corruption would not exist if many citizens did not want to prevent the enforcement of the laws, particularly in vice crimes like drugs and prostitution. Corruption arises chiefly because of our hypocrisy—we want to indulge the very vices that our laws forbid, but we do not want to revoke the laws. Corruption, moreover, commonly spreads throughout the political system; elected officials depend upon a percentage of the graft, for example, from gambling or drug operations. This has long been true in many cities in the United States, and it is currently a problem in Colombia and Mexico as well as other countries (for U.S. cities, see Chevigny 1995, chap. 4; for Mexico, see Human Rights Watch 1999).

It is equally clear that corruption, at least when it goes beyond a bribe to turn a blind eye to a gambling operation or the like, presents a threat to citizen security. The police take bribes to release defendants in ordinary criminal cases, such as thefts, or to return the proceeds of crime to its owners, as the civil police have done for decades in Brazil (Mingardi 1992). Thus corruption keeps predatory criminals in business. Moreover, police participate in serious crimes themselves for profit; in recent years, there have been scandals about police involvement in kidnapping rings in Brazil (U.S. Congress 1996, 344), Argentina (Chevigny 1995, chap. 7), Colombia (Arnson and Kirk 1993), Guatemala (Moore 1996), and Mexico (Dillon 1996). Kidnapping is one crime that most frightens middle- and upper-class people in Latin America; by participating in it, the police are creating the very fear and insecurity that governments claim they are trying to alleviate. This perpetuates the demand for more "tough police measures" and enables governments to promise that they will redouble their efforts to protect the citizens. Corruption creates an endless need for more police protection.

Corruption is connected to the physical abuse of citizens and interference with their human rights through the arrogance of office; in deciding whether to enforce a law or take a bribe instead, or whether to punish a person by beating him up, the police are saying that they are the bosses of the streets. They are legislature, judge, and executioner for the laws. Both the first and last investigative commissions in New York City, 100 years apart, recognized this. The 1894 report said "that the police formed a separate and highly privileged class, armed with the authority and the machinery for oppression and punishment, but practically free themselves from the operation of the universal law." The 1994 commission used very similar language (Clarence Lexow, *Report and Proceedings of the Senate Committee Appointed to Investigate the Police Department of the City of New York* [Lexow Commission Report, 1984] in Chin 1997, vol. 1, 31; Milton Mollen, *Report of the Commission to Investigate Allegations of Police*

Corruption and the Anti-Corruption Procedures of the Police Department
[Mollen Commission Report] in Chin 1997, vol. 6, 48–50). Such arrogance in law enforcement is the essence of a system that shows contempt
for democratic lawmaking and citizen participation; it tends to create fear
of the state and contempt for the law.

Corruption, moreover, strengthens a system of impunity; if all or most
police are implicated in crimes, then they must create a wall of silence
against investigation that will prevent the detection of violations of human
rights as well as acts of corruption. Acts of violence against citizens must
be concealed, because virtually all the official participants and observers
have secrets that they expect the others to preserve.

Even where corruption is investigated and condemned, there is nevertheless a persistent tolerance, in all parts of society, for some level of violence by
the police. The 1994 report on the New York police noted that superior officers at the middle level, such as sergeants, are tolerant of some "street justice"
as a means of social control, and Darryl Gates, former police chief of the city
of Los Angeles, claimed that his city was safer because the police were so
tough (Mollen Commission Report in Chin 1997, vol. 6, 49; Gates is quoted
in Skolnick and Fyfe 1993, 205–7). If we are to think intelligently about control of police misconduct, we have to decide whether this tolerance is justified. If some violence outside the law really is necessary to have order, then
police misconduct is a much smaller problem, and some "police brutality"
may be viewed sociologically as an unpleasant but necessary measure.

Is it a myth that being "tough" (in the sense of violent) tends to increase
order? In the case of the use of nondeadly force, it is difficult to determine
precisely as an empirical matter, because we do not have reliable evidence
about how much of this sort of brutality occurs; thus we cannot contrast it
with changes in the crime rate or anything else. The amount of deadly
force used by the police, however, is not difficult to determine in cities in
the United States. A series of respected studies have shown that there is no
correlation between the number of shootings by police and the arrest rate,
the crime rate (including the homicide rate), or the safety of officers (summarized in Skolnick and Fyfe 1993, 206). A moment's reflection suggests
that the same is probably true of nondeadly force, because the use of such
force is unsystematic and haphazard, just like the use of deadly force.

What the use of unjustified deadly as well as nondeadly force clearly
does create, in a society with an aggressive free press, is a sense that the police are not accountable to the law. For those whose rights are actually violated, and their friends, neighbors, and family, arbitrary violence creates a

fear and hatred of law enforcement. When other city dwellers see a video-
tape showing that the police have abused a person, or even read about it,
that increases a sense of alienation—helplessness in the face of power.

It is true that it has been reported in Brazil that videotapes and other reports of extreme police violence, such as executing suspects, have provoked widespread public approval (U.S. Congress 1996, 342). But such reactions are an indication of the low regard for the law as well as for the
police; the public is so desperate that it expects no legal redress, but only
violence. At the same time that they approve of official violence, Brazil-
ians have little confidence in the police, suppose that they are allied to organized crime, and report few crimes to them (Alencor and Godoy 1996;
Holston and Caldeira 1998). Respect for the law is damaged, and thus the
demand for more unlawful actions by officials is only increased. Moreover, all violence, but especially violence by officials, builds anxiety and
an air of crisis in society. People feel that their expectations are likely to be
disappointed; that they cannot rely on the regularity of official action. The
notion that people have rights for the violation of which they can demand
redress, which is essential to citizenship in a democracy, is weakened.

Control of Police Misconduct

Police violations of human rights can be controlled through many institutions and means. The government can set legal policies, chiefly thorough
the legislature and the courts. More important, administrative controls can
be imposed either by or outside the police, or both. The criminal justice
system can prosecute crimes by police, and the civil courts may award
damages or other redress. If all else fails, international remedies are available as a last resort.

Central Government Policy

If it is clear that the control of police misconduct is important, both for a
sense of security and for the consolidation of responsive government, it is
equally clear from instances like the Seabury investigation that such control cannot be seriously undertaken unless institutions in the government,
and especially in the criminal justice system, are consistent about opposing
such abuses. If politicians depend on police corruption or if high officials
believe, explicitly or tacitly, that police violence is necessary for social
control of the poor, then concentrating on institutions for control of police

misconduct is largely futile, although investigations by such institutions may help to reveal the dimensions of the problem.

For example, in Mexico there currently is pressure for reform and a halt to human rights abuses. But recent reports and studies suggest that corruption, particularly in the drug trade, has extended from the lowest police officer to the highest levels of government. The courts rely on abusive practices such as coerced confessions to conduct cases, and they appear to have little desire to exclude them. The prosecutor also often connives in such abuses and is sometimes involved, as are the police, in schemes to shake down suspects for payments. Defendants remain imprisoned even in cases where it is clear they have been framed. The National Commission for Human Rights, established to investigate such abuses, frequently conducts revealing investigations and sometimes succeeds in having officials disciplined. But that institution is unable to substantially reduce the abuses because the system appears to depend on them; a reform in the criminal justice system, including the judiciary as well as the prosecutors, to change the system of abuses, is required (Preston 1998; Human Rights Watch 1999; Chevigny 1995, chap. 8). Without a change in these policies, it would seem that programs focused on police "accountability" would not be likely to have favorable results.

It is thus the function of the central government, in the first instance, to establish standards for the police and oversee their work to bring them up to those standards. In Brazil, the federal government has advanced an ambitious human rights program, with many proposals for control of police misconduct. Although the program has not been adopted in its entirety by the Congress of the nation, it is creating an atmosphere more hospitable to the control of abuses. The federal government, moreover, has long had the additional power to investigate local abuses. Thus after a massacre in the house of detention in São Paulo in 1992, when the local officials failed to act against the perpetrators, the federal Council for the Defense of the Human Person reported that the prisoners had been summarily executed. The federal pressure, reflecting international scandal, had the effect of driving the São Paulo military police to reduce the number of killings. This has led to a program in which the São Paulo state administration has tried to train the military police to respect human rights (Cavallo 1997, 50–54).

Both the Mexican and Brazilian situations reflect the fact that governments in federal systems are reluctant to intrude on the prerogatives of state officials; they have nothing to gain by antagonizing police and politicians and they do not act lightly to correct abuses at the state level. In the

United States, for more than a century the federal government has had the power to prosecute local police for acts that violate constitutional rights, that is, in effect, for violation of some human rights standards. That power has been rarely used, and often only after a state prosecution has failed, as in the case of the Rodney King beating in Los Angeles, where the police involved were convicted in federal court after being acquitted in California state court. Nevertheless, the presence of the possibility of federal prosecution has caused some state prosecutors—in New York, for example—to look closely at police misconduct cases and to prosecute in clear cases for fear that the federal prosecutors might supersede them.

The Legislature

Until recent years, the United States federal government did not have the power to bring a case against police officials at the state or city level to force them to change their practices. In the Violent Crime Control Act of 1994, in reaction to the Rodney King beating, Congress finally gave the attorney general the power to bring a case to enjoin a "pattern or practice" of violating the federal Constitution or laws.[1] A group organized in the federal Justice Department, after investigating such patterns in several departments, has been able to establish standards for the administrative control of abuses; those standards will be discussed in more detail below in the section on oversight and discipline. This change in the functions of the attorney general illustrates that the potential powers of the legislature to control the police are enormous.

Lawmakers can limit police discretion, increase protection for suspects, and thus reduce police opportunities for abuse. In Argentina, Mexico, and the United States, the law limits the amount of time a suspect can be held before being brought before the court, thus making it more difficult to coerce the suspect. In Argentina and Mexico, recent legislation has rendered confessions made to the police alone, without the presence of other officials, inadmissible as evidence. Everywhere the law sets the standards by which an individual can be detained or arrested, and the standards for searching houses, tapping telephones, or otherwise intruding on privacy. Although the courts have sometimes seemed reluctant to give full force to these rights, the legislation is an essential tool; the courts have little to work with unless the law sets standards.

By the same token, the legislature may give the police very wide discretion. In the United States, the Constitution does not permit a person to be detained solely for purposes of identification, although a person may be detained briefly based on specific reasons to suspect him of a crime. In Argentina and Brazil, as well as very commonly elsewhere in the world, a person may be detained merely for identification; the police take advantage of the power and thousands of persons are detained for this reason every year. Sometimes they have been coerced and brutalized. In Buenos Aires, moreover, the police long arrogated to themselves the power to establish internal regulations, *edictos policiales*, for taking persons into custody, and the courts have not effectively denied them that power. Recently, these powers have been limited by the legislature after a long struggle by human rights advocates. It is interesting to see the effects created by the sudden visibility of the problem revealed in the legislature; the *edictos* have been replaced by *contravenciones* (violations) embodied in new laws, and the *contravenciones* have themselves become controversial either as too restrictive or too permissive.[2]

The legislature also has investigative powers incidental to its lawmaking powers. In every country in the Americas, the legislature has undertaken to look into police scandals concerning corruption, brutality, or other invasions of rights. The first major investigation of police corruption in New York City, in 1894, was undertaken by state legislators. Apart from ad hoc investigations, the legislature can establish ongoing institutions of accountability for the police, as Congress has done in the United States by empowering the attorney general to investigate patterns and practices of abuses. Thus in São Paulo (see Cavallo 1997, 14), the legislature has created an ombudsman (*ouvidoria*) to look into police abuses, which has been credited with reducing the amount of police violence in the state.[3]

Virtually all systems of accountability for the police are ultimately traceable to the legislature, either in the local or central government, which establishes the laws for reviewing police actions as well as for retaining or dismissing individual offenders. The decision whether systems of review shall be internal or external, and what form they should take, is commonly one for the legislature.

The Courts

The courts act as a control over police abuses first by enforcing the laws that protect the rights of suspects. Modern legal systems generally exclude coerced confessions as evidence at trial, for example, but the courts differ greatly in their willingness to enforce the exclusion. Through the famous *Miranda* decision, the U. S. Supreme Court has required the police to warn suspects of their right to remain silent, and the Court has imposed a burden of proof on the state to establish that contested confessions are in fact voluntary.[4] As these protections have been systematically applied in the local U.S. courts, the incidence of coerced confessions appears to have dropped enormously. In Mexico, laws have been adopted to limit the use of force to obtain confessions that are more stringent on paper than the rules in the United States; a confession made to the police alone, without the presence of the prosecutor or a judge, may not be used at trial as evidence.

Yet this right to remain silent has had limited effectiveness because prosecutors have not been careful to prevent coercion, and police have intimidated defendants into reaffirming coerced confessions before other officials. In effect, Mexican courts have accepted such confessions under older doctrines of law, and they have failed to release defendants even when it is clear that confessions have been coerced (Human Rights Watch 1999). If the courts are to play their constitutionally mandated role in the control of police abuses, it is essential that they protect the constitutional and statutory rights of suspects. The courts also play a role in the direct control of abuses by individual police through criminal prosecution and civil claims for damages, which will be considered in the next section.

Oversight and Administration of Police

Police abuses are often best controlled by regulations that minimize the situations in which abuses may arise or create bureaucratic records of such situations. Thus in the early 1970s, the New York City Police established stringent standards for the use of firearms; in addition, the police department established a protocol, still in effect, for reporting and investigating every time a shot is fired. Senior officers go to the scene, examine it, and prepare a report. Officers who are found to have violated the regulations are disciplined. These regulations caused the use of deadly force to drop precipitously in New York. As Fyfe (1979) found in a famous study, the decline in the use of deadly force did not adversely affect the crime rate, the arrest rate, or the safety of officers.

Although less thorough, a similar program is being used in São Paulo. There the military police have a program to retrain police involved in fatal shootings, in which police undergo evaluation and counseling for a period of 3 months. By analogy, the police may be required to file a written report every time they use force of any kind, whether in an arrest or otherwise. These force reports can then be used to track the use of violence by individual officers as well as by the police force as a whole.

Vehicle pursuits also give rise to acts of violence by the police, because they create danger and the person fleeing the police is literally defying authority. In the United States, vehicle pursuits are sometimes limited so that the pursuit cannot be undertaken without approval by superiors.[5]

Training in the rights of citizens, the use of firearms, and when and whether to use such arms, as well as in the principles of forensics for the preservation of evidence is essential to the control of police misconduct. Apparently such training is sadly lacking for the police in Argentina (CELS 1997, 61–62); training in the rights of citizens has begun in São Paulo.

Neither regulations nor training to minimize the risk of violence will be successful unless police executives and the government as a whole are determined to make it clear that standards that control corruption and protect the rights of citizens will be enforced. Police violations of the laws can be controlled in at least three ways: through criminal prosecution; through civil claims for damages or other relief; and, most important, through administrative oversight and discipline, which is addressed in a separate section below.

Prosecution

I have had occasion elsewhere to criticize prosecution as a way of controlling police discretion, because prosecutors can handle only a limited number of cases, the burden of proof in the criminal justice system of every country is very high (as it should be), and the likelihood of conviction depends on the luck of whether witnesses and forensic evidence can be found (Chevigny 1995, 98–99). In places where more sensitive instruments can be used, such as oversight bodies, or where police executives themselves are interested in controlling police abuses, prosecution is a very blunt instrument. Nevertheless, there are crimes so serious, as in the case of outright murder or torture, that criminal liability is clear and no lesser remedy is sufficient.

More important, in places where police executives themselves are not willing to control the violence, and other controls are weak, prosecution is the most important means of accountability. In such jurisdictions, it is necessary to protect the state's witnesses against retaliation, and a program of witness protection should be established. An example is Argentina, where criminal matters are pursued by an investigating magistrate. There the courts have grown stronger in recent years in pressing cases for torture and homicide against the police, as well as for more complex crimes linked to corruption. Most notorious is the continuing investigation into the terrorist bombing of a Jewish center (the AMIA) in Buenos Aires, in which high-ranking police in the province are accused of having participated in return for payoffs (CELS 1996, 91–111). In Argentina and Brazil, nongovernmental organizations play an important role in assisting the courts, because private parties may press a prosecution in Argentina, and in Brazil a private party may assist the prosecutor.

In federal systems like the United States and Brazil, criminal cases for violations of human rights may be used as a way of trying to bring state police up to a minimum standard, when state prosecutors will not act or have not been able to make a difference. In the United States, the federal government has the power to prosecute deliberate violations of federal civil rights, including excessive force and invasions of privacy such as unlawful searches. The government has acted in cases where the local prosecution has failed, as in the case of the beating of Rodney King, when the local prosecution was unsuccessful. In a recent report, Human Rights Watch has advocated that Brazil adopt a similar system, federalizing crimes that violate international standards of human rights (Cavallo 1997, 22).

In some countries, the courts have been structured so that it is very difficult for them to act as effective instruments of accountability for the police. In Brazil the military police, which are not really military but are organized along military lines and act as patrol police in many states, have been prosecuted in special military tribunals largely staffed by senior officers. These tribunals have shown themselves reluctant to convict police for acts performed in the line of duty, even in cases of extreme violence. Moreover, they are understaffed and underfunded, so that they are unable to dispose of the cases fast enough to act as an effective control on police violence even if their decisions were less lenient (Cavallo 1997, 22). The system of military justice is under attack in Brazil, and the legislature was asked to abolish it as this was being written.

Civil Liability

In addition to protecting the rights of suspects or trying police for crimes, the courts play a separate role in accountability when they hear claims for damages or other relief due to the abuses of police. Damage claims are available everywhere in the Americas; if it can be proved that an official has committed a tort (a noncriminal wrong) against another person, the courts will award damages. In the United States, such cases have helped establish minimum standards for police conduct. The *Garner* case held that shooting a fleeing suspect who is not armed, has not committed a dangerous crime, and does not otherwise threaten life is not justified.[6] Nevertheless, although it is important that injured parties should be compensated, with a few exceptions the civil remedies have proven to be surprisingly ineffective as an instrument of accountability. In Los Angeles, New York, and other localities in the United States, as well as in Argentina and Brazil, damages have been awarded for police abuses, but the total amount of the damages usually has not been large enough to affect the policies of the police (Chevigny 1995, 101–5, 173, 196).

This need not be the case. In Los Angeles and New York, the damages, which total many millions of dollars, are paid out of the budget for the entire municipality. If the damages were paid out of the police budget, the management response might be to change practices so as to minimize the damages. Moreover, the decision to ignore patterns of abuse disclosed in the damage cases is a policy decision by the city administrations. The lawyers for the cities have, for the most part ,simply defended the cases, without giving thought to changing practices so as to minimize the damages; this is in effect a decision to leave all police policy to the police themselves. It is certainly possible for the cities and states to use the cases as a means for drawing up new regulations for the police so as to minimize damages. This has begun to happen in Los Angeles County since the Rodney King case, where the civil claims are being monitored in an effort to reduce damages and control abuses.[7] And of course, the same can be done elsewhere in the Americas. The point is that civil damage claims cannot be part of a system of accountability unless the government and the police administration make use of them. Patterns of abuse that appear in civil cases must be stopped and individual police must be disciplined for abuses that appear in the civil cases.

In the United States, the courts have the power not only to award damages but also to order public officials to cease an abusive practice. This power seems at first glance to offer greater scope than a damage action for using the courts as an institution of accountability; lawyers in the United States have been trying for decades to bring this equitable or injunctive power to bear against police abuses on behalf of individuals or classes of private plaintiffs, with very mixed success. The courts have shown themselves extremely reluctant to act as effective sources of accountability. Congress has, however, recently given the federal attorney general, acting for the government and not as a private plaintiff, the power to bring cases to put an end to a pattern or practice of abusive police actions. Such cases have been used to set standards for adequate police administration and discipline of police personnel, thus emphasizing that the most important controls of police abuse lie in a proper system of accountability and discipline.[8]

Police Discipline and Outside Oversight

A merit-based system of advancement and a system of discipline that makes it clear that violations of rules (including rules against corruption) will be enforced are both indispensable to the control of police misconduct. In some cases in Latin America, the discipline and promotion systems appear to be arbitrary and are in any case not transparent. Discipline may be meted out, even to many officials, when there is a scandal, but the basis for the discipline is not clear. In Buenos Aires, it appears that the police disciplinary system, like the promotion system, depends on the whim of superiors and does not afford due process to the accused official. Instead, a stated system of charges and trials must be established that ensures due process to officials as well as justice to citizens. These are the minimum without which no disciplinary reform is possible.

In Brazil, police discipline has been more systematic at least in the civil police; the disciplinary officer (*corregedor*) of the São Paulo civil police worked for years in the 1980s to reduce the incidence of torture, and finally began to enjoy some success in the 1990s; the process was tolerably clear and the results were recorded (Chevigny 1995, chap. 1). Police discipline, however, is too closely connected to the criminal process in Brazil. Officers who are accused of misconduct will often be criminally prosecuted, and if the prosecution is not successful, the acquittal may act as a bar to dismissal from the police. And the criminal process, as we have seen, has often been ineffective in the case of the military police.

In the United States, the minimum exists; disciplinary procedures are clear and transparent, affording protections to the accused. Police unions are strong and have protected the rights of their members in such proceedings. Discipline is often ineffective, however, as a means of accountability. In Los Angeles, for years before the Rodney King case, there was almost no discipline for acts of violence. In New York, the system of discipline has been called "insular and arbitrary." Penalties for serious acts of brutality may be very small, whereas officers who are critical of their superiors are sometimes subjected to endless disciplinary proceedings for technical infractions.[9] Disciplinary proceedings do not yet send a clear signal that brutality against citizens is condemned as illegal and unprofessional.

In the United States, nevertheless, the politics of control of police violence has centered on disciplinary proceedings for individual wrongdoers. For decades, critics of the police have been pushing for reviews of police misconduct by an external board, a system that is commonly referred to as "civilian review." Although the controversy surrounding external review has been enormous, during the past 30 years such systems of review have become increasingly popular; in 1997 more than half of the police in the largest cities had systems of external review. It seems clear that during the same period, police practices improved; the use of deadly force decreased by half; and complaints of coerced confessions became matters of occasional scandal rather than the commonplace of police work that they once had been.

Yet these changes appear to have been either the result of oversight by the courts, in the case of confessions, or the result of changes imposed from within. The decrease in the number of shootings was brought about by stringent regulations that commanders imposed, partly to mute the constant chorus of protest against police brutality from minority communities, and thus to reduce social unrest. The external systems of review are thus part of a movement toward improved police practices, as much as a cause of them; the review boards are tolerated because police officials need better relations with their communities, and because police do not have as much to fear from review as they once had.

Although police practices have improved in the United States, it is also clear that police brutality—in the form of summary punishment meted out in the streets—as well as the abuse of deadly force have not disappeared. Incidents tend to arise when people defy the authority of the police, as the police see it (sometimes called "contempt of cop" in the United States) by arguing or starting a fight, or even by fleeing. The beating of Rodney King after a vehicle pursuit in Los Angeles in 1991 and the torture of Abner Louima, apparently after a quarrel or a fight in New York in 1997, are among the most notable examples. The persistence of abuses such as these has proved to be stubbornly resistant to systems of administrative discipline, even when those systems are external to the police.

External review boards are sometimes created during a period of scandal about the police, or during an administration in the city that is critical of the police, as in the case of New York's review board, established during the administration of David Dinkins, long a critic of the relations between the police and minority communities. They are not elected bodies; their members are usually appointed by city officials outside the police department. When the political atmosphere changes, the support for the review board weakens; thus the boards are perennially underfunded. If they become too aggressive in criticizing the police, they may be weakened still further or find that their aggressive staff members are replaced, as happened with the review board in San Diego County. If relations between the board and the police become very antagonistic, the police can virtually immobilize the board by refusing to supply any information or carry out any of the recommendations of the board.

Furthermore, in most places in the United States, the review boards only have investigative powers. In almost all places, civil service laws prescribe an administrative trial for the discipline of police, just like other public servants. Thus the review board may recommend discipline, but the department may refuse to administer it, as has happened under the review system in New York City. The systems of internal departmental discipline have all the defects noted above; superior officers are reluctant to find policemen at fault and are equally reluctant to impose severe sanctions. And even when the department decides that it wants to dismiss a police officer, the process can be very difficult. In Philadelphia, for example, officers who have been dismissed have often retained their jobs through an arbitration process that is guaranteed by their contract (Collins 1998, 331–32).

Administrative review of police misconduct confronts a dilemma. If it is external, it tends to form an adversary relationship with the police and thus becomes isolated and ineffective. If it is internal, then it tends to become socialized to police mores, and to try to protect the department from scandal. On balance, external review is the more promising approach, and in the long run it may become more effective, as departments realize that the external review system is not going to disappear and that they may actually be able to avoid scandal if they have neutral means of investigation.

Any system of discipline that is based on a case by case review of incidents involving individual officers, moreover, confronts difficulties that are characteristic of the police function. The use of force is part of police work; the police are supposed to use force when it is necessary and they cannot carry out their duties without it. In virtually every case where police brutality is alleged, the accused police officers are going to claim that the force was justified. Thus they will claim that the person injured committed some offense, if only a breach of the peace, that provoked the police to act; having done that, then they will go on to say that the person resisted arrest. The trio of charges—disorderly conduct, resisting arrest, and assault on an officer—are characteristic in the background of police brutality allegations in the United States. A version of the pattern appears everywhere; in all places, including Argentina and Brazil as well as the United States; when a suspect is shot, for example, there is invariably a claim that the suspect was armed and perhaps that there was a "shootout."

In virtually every disciplinary proceeding for an act of violence, it is necessary to determine the validity of the police claim of justification, and often to clear away the criminal charges against the person injured as well. In many cases, this is going to be impossible, because the burden of proof is inevitably on the complainant and the facts are often unclear. Thus the number of unsubstantiated cases will always be high; in the United States, only a small percentage of complaints made to review bodies, whether internal or external, are found substantiated (Chevigny 1995, 92). This creates an unfortunate situation in which police officials can publicly minimize the problem of abuse of citizens because so few complaints can be substantiated.

Discipline of individual officers, then, does not by itself offer a very effective way to control police violence. It does not follow, however, that the police complaint system is not useful in a program of control. In every case where there has been a scandal about police violence and a resulting investigation, usually by a special commission—as in Boston, Los Angeles, and New York—the investigation has found that a relatively small percentage of the police account for virtually all the complaints (Collins 1998). Thus the complaint system can be used as an "early warning system" that an officer may be headed for trouble. An early warning system is a simple administrative device; when a police officer receives a certain number of complaints within a set time—3 years, for example—then that officer is scheduled for a review, counseling, and possibly retraining.

Whether or not complaints are substantiated, then, they can be the source for monitoring particular officers and retraining them if necessary. The work of the complaint system may reveal other problems, such as recurrent patterns of actions in particular neighborhoods, or police inquiry concentrating on particular groups such as black youths. When those patterns are found, the information can be used to change the patterns of behavior. But the patterns, either of an individual or of groups of officers, cannot be used for management purposes unless the department is willing to use them.

Thus an effective review system needs to have powers beyond the mere processing of complaints. It has to have the power to collect information and to make recommendations to the department. The department has to be willing, for example, to set up an early warning system if the review body recommends it. Thus effective review requires a body that can hear complaints as well as recommend changes to the department and bring pressure to see that they are implemented. In some cities in the United States, these functions are separated. Seattle and San Jose have auditors (outside oversight boards) that can review complaints systematically and make recommendations for changes in the system. In addition, an official should be established inside the police who can explain the recommended reforms and assist the police in bringing them about. Los Angeles now has an inspector general inside the department who answers to the police commission outside the police department.

Outside oversight boards and complaint review boards that are empowered to hear and investigate complaints, and to recommend systemic changes and see that they are carried out, ought to be centered outside the police, as external bodies. They ought to have a liaison officer, like an inspector general, to see that the police carry out reforms. Moreover, their mandate ought to be extended to cover issues of corruption as well as violence, because the two are so closely associated. In New York, the City Council repeatedly tried after the most recent corruption report of 1994 to institute outside oversight of corruption in the police department, but then-mayor Rudolph Giuliani persistently resisted this change.

It is significant that police in the United States generally are opposed to the institution of inspector general or similar oversight officials answerable outside the police. The brave inspector general in the Los Angeles Police Department was recently forced to resign because of a lack of support from the civilian police commission, which wants to give a supposedly strong police chief a chance to reform the department. This is an error; police chiefs have been failing to reform from within for decades. It is a basic principle of management that an independent inspector of some sort is required; yet police in the United States have successfully avoided the requirement. It is striking that in New York City every agency headed by a mayoral appointee has an inspector general for abuses in his or her department *except for the police*. Here we see clearly that, in effect, cities perpetuate the conditions for police abuses.

It should be emphasized that reforms such as those discussed above will be possible only where there is a reasonably well-organized and transparent system of administrative discipline for police, regardless of whether it is very effective. Where, as in Buenos Aires, there is an irrational system with ill-defined procedures, it is all but impossible to use the system as a basis to develop an early warning system or other management techniques that would make it possible to control abuse. A well-organized system for taking complaints, which is known to the citizenry, is the essential first step.

The U.S. federal Justice Department has been using its power to bring cases against police departments that engage in patterns or practices of abuse, to establish standards for administrative discipline and oversight. As of this writing, the department has entered into consent decrees (negotiated court orders) for the reform of departments in two cities. These consent decrees, which are apparently intended to act as a model for other departments, establish high standards of accountability. Among the provisions are: (1) a computerized early warning system about officers, including information about civilian complaints, the use of force, and civil lawsuits—this standard will be used to collect information from civil damage claims in the courts, from internal police documents as well as from the civilian complaint board; (2) a requirement that the police prepare reports about the use of force and establish a system for tracking such reports; (3) a user-friendly and consistent system for taking and investigating civilian complaints; (4) periodic departmental audits to see that proposed reforms are being complied with; and (5) appointment of an outside oversight officer to monitor compliance with the reforms.[10] At present this relatively simple system of oversight and administration exists almost nowhere, outside the cities where the federal cases have been brought, in the United States or elsewhere in the Americas.

International Oversight

International standards exist for the use of force by police, embodied in the Code of Conduct for Law Enforcement Officials of 1979, the Basic Principles for the Use of Force and Firearms by Law Enforcement Officials of 1990, and the Convention Against Torture and Other Cruel, Inhuman, or Degrading Treatment or Punishment. In general, the use of cruel or degrading investigative methods, the use of force that is not absolutely necessary, and the use of deadly force except as a last resort, are condemned.[11]

The Convention Against Torture contains provisions for investigating allegations of torture, whereas the other two instruments have no enforcement procedures. The importance of the instruments, however, is primarily that they establish minimum standards; thus if a police department violates them, the international community may criticize it for not living up to international standards. United Nations rapporteurs as well as nongovernmental organizations periodically write reports about all the countries in the Americas, criticizing police practices under international standards. These reports exert pressure for reform, through diplomacy and publicity. Thus after the massacre at the detention facility in São Paulo in 1992, the criticism of the international community drove the federal government of Brazil to criticize the state of São Paulo, which subsequently tried to reduce the amount of police violence. In addition, claims can be brought before the U.N. Human Rights Committee against countries (not including the United States) that have accepted its jurisdiction over individual complaints. In addition, complaints can be brought to the Inter-American Commission on Human Rights of the Organization of American States. Both organizations require that domestic remedies be exhausted. Thus they are the places of last resort, if none of the remedies discussed above can be made to work in the country where the abuse has taken place.

Conclusions

The key to the control of police abuses lies, most naturally, in the management of the force. Clear guidelines for the control of force, including deadly force—with requirements that officers account in writing for every use of force—are necessary. Moreover, a well-defined, transparent system of discipline must be put in place to make sure that guidelines are complied with and that a penalty is imposed when they are violated. Even though such a system of discipline may not be very effective at first, its establishment is one of the most basic steps to control; as long as discipline remains arbitrary, vague, or political, its reform is almost impossible.

A body outside the police should investigate serious complaints of both corruption and abuse of power. But that body should never be limited to case-by-case investigation; it must look for systemic problems and patterns and make recommendations to correct them. As a simple example, such a body can usually find the police officers who are persistent violators and set them aside for special training and attention. An outside oversight board, either part of the investigative body or separate, should exist to make sure that the police respond to demands for reform. Even though it is to the long-run advantage of the police that such systemic problems should be detected and corrected, the police do not usually see the outside oversight as an advantage, and the necessary institutions will likely have to be established by the legislature.

The legislature must also act to establish limits on police discretion and criminal procedure that will balance citizen security with citizen rights. The courts must enforce the limitations on police discretion that the legislature establishes. If the Constitution protects citizen rights, moreover, the courts must protect human rights even when the legislature fails to act. The courts should always be particularly careful to exclude coerced confessions. The burden should be on the state to establish that a confession is voluntary and that human rights against unlawful searches and police violence have not been violated.

Damage recoveries against the state or the municipality or even against the individual officer should be managed so as to function as a control on police misconduct. The damages should be paid out of the police budget, and an independent investigative body should analyze the results of lawsuits systematically to see whether patterns of abuse can be stopped, or if police practices can be changed to minimize the damages. Injunctive actions against broad patterns of abuse should be authorized by the legislature and heard by the courts.

The central government should establish oversight, through the executive, to ensure that local officials observe the standards of human rights. The central government should require reports from the local governments, and it should use its power to intervene to criticize or bring an action against the local government if it does not do enough to protect local citizens. The new power of the U.S. attorney general to bring federal action against local officials for patterns of abuse should serve as a model.

Abusive officials should be prosecuted, at least when managers at the state level fail to act or when the disciplinary system fails. If lower officials will not prosecute, central or federal government officials should be authorized to bring the case. Adequate resources should be allocated for the work, including funds to protect witnesses from assault or harassment.

Notes

1. The statute granting the new power to the U.S. Attorney General is 42 US Code secs. 14141–42. See also Curriden 1996, 62–65.

2. The case of José Luis Ojeda, who was beaten, apparently for corrupt reasons, after being detained in a sweep for identification, see CELS 1997, 99–103; for the *edictos policiales*, see CELS 1998, chap. 2.

3. As was stated in note 1 above, the statute granting the new power to the U.S. Attorney General is 42 US Code secs. 14141–42. Also see Curriden 1996, 62–65.

4. *Miranda v. Arizona* 384 US 436, 1966. The leading case placing the burden on the prosecution to prove the voluntariness of confessions is *Lego v. Twomey* 404 US 477, 1972.

5. Police regulations are discussed by Walker (1993); the São Paulo regulations are discussed by Cavallo (1997, 52).

6. *Tennessee v. Garner* 471 US 1, 1985.

7. "Los Angeles Board Saves City $30M in Litigation" (Wells 1997); the reference to "city" is a misnomer; actually Los Angeles County is being discussed. Also see the semiannual reports of Special Counsel Merrick J. Bobb for the L.A. County Sheriff, 1994–98.

8. See note 3. With respect to proving a "pattern or practice," see *Rizzo v. Goode* 423 US 362, 1976; with respect to standing to challenge an abuse to which one may be subject only once, see *City of Los Angeles v. Lyons* 461 US 95, 1983. Lyons sought to enjoin the use of a potentially deadly chokehold as a police practice and was unsuccessful largely because he was unlikely to be choked again by the police.

9. For Los Angeles, see Chevigny (1995, chap. 1); for New York, see Kocienewski (1997, 1998a, 1998b).

10. *U.S. v. City of Pittsburgh, et al.* U.S.D.C. W.D.Pa. civil case # 97-0354 consent decree.

11. These instruments are set forth in United Nations 1994, vol. 1, part 1, pp. 312, 318, and 293, respectively.

References

Alenco, K., and M. Godoy. 1996. Policia de medo e corrupta, diz pesquisa. *Folha de São Paulo*, January 14.

Arnson, Cynthia, and Robin Kirk. 1993. *State of War: Political Violence and Counterinsurgency in Colombia*. New York: Human Rights Watch.

CELS (Centro de Estudios Legales y Sociales). 1996. *Informe Anual 1995*. Buenos Aires: CELS.

———. 1997. *Informe Anual 1996*. Buenos Aires: CELS.

———. 1998. *Informe Anual 1997*. Buenos Aires: CELS.

Chevigny, Paul. 1995. *Edge of the Knife: Police Violence in the Americas*. New York: New Press.

Chin, Gabriel, ed. 1997. *New York City Police Investigation Commissions, 1894–1994*. Six volumes. Buffalo: W. S. Hein.

Collins, Allyson. 1998. *Shielded from Justice; Police Brutality and Accountability in the United States*. New York: Human Rights Watch.

Curriden, M. 1996. When Good Cops Go Bad. *ABA Journal* (May): 62–65.

Dillon, Sam. 1996. In Shake-Up, Army Officers Fill Top Police Posts in Mexico City. *New York Times*, March 21, A3.

Fyfe, J. 1979. Administrative Interventions on Police Shooting Discretion: An Empirical Examination. *Journal of Criminal Justice* 7: 309–23.

Holtson, James, and Teresa Caldeira. 1998. *Law and Violence: Disjunctions of Brazilian Citizenship in Fault Lines of Democratic Governance in the Americas*, ed. Felipe Aguero and Jeffrey Stark. Boulder, Colo.: Lynn Rienner.

Human Rights Watch. 1999. *Justice Undone: Human Rights Violations and Mexico's Justice System*. New York: Human Rights Watch.

Kocienewsky, D. 1997. System of Disciplining Police Is Seen as Insular and Arbitrary. *New York Times*, December 19, A1.

———. 1998a. In Police Brutality Case, Penalty was Lost Vacation Days. *New York Times*, April 23, B1.

———. 1998b. A Police Prosecutor Asserts a Cover-Up in a Beating Inquiry. *New York Times*, April 9, A1.

Mingardi, G. 1992. *Tiras, gansos e trutas; Cotidiano e reforma na policia civil.* São Paulo: Scritta.

Moore, M. 1996. Crime Bedevils Guatemala. *Washington Post*, June 17, A10.

Preston, J. 1998. Size of Raul Salinas Secret Funds Is Doubled. *New York Times*, October 3, A3.

Skolnick, J., and J. Fyfe. 1993. *Above the Law: Police and the Excessive Use of Force.* New York: Free Press; Toronto: Maxwell Macmillan Canada.

United Nations. 1994. *Human Rights: A Compilation of International Instruments.* New York: United Nations.

U.S. Congress. House. Committee on International Relations. 1996. *Country Reports on Human Rights Practices for 1995*. Washington, D.C.: U.S. Government Printing Office.

Walker, Samuel. 1993. *Taming the System: The Control of Discretion in Criminal Justice, 1950–1990*. New York: Oxford University Press.

Wells, T. 1997. Los Angeles Board Saves City $30M in Litigation. *North County Times* (San Diego County), May 23, 1.

4

Citizen Security and Reform of the Criminal Justice System in Latin America

Mauricio Duce and Rogelio Pérez Perdomo

This chapter examines certain aspects of the relationship between citizen or personal security and the reform of the criminal justice system in Latin America. There is an abundant literature on citizen security and its associated problems of violent crime and fear of crime, as well as on judicial reform. The chapter, which falls within the tradition of "law and society" or the "sociology of law," addresses the relation between the two topics, a matter that has been explored less extensively.

Criminal justice—or, more broadly, the penal system—is generally considered to be an important part of the *social reaction* to crime and to insecurity. From a didactic point of view, such a relationship may be justified. Nevertheless, in the perspective of this chapter, the proposition that criminal justice reform is a reaction or response to what is occurring in the area of crime would be an oversimplification, and it would ignore the complexity of relatively independent social processes. What is postulated here is that both are social phenomena that, to a degree, have their own dynamics. Thus, criminal justice consists not only of law (including both principles and regulations), but also of complex social and organizational processes, and criminal activity is a social process that can only be understood in the context of legal regulations, processes, and institutions.

In the first section of the chapter, the status of the criminal process in Latin American before reform will be analyzed. To explain the current process of change in the criminal justice system in the region, it is indispensable to have a perspective on the object of reform. Further on, consideration will be given to the current status of reform and to its principal components. One of the objectives of this first section is to highlight the fact that criminal justice reform is not simply a reaction to changes in criminal activity. In the second section, a presentation will be made of the current state of knowledge regarding personal security, along with an analysis of the possibilities of reforming the criminal justice system aimed at solving some of the related social problems. Though the present authors will not attempt to analyze the reaction to reform, this will be covered briefly in the conclusion.

Reform of the Criminal Justice System

Latin American lawyers usually distinguish two elements within the general subject of criminal justice. One, which has traditionally drawn the greatest attention, is what is referred to as *criminal law*, which includes the principles and rules related to offenses and punishment. Its basic legislative text is the penal code, on which there is ample scholarly output; lawyers call this academic production *doctrine*. The other topic relates to processes or actions, ranging from the discovery of a crime to the punishment phase, the study of which is referred to as *criminal procedural law*. Its basic legislative text is the code of criminal procedure (código de enjuiciamiento criminal or código de proceso penal). In the civil law tradition, the study of this topic has traditionally been a "poor relation" of criminal law, with much less doctrine.

Both codes derive from the European tradition. They were developed in their modern form in the nineteenth century, almost simultaneously in Europe and Latin America. European penal codes quickly had repercussions in Latin America, and the concept of offense and punishment closely followed these changes, to the point that there could be considered to be a commonality of thinking on criminal law on the two continents (Jiménez de Asúa 1950). As will be seen further on, the same did not occur with codes of criminal procedure, where a dynamic completely different from the European one exists—a subject on which there continues to be confusion in traditional legal doctrine in the region, and even in comparative studies.

From the perspective of this chapter, the procedural aspect of the law is more important, because it involves the law in action. The present authors highlight the elements of the process not found in legal texts (or case files) or in what can be gleaned from courtrooms. The process that is of interest here has a broader dimension: It relates to the criminal process that begins with police action, as well as to what occurs after sentencing—the treatment of the criminal. Therefore, when reference is made to the reform of the criminal justice system, this concerns the process in the broad sense mentioned above. Criminal law, in the sense of the principles and rules that appear in the Penal Code or that have been formulated by academics or by the highest courts, is far less important than the daily actions of the police and lower court judges. These actors, in practice, define what is a crime and how to treat people accused of one.

Criminal Process before Reform

The Latin American criminal process has traditionally been defined as an "inquisitorial" process, in which the judge and the prosecutor are one. The term refers to the general design of the system and, particularly, to the role within this system of the judge, who not only is charged with trying the case, but also with directing the investigation that seeks to elicit the truth regarding the wrongful acts (Merryman 1985, 126).

In the inquisitorial process, the key individuals are the person who is accused of a crime (the *defendant*), who is being criminally prosecuted, and the judge himself. Other important roles are that of the police, who are seen as collaborating with the judge in the investigation, and that of the public prosecutor. The prosecutor is theoretically independent and represents society. His role is to formulate charges, if he believes that the accused has committed the crime, and to request a sentence. Finally, there is the person defending the accused. The role of the defense in the inquisitorial process, however, is limited. The accused is conceived as an object of the process more than a subject with rights. Thus, the investigation (*sumario*, or pretrial proceeding) is secret, even to the accused. The suspect may be detained and questioned, even though he may not be informed of the crime of which he is being investigated. The length of time for which he may be detained is limited, and the investigation must end in a committal order, which may be designated as an arrest order if the judge orders so-called preventive detention.

In the inquisitorial process of the late Middle Ages, and the so-called *ancien régime* in Europe, torture was commonly used to obtain reliable information, and the judge could issue a sentence without the accused having any real opportunity to defend himself (Tomás y Valiente 1969, 182ff.). Subsequently, such an opportunity was established during a stage in the process at which the suspect was informed of the reasons for his arrest, charges were made, and the defendant was permitted to present arguments and evidence.

This second phase, which theoretically includes trying or arguing the case, is referred to as the trial (*plenario*). Unlike the pretrial proceeding, it is public. Nevertheless, in practice, the extent to which this is "public" in nature is confined to the ability of the defendant to obtain limited access to the case documents. The public may also, except in certain cases, attend court proceedings and review official case records and documents. In many of the region's countries, this phase of the process consists of dealing with a set of written records, with no real confrontation between the parties in the presence of the judge, and with no real opportunity to examine and cross-examine witnesses. In most Latin American countries, there is no provision for oral proceedings in the sense in which that concept is generally understood today (Binder 1993a, 69; 1993b, 219).

The common-law criminal process was quite different. It did not include the inquisitorial process, which was a European innovation that began in the fourteenth century. The process that developed in England has been called "accusatorial." Originally, it began with an accusation by a private individual, though today a representative of society (a prosecutor) may also initiate it. The judge acts as a director or referee of the oral, public, adversarial proceeding, and the jury makes the decision. It should be noted that the prosecutor plays a very important role: He initiates the process with lodging charges, and he is responsible for providing proof.

In the wake of the French Revolution and liberalization in Europe during the early nineteenth century, the European criminal process introduced important changes. These provided better guarantees of the right to a defense, creating the modern prosecutor, establishing the adversarial oral proceeding as a central part of the process, and instituting the use of juries in many cases. Hence, reference is made to a "mixed" process, with inquisitorial and accusatory elements. Inquisitorial elements dominated in the investigative (*sumario*) phase, whereas accusatory aspects prevailed in the *plenario* phase.

Latin American codes of criminal procedure, though adopted by most of the countries in the second half of the nineteenth century—that is, after the reform in Europe—remain more closely linked to the previous inquisitorial tradition. In most of the region's countries, the prosecutor has (or had) a very minor role. Although the prosecutor presents the charges, the judge is not limited by them. The prosecutor may also present new evidence, and the judge is also empowered to do this, because it does not conflict with his role as a truth seeker. The limited role of the prosecutor in the context of the Latin American inquisitorial process led Chile, in 1927, to eliminate this institution and give the judge the entire responsibility for investigating, formulating, and deciding the case. In other countries, the existence of prosecutors has remained little more than a formality (Duce 1999, 56ff.).

In a number of countries, such as Chile, Paraguay, Uruguay, and Venezuela, no distinction was made between the examining magistrate, who is responsible for the investigation, and the judge, who issues the ruling. This distinction was considered very important in Europe, where these functions were separated to promote the impartiality of the court (Duce 1999, 37ff.). Only a very few countries (including Colombia and the Dominican Republic) have institutionalized juries in a more or less permanent fashion, though a number of countries have used juries, or had legislation calling for them, for certain periods of time. These factors have led to a concentration of functions in the person of the criminal judge, a situation to which it is difficult to find a parallel in other regions.

Another feature of the Latin American criminal process is its written nature. Judicial proceedings are formalities that often merely involve reading or obtaining documents prepared by the parties or by the judge. Thus, the case records are the central element of the process, and in practice there is very little contact between the accused and the judge. Indeed, many sessions that, according to the code, are supposed to be presided over by the judge are not, but instead take place before a court employee. The judge later signs his name as if he had been present. This is what is known as the "delegation of judicial functions," and it has been one of the most extensive problems of the inquisitorial process in Latin America (Binder 1993b, 205).

This emphasis on written formalities gives the process an extremely formalistic character. If the judge does not sign the transcript of the proceeding, the hearing is null and void. The absence of the judge from the hearing, however, does not affect its validity (as long as he signs the transcript;

Duce 1999, 49). The process primarily involves voluminous documents (the case file), rather than oral proceedings. As we have indicated, there generally has not been an oral, public, adversarial trial process in Latin America, even at the trial phase itself. This is a fundamental difference with the reform process that began to be implemented in Europe in the nineteenth century.

One final feature that should be pointed out is the ability to appeal the many decisions that are handed down during the process. This is, to an extent, a way of checking the power of the presiding judge, giving greater power to the higher-court judges. For the most important decisions, the higher-court judge plays an obligatory role through a process called "consultation," even if the parties do not appeal. This is also typical of the more traditional inquisitorial process and reflects a preference for having in place a hierarchy that provides monitoring of judges by their superiors, emphasizing the hierarchical, pyramidal structure of the system in the region.

An inevitable question is why Latin American countries remained so linked to the inquisitorial tradition and did not adopt the innovations of European countries, which in other respects often served as their models— particularly with regard to substantive criminal law. The differences in Europe, as has been noted, involved guaranteeing greater right to a defense, relative limitations on the power of judges, the introduction of oral proceedings, and rules providing for juries or citizen participation in the trial process.

The answer to this question may vary somewhat from country to country. But in general, the differences between Latin American and Europe show the relatively minor importance or effect of the penal code on the criminal process itself, with regard to punishment. For example, in 1924, Peru adopted the Swiss penal code, which was the most innovative and liberal in Europe. However, the two societies were very different. Specifically, Switzerland did not have Peru's extensive illiterate, indigenous population (which the code classified as savages, semicivilized, and civilized for the purposes of criminal responsibility), nor did Peru have the capacity to make major investments in the treatment of convicts, as did Switzerland. Consequently, the penal code, as understood and applied in Peru, became much more repressive than it had been as understood and applied in Switzerland (Hurtado Pozo 1997).

With regard to codes of procedure, proponents in several countries explicitly stated that, due to the difference in the level of civilization in the respective societies, innovations that were common in Europe could not be introduced in Latin America. What, precisely, was the nature of this difference? The answer centers on the fact that, due to the composition of Latin American society, the small Europeanized elite felt that providing too many guarantees to protect the rights of suspects—who were generally from less-educated social groups and supposedly had a greater propensity for criminal activity—could be a hindrance to ensuring social order.

Similarly, the elite feared that instituting juries in which common people—who would likely be less educated and more prone to criminal activity—would render judgments on the accused could result in excessive leniency for those guilty of criminal activity. The numerous avenues for appeals or consultation also reflect a desire to exert control, even over judges, to prevent them from deviating from the standards. These motives were disguised in various ways. In Chile, for example, it was argued that the country's poverty and the isolation of vast portions of its territory made it impossible to implement a more civilized system.

Two things should be noted here. First, the basic system involving an inquisitorial phase, adopted by Latin American countries during the codification process in the nineteenth century, is an extension of the system employed during the colonial period. Second, this system has prevailed in the region without major modification up until the current process of reform, in which substantial changes have been introduced, as will be seen below. This is not simply the result of inaction or neglect. In fact, during the twentieth century, most countries of the region implemented reforms, which generally did not involve significant changes in the inquisitorial system that was in effect. The inquisitorial system thus can be said to have been in effect in Latin America for nearly 500 years.

The discussion above sketches the broad outlines of the Latin American penal system and offers a general sociopolitical explanation for why the most repressive features of the inquisitorial system were retained. The divergence of the Latin American penal system from the European normative model is related to the sociopolitical factors mentioned. Two specific features, which could be considered dysfunctional, should be noted: the excessive length of trials and the high number of persons who are imprisoned without having been sentenced. These features are not exclusive to Latin America, because many countries in other parts of the world, including those with different types of systems, are subject to the same criticism.

However, the design of the inquisitorial system represents one important cause of the penal system's dysfunctional features. Along with this ideological element, the dysfunctionality may, to a great extent, be explained by the way trials in the region are conducted. Trials are presided over by judges and others within the system according to a routine characterized by negligence and slowness, which may even ignore the time frames formally established in the codes. This situation is altered only when there are lawyers or others capable of exerting pressure to expedite particular cases (Pérez Perdomo 1989, 1995).

The high number of defendants in detention (generally above 50 percent), referred to as "unconvicted prisoners" (Carranza et al. 1983), is another factor partially associated with this circumstance. Technically, these are innocent persons, because they have not been convicted. It should be noted, however, that at any given time in any criminal justice system, a number of persons being processed by the courts are in detention because they are accused of serious crimes and the authorities believe there is a risk that they may not appear for trial. The anomaly is that the vast majority of those in prison are defendants, not convicts. This demonstrates that there is a highly repressive mentality in the legislation and among judges, one that favors prison rather than other guarantees and involves a lengthy trial process.

The confluence of these two factors is inevitable: A highly repressive but expeditious system will produce far more convicts than defendants, whereas an inefficient process will only produce a large number of defendants in prison if judges frequently resort to preventive detention. These features are not exclusively the result of the inquisitorial system. Rather, they relate to the central belief that those being processed by the criminal justice system are dangerous to society, unless their social connections prove otherwise, and they must therefore be disciplined beyond the strict provisions of the law.

Another important dysfunctional element, which indicates the extent to which this judicial model is removed from everyday reality, is the central importance of the police—for in practice, the police, not the judge, direct the investigation. The police only appear before the judge to justify a detention already in force or to obtain authorization for some future action, such as the search of a home. Otherwise, the police gather circumstantial and other evidence and—at the point the police consider the case to be "solved"—present the case to the judge and the defendant. The system creates a certain solidarity between judges and the police in carrying out their respective duties. A number of empirical studies indicate that judges exercise little or no oversight of police activity, even in cases where there are complaints of psychological or physical pressure being applied (Rico

1985; Jiménez 1994, 212ff.). As will be seen, this police role, along with the relation between the work of the police and that of judges, results in major abuses.

Reform of Criminal Procedure

The foregoing describes the criminal trial system, which most Latin American countries are changing or anticipate changing in the near future. There has been an accumulation of criticism of the criminal courts, coming from experts in the field, who are concerned about its backwardness compared with that of Europe, and from human rights advocates, who are concerned with abuses and a lack of guaranteed rights, both in trials and in detention centers (Zaffaroni 1986).

The first code of criminal procedure in the region to undergo significant change affecting the prevailing inquisitorial system was that of the province of Córdoba, Argentina, which introduced oral proceedings in 1939. Other Argentine provinces followed this example in subsequent years. In 1972, Costa Rica reformed its criminal justice system, largely following the Córdoba model. In 1986, Argentina's proposed federal reform of criminal procedure (known as the Maier reform) was published, and it has been extremely influential, serving as the basis for a model code proposed in 1988 by the Instituto Iberoamericano de Derecho Procesal. Both of these texts have been used as the basis for new codes in the region.

The reform movement accelerated greatly in the 1990s. Colombia's reform and the federal Argentine reform entered into force in 1992, and that of Guatemala took effect in 1994. Reforms in Costa Rica and El Salvador entered into force in March and April 1998, respectively, and Venezuela's reform took effect in July 1999. Bolivia, Chile, and Paraguay and have proposals awaiting legislative approval, and almost all other Latin American countries have ongoing debates and various types of proposals (Duce 1999, 70ff.).

It should be noted that in many countries reform is not seen simply as a legislative change in criminal procedure but also as a change in the entire criminal justice system. Thus, there are reforms or adjustments to the reforms. Colombia and the federal Argentine system, for example, have reached this phase, which can be conceived of as one of further reform and corrective adjustments to the initial reforms.

These reforms in the different countries are not independent of each other. The central ideas are the same: to shift from the inquisitional system to one with prominent elements of the accusatorial system—with oral proceedings; an enhanced role for the prosecutor; the recognition of suspects', defendants', and victims' rights; inclusion of the principle of timeliness; and so on. It is not a coincidence that this commonality exists. There is a broad awareness among reformers of the ideas and text of the model code proposed by the Instituto Iberoamericano. Various countries in the region have customarily called upon such widely recognized intellectual authorities as Julio Maier and Alberto Binder to help design reforms, and thus these experts have had a major impact on the reform movement in the region.

The reform movement does not draw only on intellectual strengths. A number of international and multilateral organizations have been providing economic support and technical assistance. In the 1980s, the United Nations Latin American Institute for the Prevention of Crime and the Treatment of Offenders (ILANUD) became a center of support for judicial reform. In a number of countries, the U.S. Agency for International Development has collaborated actively, whereas in other countries European cooperative organizations have been the most active in providing technical assistance and financial resources. Recently, the World Bank and the Inter-American Development Bank made large investments in or loans to countries to accelerate the reform process (though their cooperation has focused generally on the region's legal system, not specifically on criminal justice).

Reform is not concentrated exclusively on criminal court procedures. Prosecutors, public defender systems, the police, and prisons receive increasing attention. Furthermore, this reform is seen as part of a more general reform involving civil justice, and even the legal system as a whole (Frühling 1997). One of the central ideas underlying the reform process is that the world economic order, with its market orientation and with foreign investment as a driving force behind the development of the so-called emerging markets, requires this integral reform of the legal system to ensure the juridical security of citizens and, more specifically, of investors (Pérez Perdomo 1995). This thinking has clearly motivated multilateral banking institutions to become involved in the region's legal systems.

However, there are also other important factors and forces at work. These include the democratization process in various countries following decades of dictatorial or authoritarian rule, criticism of obsolete political systems in other countries, pressures to modernize the state overall, reassessment of the role of human rights, negative perceptions of the judicial system, and, particularly, negative perceptions of the criminal courts. It is difficult to identify reform with any single one of these factors, for it represents a response to all of them, with varying emphases in each country of the region.

Citizen Security and the Impact of Criminal Justice Reform

The objective here is not to analyze this vast legal reform process, but rather to pose a question: To what extent can criminal justice reform influence personal security in the Americas? This section examines the relationship between the reform of the criminal justice system and citizen security in Latin America. As has been indicated, the literature on this subject referring to the region, is not extensive. This is particularly true in relation to the potential impact that reform can have on problems of citizen security, such as an increased fear of crime on the part of the people and attempts to combat some of the more violent forms of criminal behavior.

The analysis is divided into two subsections. The first examines the various and complex dimensions of citizen security in the region, looking at the overwhelming scope of the issue and some of its main features. The second presents a number of ideas on the relation between criminal reform and citizen security.

The Complex Nature of Citizen Security

It is safe to say that personal or citizen security is perceived as an important problem in Latin America, though the intensity of the concern varies according to the country. The first element involved is the amount of crime, particularly violent crime. There are numerous national or city-specific studies on this subject. It is sufficient here to emphasize the concept that citizen security (or more precisely, insecurity) is determined by the number of incidents of violent crime. A small number of studies take the opposite approach, in which the perception of security is socially constructed. Thus, it is not simply the number of violent criminal incidents that creates the perception. This chapter attempts to examine both of these issues in relation to criminal justice reform.

On the basis of the volume and extent of criminal activity shown in both published studies and work in progress, in can be stated that Latin America, as a region, is extremely violent compared with Asia, Australia, Europe, and North America (e.g., see chapter 5 of this same volume). The comparison is generally based on average homicide rates—the violent crime that is used as a primary indicator—because statistics on homicide tend to be more reliable than do those on other crimes. The regional average is 20 homicides per 100,000 inhabitants a year, approximately three times the figure for the United States—which, in turn, is double that of Western Europe. There is a huge spread within the region. Figures for Argentina, Chile, and Costa Rica are comparable to those for Europe, whereas those for Colombia and El Salvador are several times the regional average. Those for Brazil, Mexico, and Venezuela are close to the regional average (Frühling 1997; Ayres 1998).

One important feature of violence in the region, vital to understanding the complexity of the issue, is the institutional or institutionalized aspect of the phenomenon. Police in the region are well known for persistent excesses that generally constitute serious violations of human rights (Chevigny 1995; Jiménez 1994). In periods of dictatorship, these excesses are the result of government policy designed to eliminate or control the opposition, but abuse also exists in relation to common criminals in both democratic and dictatorial regimes. Deaths in "confrontations" with police are frequent, as is torture. So-called confrontations with police are actually ways of disguising extrajudicial executions, as is reflected by the fact that the criminals (or supposed criminals) are rarely wounded, and the police are rarely killed or wounded. Torture and abuse continue to be a frequent investigative tool for common crimes. Their purpose is to obtain confessions that make it easier to obtain a conviction.

This type of violence has been called institutional because it is carried out by a government institution and is consonant with the policy (generally not explicit) of the police and the political elements that oversee them. One type of nonviolent institutional crime is the bribe (*mordida*, as it is known in Mexico, or *matraca* in Venezuela). In general, this involves modest sums of money, which the police demand from citizens to forgive real or imaginary violations, and which technically constitute extortion. Superiors are aware of these practices, and agents must sometimes share the money with them. There was a practice among the Buenos Aires police, for example, where court files were overseen by the police and were sometimes sold to the parties involved. Such situations, along with other corruption and abuse, have motivated a series of restructuring and reforms, which have not always been entirely successful.

Apart from these clearly institutional cases, or cases where institutions are being subverted, a number of crimes are committed directly by police groups, generally without authorization from their superiors. Police groups form death squads that carry out what they consider social cleanup operations in their free time. They murder small-time criminals, including children and young people. Police crimes also include kidnappings, drug trafficking, and auto theft. Obviously, this is organized crime that, to a degree, uses the police organization, its weapons and privileges; however, there is less institutional responsibility in these cases than, for example, in cases of torture, where there is an *institutional* purpose.

Police crime is not limited to Latin America. Many, if not all, societies, have or have had such problems (Chevigny 1995; Henshel 1996). It is the extensiveness of the phenomenon that is unique to Latin America. Possible explanations include the complicity of judges, which can be caused by the type of inquisitional process described above, and the inefficiency of the system in carrying out formal punishment of criminal activity. Marked social stratification, where the welfare and lives of disadvantaged social groups are devalued, and a lack of democracy and civility may also be explanatory factors. In many cases, there is also a legacy of nondemocratic periods of government when the police had carte blanche to carry out these practices or were expressly ordered to do so.

This brings us to the second element or dimension of citizen insecurity to be examined. Insecurity is a function not only of the number of violent crimes committed, but also of the manner in which the phenomenon of crime is experienced in the society. Fear is socially constructed (Zubillaga and Cisneros 2001; Pérez Perdomo 1997). The relative independence of insecurity as a function of the incidence of crime and insecurity as a social construction can be seen in a study showing similar levels of insecurity or fear in parts of Venezuela that have very different incidences of crime and violent crime (Navarro and Pérez Perdomo 1991). The image of the criminal is also significant. From the standpoint of middle- or upper-class Caracans, criminals (*malandros*) live in the *barrios* and have the look of lower-class people, and thus the fear of crime is largely fear of those who are perceived as "not one of us." To people of a lower class, the *malandros* live in the *barrios*, just as they do, but are perceived as dressing better, with brand-name clothes (Zubillaga and Cisneros 2001). In Chile, the view of experts is that increased fear of crime in recent years is not related to an objective increase in crime (Mera 1992, 12; Riego 1999). Thus, the perception of insecurity is not necessarily associated with the statistical probability of being the victim of a violent crime, but rather with the social construction of the problem and with citizens' perception of the probability of being victimized.

This construction can come about in various ways—through interpersonal communication, the social communications media, and in the same way that society produces crime itself. This last factor deserves special emphasis. When a large segment of the population believes that the police are not interested in responding to the collective needs of the people or, worse, when the police themselves are involved in criminal activity, confidence in the institution is negatively affected and the police themselves become a source of insecurity. This is certainly the case in a number of Latin American countries. In at least three cities with high violent crime rates—Cali, Caracas, and Rio de Janeiro—more than a quarter of those interviewed considered the police to be "bad" or "very bad" (Briceño León, Carneiro, Vélez, Oviedo, and McAlister 1997).

Further, the people do not view judges as protectors of their rights nor as monitors of potential police abuse, because they do not, in fact, act as such. Judges are distant figures who speak a strange language and whose rulings are incomprehensible. They can allow dangerous criminals, who have been convicted in the media, to go free, while at the same time they can impose severe sentences on people who are regarded sympathetically. Opinion polls in Latin American countries show very low confidence in judges—generally less than 30 percent—whereas industrial countries generally have confidence levels above 40 percent, and sometimes more than 60 percent (Martínez 1998).

Two recent surveys in Venezuela and Chile are striking in this respect. According to a United Nations Development Program survey carried out in Venezuela during January and February 1998, 85 percent of the population lacks confidence in the administration of justice (UNDP 1998, 147ff.). According to another Venezuelan study, half of the population of Caracas considers the courts to be ineffective or extremely ineffective, and 36 percent consider them moderately effective. Half of the population also felt that people should take justice into their own hands (Briceño León, Camardiel, Avila, DeArmas, and Zubillaga 1997).

A prolonged conversation that one of the present authors had with a prisoner in Caracas is indicative of this feeling. The prisoner indicated that he knew he would not be in prison if he had money. In response to the question of how he would use money to gain his freedom, he said he had no idea, but that he knew he could solve his problems with money. In other words, he did not understand how the machinery of the system functioned, but he believed that it was a system in which money could make things happen. The general population also lacks an understanding of the purpose of the process and of its basic rules.

This explains the ambivalent social reaction to crime and to the police. In general terms, the populations of various Latin American cities with high violent crime rates are willing to accept illegal conduct by the police, such as searches of homes and detention on the mere suspicion that a person may be a criminal. This is not universal, however. In those countries that most recently have had military dictatorships, illegal conduct by the police is less accepted than in countries with a stronger democratic tradition. In other words, the memory of excessive repression counterbalances the desire for order at any cost.

Attitudes toward capital punishment are similar. In most Latin American countries, capital punishment is prohibited by the constitution but enjoys considerable popular support. The degree of this support would appear to be incompatible with the lack of confidence in judges and courts, which would be responsible for administering the death penalty. One wonders whether this support is actually support for extrajudicial execution (Holston and Caldeira 1998). The fact that the population is also distrustful of the police only increases the perplexity engendered by this phenomenon. The present authors' hypothesis relates, above all, to people's inconsistent reactions to social problems. Faced with an increase in violent crime, the death penalty solution seems appropriate. But delving deeper, one sees that there is a lack of confidence in any institution regarding the application of the death penalty. To the thoughtful observer, the contradiction is clear, but it does not appear to pose any problem to those answering questions spontaneously and without reflection.

Evidently, the problem of citizen security has various dimensions that go beyond the responsiveness of the criminal justice system. Hence, one could conclude that reform of the criminal justice system cannot satisfy all the social demands created by the problems of objective and subjective insecurity. This does not mean, however, that reform cannot produce significant improvements in the current situation, an issue to which we now turn.

Procedural Reform of Criminal Justice Systems as a Response to Citizen Security

In the context given above, what are the implications of reforming the criminal justice system for the problems associated with citizen security? Because there is such widespread discontent regarding lack of security and the functioning of the courts and of the police, reform is welcomed. Reform enlists distinguished jurists, who propose modernizing criminal justice procedures, introducing rights for suspects and defendants, promising greater efficiency in criminal prosecution, and attempting to dissociate the bench from the police. Reform is based not only on the intellectual prestige of its proponents but also on the support of international organizations and multilateral banking institutions. The situation is—to indulge in a metaphor—like a honeymoon where the newlyweds are happy and have high expectations of each other. As we shall see, inflated expectations constitute one of the most serious obstacles to achieving reform in the near future.

One common phenomenon in recent years in the region is citizens' increased demands on the authorities in problems relating to citizen insecurity. The topic has become one of the most important elements in public discourse and political debate. The press has adopted it as one of its favorite subjects. Almost all the governments in the region have agendas that include policies to combat the problem. Opposition parties, which generally blame the government for not being able to deal with the problem of crime, exploit the discontent of large segments of the population. In this context, governments and politicians of all political persuasions are beginning to use the reform of criminal justice procedures as one of the major issues for institutional action. Faced with social pressure, politicians and people in power are turning to a new institutional response to solve the problems: reform of criminal justice procedures, which thus conveys to the public that they are concerned with solving the people's problems through the implementation of effective mechanisms.

This should not be considered an entirely false response. The improvement of criminal justice procedure is one of the most important institutional reforms being undertaken by governments in the region. Its importance relates not only to the changes in institutional architecture involved, but also to the extensive human and material resources being invested in the effort and its potential impact on the institutional system. In this sense, it is understandable that politicians would attempt to gain the greatest possible advantage from such reform. In terms of modern policymaking, it is also reasonable to try to solve various social problems with more holistic approaches that include the criminal justice system. This is particularly relevant in light of the fact that at least some of the problems regarding citizen security are related to the criminal justice system, and it therefore seems justified to demand that this subsystem of the government address the issue.

Problems arise, however, when officials claim that reform of the criminal justice system is "the answer" or when reform is presented by officials, and by politicians in general, as a panacea that will solve all the problems.

Unfortunately, this seems to be the prevalent attitude in the region. One indication of this is when officials say that the reforms will make it possible to punish more criminals more quickly, thus increasing the cost of crime and reducing crime rates—for example, in the Explanatory Introduction to the Organic Code of Criminal Procedure in Venezuela (analyzed in Pérez Perdomo 1998). This does not mean that reform should not legitimately seek to make the criminal justice system more efficient in prosecuting and punishing crimes. The point being made here is that the reform of rules alone does not necessarily increase efficiency, nor does it automatically translate into a significant improvement in citizen security, as will be seen below.

The main negative result of this attitude is the unduly optimistic expectations it creates as to the real possibility of bringing about significant change in the short term. These high expectations can lead to frustration when the reform fails to produce the quick results that people had expected, creating a serious risk that the reform process will be reversed. Reform requires major efforts regarding implementation and substantial support from the community and political authorities. If citizens are dissatisfied with the lack of significant progress and thus exert pressure on politicians and the government, counterreform will rear its head precisely at the point when the reform process is most vulnerable.

As has been shown, reform has a limited ability to solve the social problems that surround citizen security, since the causes of these problems clearly exceed the reach of the criminal justice system. Even within the sphere of the criminal justice system, where reform can make important contributions, there are at least three obvious obstacles. First, experience in various countries of the region, where reforms have been in place for some years, demonstrates that the process of change is slow and that immediate results cannot be expected during the period of adjustment. Because of the magnitude of the institutional, legal, and cultural change involved in bringing about reform, it would be naive to expect the system to produce dramatic results overnight. The process takes time and requires changes in attitudes, as well as the retraining of judges, judicial system employees, and members of police organizations (Pérez Perdomo 1998).

Second, the chances that reform will produce concrete improvements in citizen security depend on structural changes in the criminal justice system, on designing and implementing specific programs to achieve highly circumscribed objectives, and on reorienting institutions within the new structure to address the specific objectives. Reform in the countries of the region appears, however, to have been designed, implemented, and adjusted without taking these factors into consideration. Thus, even with rationally implemented reform, the new system will do less to solve the problems than if efforts were directed more specifically at this issue. The result may even be counterproductive, increasing inefficiency and contradictions within the system.

Third, reform has not included changes to the police, the part of the institutional system that has been identified as one of the sources of the problem of citizen insecurity. Unfortunately, police reform has not been a focus of attention in criminal justice reform in the region (Rusconi 1998, 189; Duce and González 1998, 51), thus substantially limiting the likely effects of changes in the judicial system. There has also been insufficient attention to problems of treatment and punishment.

In short, certain sectors offer unrealistic expectations of what they can deliver in terms of reform. With regard to the reform that can realistically take place, there also has been a lack of real support. In this sense, reform is caught in a very difficult situation.

Can reform actually contribute to citizen security? In the present authors' view, reform can make important contributions, within the limited sphere of action of the criminal justice system, in combating the problems of citizen insecurity and crime. However, this is not a direct, immediate consequence of reform, but rather it requires a number of other elements.

First, as Currie (1998, 163) has stated, despite the limited ability of the criminal justice system to prevent crime, its potential for reducing crime rates is greater than results achieved so far would indicate. Currie's view is that the criminal justice system must be reoriented to include greater efforts toward prevention, rather than the current punishment-oriented approach, as well as toward a policy of reintegrating criminals into society, rather than segregating them. According to Currie, a criminal justice system based on these principles has a greater chance of providing effective alternatives for citizen security than the traditional strategies based on the suppression of crime and criminals, which have prevailed in the United States during the past few decades, without any significant success.

Currie develops these ideas in detail, arguing that three vital areas of the system must be reoriented to achieve results: increasing investment in rehabilitation programs, reformulating the objectives and forms of sentencing, and reducing violence in the community by designing more effective policing strategies. For each of these areas, Currie gives extensive examples of various programs implemented in the United States that show the success of an alternative to the punitive approach. Without detailing each of these proposals, it is important to emphasize that with a different concept of the system and with programs designed specifically to achieve concrete and measurable results, modest but highly significant advances can be achieved in the area of prevention.

By transposing Currie's proposals to the context of reforms in criminal justice procedure in Latin America, progress could be expected, provided that there is an appropriate reformulation of the roles played by the various protagonists in the new criminal justice system. Thus, for instance, reorienting the system to emphasize the reintegration of offenders into society requires commitment and coordination on the part of prosecutors and judges, keeping these objectives firmly in mind. Procedural mechanisms—such as alternative release programs—which have a role in most of the region's reforms, must also be implemented and utilized in a manner consistent with the objective of social integration. The system must have a much more sophisticated ability to differentiate between various types of offenders and crimes, so as to provide more varied and flexible alternatives for offenders with a high likelihood of being successfully reintegrated. If the system is unable to make this differentiation at a very early stage, there is far less chance of achieving positive effects from proactive intervention.

Another study deserving of attention is that of Riego (1998). Though it deals specifically with Chile, the ideas it presents can readily be extended to most countries of the region. According to Riego, the reform of criminal procedure can have a positive effect by attacking the principal factors responsible for people's perception of insecurity. As has been mentioned, perceived insecurity is not caused only by objective crime conditions but also by a number of other factors.

Riego suggests two lines of action for reform to pursue in combating this social perception of the insecurity phenomenon. First, to a great extent, the problem relates to a perception of disorganization, corruption, and ineffectiveness in the criminal justice system, as regards its basic ability to deal with crime. This increases people's sense of vulnerability to crime. Riego argues that improving organization and professionalism in the system and facilitating the effective processing of complaints—with authorities responding to each complaint—could substantially improve the perception. Closely connected to this is Riego's argument that another source of the problem is how crime victims perceive their experiences within the judicial system. Riego suggests that improving the treatment of victims could produce substantial improvement in how the system is perceived.

Reform offers ample opportunity to develop programs providing information, protection, and reparation for victims, features absent from the region's traditional inquisitorial systems. Nearly half of the criminal codes that have been approved or are in the process of being approved in the region include such provisions. Efforts must be made to refine the implementation of such measures, so that they do not become mere rhetoric by legislators.

A second suggestion by Riego is to involve prosecutors in formulating local crime prevention policy. On the basis of experiments in the United States and acknowledging that the prosecutor is not the key player in these efforts, Riego (1998) proposes that prosecutors be involved in designing and conducting local crime prevention programs. He argues that the most successful experiences in preventing crime involve working in particular locations and addressing specific social and urban conditions that lead to crime and citizen insecurity. Prosecutors can reinforce the work of local communities in identifying conditions and places that are a source of problems. They can also collaborate by using the system's punitive resources, as necessary, in the most extreme cases, as a complement to prior action taken by local authorities and communities.

As with Currie's proposals, this second line of action suggested by Riego presupposes a change of orientation on the part of the criminal justice system, particularly in the policy of the public prosecutor. Prosecutors must consider community-based prevention a priority in investing economic and human resources.

Beyond the specific content of the proposals briefly summarized here, the proposals suggest three important factors to be considered in future reform of the region's criminal justice systems. First, they demonstrate that reform can improve citizen security. Second, they highlight the fact that these contributions become especially important if the role of the system and of its protagonists is conceptualized within a broader framework than the traditional one. Third, they illustrate that results only can be achieved through specific planning and implementation; that is, reform does not automatically produce results.

Conclusions

The criminal justice reform movement is a complex, relatively recent social and political development that is still evolving and whose results cannot yet be assessed. Yet the problems of citizen security are also the result of several social variables that go beyond the limited sphere of the criminal justice system. Therefore, judicial reform alone, even in conjunction with police reform or other specific reforms, cannot be expected to have a decisive impact on the problems associated with a high incidence of violent crime or on its social construction. It is well known that crime is a complex, multifactor phenomenon that must be viewed in its totality.

In this context, the potential impact of reform can be destroyed by media scandals. These are inevitable when a reformed court releases someone the media or public opinion considers to be a dangerous criminal guilty of perpetrating a horrible crime, and there is bound to be pressure to return to a more repressive system. Reform may fail because of a lack of understanding of its purpose. Unfortunately, there are no databases that would make it possible to analyze the impact of reform on public opinion, nor are the present authors aware of any work being done in this regard. Informal conversations in Caracas with Adolfo Binder and William Evans (who have worked on criminal justice reform in various Latin American countries) suggest the hypothesis that reform is not well received primarily because it is regarded as weakening the ability of the police and of the criminal justice system to deal with crime.

The entry into force of Venezuela's reform, in July 1999, is a significant example. The main protest came from the police, particularly the Judicial Technical Police, who felt restricted by not being able to imprison suspects to interrogate them and who felt limited by the fact that inspectors from the prosecutor's office were to oversee their actions. The reform is also said to have increased insecurity by being advantageous to criminals. Police chiefs and Interior Ministry officials, as well as conservative figures, proposed that the national legislature (which at the time of this writing was still in session) suspend the entry into force of the new code of criminal procedure. The reaction of nongovernmental organizations concerned with human rights seems to have neutralized the virulence of the attack coming from authoritarian quarters. To date, no statistics are available to indicate that the reform has increased crime, as some police officials and journalists claim.

The great challenge is for the authorities, politicians, technical personnel, those participating in the system, and the population as a whole to understand what is at stake. The issue is not simply a problem of combating crime and increasing security, but rather one of respect for the human rights that are the basis for our civilization. At the same time, reform of the criminal justice system is being touted as a solution to the problems of citizen insecurity and of inefficiency in the administration of justice, thus creating expectations that cannot be fulfilled through penal reform alone. To prevent the disillusionment that threatens to ensue, modest, realistic goals for reform must be proposed.

If more temperate police forces, relatively efficient judicial systems, and a better understanding of them on the part of the public are achieved, an important step forward on the road to civility—indeed, to civilization itself—will have been taken. If, however, Latin American countries remain mired in specific legislative or institutional reforms, without proper coordination and evaluation, they will have squandered an unprecedented opportunity to bring about institutional changes offering their citizens a higher quality of life.

References

Ayres, Robert L. 1998. *Crime and Violence as Development Issues in Latin America and the Caribbean.* Washington, D.C.: World Bank.

Binder, Alberto. 1993a. Crisis y transformación de la justicia penal en Latinóamerica. In *Reformas procesales en América Latina,* ed. Julio Maier et al. Santiago: Corporación de Promoción Universitaria.

———. 1993b. *Justicia Penal y Estado de Derecho.* Buenos Aires: Ad Hoc.

Briceño León, R., A. Camardiel, O. Avila, E. De Armas, and V. Zubillaga. 1997. La cultura emergente de la violencia. *Revista Venezolana de Economía y Ciencias Sociales* (Caracas) 3: 2–3.

Briceño León, R., L.P. Carneiro, L. F. Vélez, J. M. Cruz, E. Oviedo, and A. McAlister. 1997. Comparando violencia y confianza en la policía en tres ciudades de América Latina. *Revista Venezolana de Economía y Ciencias Sociales* (Caracas). 3, No. 2–3.

Carranza, E., M. Houed, L.P. Mora, and E.R. Zaffaroni. 1983. *Los presos sin condena en América Latina.* San José: U.N. Latin American Institute for the Prevention of Crime and the Treatment of Offenders.

Chevigny, Paul. 1995. *Edge of the Knife: Police Violence in the Americas.* New York: New Press.

Currie, Elliot. 1998. *Crime and Punishment in America.* New York: Metropolitan Books.

Duce, Mauricio. 1999. Criminal Procedural Reform and the Ministerio Público: Toward the Construction of a New Criminal Justice System in Latin America. J.D. thesis, Stanford Law School, Stanford University.

Duce, Mauricio, and F. González. 1998. Policía y estado de derecho: Problemas en torno a su rol y organización. *Pena y Estado* (Buenos Aires) 3: 51–62.

Frühling, Hugo. 1997. La prevención del crimen: Notas sobre la justicia penal y la reducción de oportunidades para la delincuencia. Unpublished.

Henshel, Richard. 1996. The Study of Police Crime. In *Social Control and Justice. Inside or Outside the Law?* ed. L. Sebba. Jerusalem: Magnes Press, Hebrew University.

Holston, James, and T. Caldeira. 1998. Democracy, Law, and Violence: Disjunctions of Brazilian Citizenship. In *Fault Lines of Democracy in Post-Transition Latin America*, ed. F. Aguero and J. Stark. Miami: North–South Center Press.

Hurtado Pozo, Luis. 1997. *La ley importada: Recepción del derecho penal en el Perú.* Lima: Cedys.

Jiménez, María Angélica. 1994. El proceso penal chileno y los derechos humanos. *Cuadernos de Análisis Jurídico* (Universidad Diego Portales, Santiago), special series 2(4): 1–276.

Jiménez de Asúa, Luis. 1950. *Tratado de derecho penal*, vol. 1. Buenos Aires: Losada.

Martínez, Néstor Humberto. 1998. Rule of Law and Economic Efficiency. In *Justice Delayed, Judicial Reform in Latin America*, ed. Edmundo Jarquín and Fernando Carrillo. Baltimore: Johns Hopkins University Press.

Mera, Jorge. 1992. Seguridad ciudadana, violencia y delincuencia. *Sistema penal y seguridad ciudadana, Cuadernos de Análisis Jurídico* (Universidad Diego Portales, Santiago) 21: 11–25.

Merryman, John H. 1985. *The Civil Law Tradition*, 2d ed. Stanford, Calif.: Stanford University Press.

Navarro, Juan C., and R. Pérez Perdomo. 1991. *Inseguridad personal: Un asalto al tema.* Caracas: Ediciones IESA.

Pérez Perdomo, Rogelio. 1989. La durata dei processi penale e i diritti umani: Un problema per l'indagine sociologica-giuridica nell'America Latina. *Sociologia del Diritto* 17(1): 117–30.

———. 1995. *Políticas judiciales en Venezuela.* Caracas: Ediciones IESA.

———. 1997. Medios de comunicación y crimen. Unpublished.

———. 1998. El Código Orgánico Procesal Penal y el funcionamiento de la administración de justicia. *Capítulo Criminológico* 26(1): 19–43.

Rico, José María. 1985. *Crimen y justicia en América Latina*, 3d ed. Mexico City: Siglo XXI.

Riego, Cristían. 1998. La reforma procesal penal chilena. *La reforma de la justicia penal, Cuadernos de Análisis Jurídico* (Universidad Diego Portales, Santiago) 38: 15–54.

———. 1999. Las reformas judicíales y la seguridad ciudadana. *Perspectivas* (Santiago) 3(1): 43–61.

Rusconi, Maximiliano. 1998. Reformulación de los sistemas de justicia penal en América Latina y policía: Algunas reflexiones. *Pena y Estado* (Buenos Aires) 3: 189–98.

Tomás y Valiente, Francisco. 1969. *El derecho penal de la monarquía absoluta.* Madrid: Tecnos.

UNDP (United Nations Development Program). 1998. *Venezuela: Una reforma judicial en marcha.* Caracas: UNDP.

Zaffaroni, Eugenio R., coordinator. 1986. *Sistemas penales y derechos humanos en América Latina.* San José: Inter-American Institute for Human Rights; Buenos Aires: Depalma.

Zubillaga, Verónica, and Angel Cisneros. 2001. El temor in Caracas: Relatos de amenaza en barrios y urbanizaciones. *Revista de Mexicana Sociología* 63(1): 161–76.

5

The Violent Americas: Risk Factors, Consequences, and Policy Implications of Social and Domestic Violence

Andrew Morrison, Mayra Buvinic,
and Michael Shifter

The Latin American and Caribbean region has the reputation of being one of the most violent in the world, and the available data confirm this perception. In the most recent year for which comparable homicide data are available for regions of the world (1990), Latin America and the Caribbean had a homicide rate of 22.9 per 100,000 people, more than twice that of the worldwide average of 10.7.[1] Only Sub-Saharan Africa had a higher rate (40.1), and no other region of the world had a homicide rate in excess of 9 per 100,000. The most recent estimates for Latin America and the

This chapter is a modified version of the working paper "Violence in Latin America: A Framework for Action," which was published in 1999 by the Sustainable Development Department of the Inter-American Development Bank. The authors thank those whose comments improved the quality of this document. Isolde Birdthistle, Edward De Vos, Ronald Slaby, Joan Vaz Serra Hoffman, Cheryl Vince-Whitman, and Debbie Whitcomb of the Educational Development Center made valuable suggestions. Rafael Lozano of the World Health Organization and Carlos Castillo of the Pan American Health Organization facilitated access to valuable data. The views expressed in this chapter are those of the authors and should not be attributed to the Inter-American Development Bank.

Caribbean put the homicide rate at 28.4 in 1994 and show that the homicide rate for the region rose more than 44 percent during the 1984–94 period.[2]

International comparisons of levels of violence are fragile exercises. Data may be more trustworthy in one region than another, samples on which regional means are based may change over time, definitions of particular types of violence may vary over countries, and an individual country may be quite violent when measured by one yardstick (e.g., homicide) and quite peaceful when measured by another (e.g., armed robbery). Moreover, a national government's policy response to violence generally hinges not on a country's place in an international ranking, but on the level of violence that a particular society deems intolerable. In this sense, the level of insecurity felt by the populace may be an especially good measure of the impact of violence on a nation's psyche, polity, and economy, because it is insecurity (or a sense thereof) that affects variables such as social capital, human capital, and investment.

Violence produces insecurity, but not in any simple linear fashion, because the degree of insecurity that results from any given level of violence depends upon how this violence is perceived by the populace. Perceptions, in turn, are heavily influenced by the way the media cover violence. This chapter focuses on the underlying source of insecurity—levels of violence—rather than on the role of the media in shaping perceptions of this violence. The second section documents the extent of violence in the region by presenting data on homicides, the health effects of violence, and estimates of the prevalence of domestic violence. The third section attempts to bring order to this complex topic by presenting a typology of violence. The fourth section identifies the principal risk factors for violence at the individual, household, and social and community levels.

The fifth section presents research that has attempted to estimate the socioeconomic costs of violence in the region; it distinguishes among direct, nonmonetary, economic multiplier, and social multiplier costs and effects. Finally, the sixth section offers a discussion of the choices that confront government policymakers who wish to reduce levels of violence: integrated versus targeted programs, national versus local initiatives, and—perhaps most contentious—prevention versus remedial or treatment measures. It argues that preventive policies are generally more cost-effective than treatment options and identifies several especially promising options for preventing violence.

How Violent Is the Region?

Latin America is one of the most violent regions in the world, according to available data; it has a homicide rate of almost 18.4 per 100,000 people

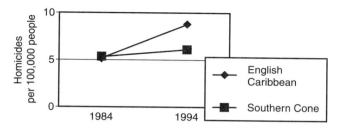

Figure 5.1. *Homicide Rates in Low-Violence Regions, 1984 and 1994*

(PAHO 1998). Hidden within this aggregate is substantial intraregional variation; for 1994—the most recent year for which comprehensive data are available—homicide rates were 51.9 per 100,000 in the Andean region, 30.1 in Brazil, 21.1 in Central America and the Hispanic Caribbean, 19.5 in Mexico (1995 data), 8.7 in the English Caribbean, and 6.2 in the Southern Cone.

Perhaps even more troubling, in each and every one of these areas—including the relatively less violent ones—the homicide rate increased between 1984 and 1994. The non–population–weighted rate of increase was 40.9 percent during the 10-year period, or approximately 3.4 percent a year (authors' calculations based on Pan American Health Organization data). The highest rates of increase were recorded in the Andean region and the English Caribbean, where homicide rates more than doubled and increased by more than 67 percent, respectively. Brazil and Central America (including the Hispanic Caribbean) increased by 29.7 and 20.6 percent, respectively, whereas increases in the Southern Cone and Mexico were 14.8 and 7.1 percent. Figures 5.1 and 5.2 show the evolution of homicide rates for low- and high-homicide countries.[3]

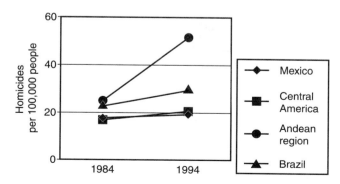

Figure 5.2. *Homicide Rates in High-Violence Regions, 1984 and 1994*

The variation is even more striking at the country level. Recent estimates for Latin America and the Caribbean put the regional homicide rate at 28.4 in 1994;[4] homicide rates exceeded that regional average in Colombia, El Salvador, Guatemala, and Jamaica; at the same time, Argentina, Chile, Costa Rica, Honduras, Paraguay, and Uruguay all had homicide rates below (or well below) the worldwide average of 10 per 100,000 residents.

Homicide, of course, is only one measure of the level of violence in a society. Another measure is victimization by any type of violent crime. Ideally, data on victimization should come from victimization surveys rather than police records, because underreporting is a serious problem in many countries. Furthermore, because the degree of underreporting varies significantly by country, cross-country comparisons made on the basis of statistics generated by the police will be quite unreliable. Figure 5.3 shows victimization rates by violent crime for six world regions, based on the International Crime Victimization Surveys (United Nations 1999).[5] As can be readily seen, there is large variation among the regions of the world, and frequently between the victimization rates of males and females in a given region.[6]

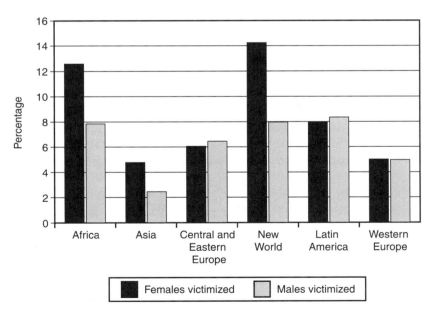

Figure 5.3.   *World Victimization Rates from Violent Crime*

Another useful measure of the severity of violence, but one which is much less widely available, is disability-adjusted life years (DALYs) lost due to violence—a measure of the number of years lost or lived with disability as a result of violence. This measure is distinct from the preceding ones in that it does not purport to capture the prevalence of violence, but rather its health effects. In the Global Burden of Disease study (Lopez and Murray 1996)—sponsored by the World Health Organization, the World Bank, and the Harvard School of Public Health—violence was found to be the third leading cause of death in the world for males between the ages of 15 and 44 years.[7] It is not surprising that the burden represented by violence varies significantly by region (table 5.1).

Per capita DALYs lost due to violence are a shorthand measure of the seriousness of violence as a public health and economic development issue. According to this measure, Latin America and the Caribbean is the region with the second highest burden associated with violence, trailing only Sub-Saharan Africa, with almost 4.5 days per person per year in 1990, more than twice the world average. Once again, aggregate numbers hide substantial heterogeneity, this time by sex. Males lose substantially more DALYs due to violence (0.0124 DALYs, or 4.52 days, in 1990, compared with 0.0019, or 0.69 days, for females—a ratio of more than 6.5 to 1; authors' calculations based upon Murray and Lopez 1996). With DALY losses so strongly concentrated among males, it is no surprise that violence is responsible for 16 to 17 percent of all male deaths (Murray and Lopez 1996, 185) and thus is a more important killer than many well-known diseases.

Table 5.1. *Disability-Adjusted Life Years (DALYs) Lost to Violence in 1990, by Country or Region*

Country or Region	Total DALYs Lost (in thousands)	Population (in thousands)	DALYs Lost per Capita
Established market economies	1,713	797,790	0.0021 (0.77 days)
Formerly socialist economies of Europe	1,447	346,237	0.0042 (1.53 days)
India	2,951	849,514	0.0035 (1.28 days)
China	3,163	1,133,693	0.0028 (1.02 days)
Other Asia and Islands	2,695	682,534	0.0039 (1.42 days)
Sub-Saharan Africa	11,336	510,274	0.0222 (8.10 days)
Latin America and the Caribbean	5,447	444,295	0.0123 (4.49 days)
Middle Eastern Crescent	2,366	503,075	0.0047 (1.72 days)
World	31,118	5,267,412	0.0059 (2.15 days)

Source: Authors' calculations based on Murray and Lopez 1996.

Table 5.2.   *The Prevalence of Violence against Females in Latin American and Caribbean Countries*

Country or City	Type of Violence Found (percent)
Santiago, Chile, 1993[a]	33.9 psychological
	10.7 physical (severe violence)
	15.5 physical (less severe)
Colombia, 1990[b]	33.9 psychological
	20 physical
	10 sexual
San José, Costa Rica, 1994[b]	75 psychological
	10 physical
Paraguay, 1996[c]	9.4 physical
	31.1 psychological
Monterrey, Mexico, 1995[b]	45.2 abused
	17.5 physical and sexual
	15.6 physical and psychological.

[a] In the past year.
[b] The period not specified in study or review article.
[c] In her lifetime.
Sources: Santiago, Chile: Larraín 1993. Colombia: Heise, Pitanguy, and Germain 1994. San José, Costa Rica: Quiróz and Barrantes 1994. Paraguay: Centro Paraguayo de Estudios de Población, Centers for Disease Control and Prevention, and U.S. Agency for International Development 1996. Monterrey, Mexico: Granado Shiroma 1995.

Although social violence (which involves individuals not currently or formerly living in the same household) primarily affects males, domestic violence (which involves people related to each other) primarily affects females (see below).[8] Table 5.2 provides information on the prevalence of violence against females for those countries where there is available data. Although the survey instruments are not always comparable between countries, the findings in the table are representative of—and therefore can be generalized to—the country or city cited.

Because of the high prevalence of domestic and social violence and their links, the focus of this analysis is the broader subject of violence rather than the narrower one of criminal violence. A violent act may or may not contravene existing legislation and consequently may or may not be labeled as "criminal" by the criminal justice system. A case in point is domestic violence, some types of which even today are not considered criminal behavior in some countries of the region. Nor need all criminal acts be violent; such "victimless" crimes as prostitution and bribery usually do not involve violence (see table 5.3). By including both criminal and noncriminal violence, this chapter considers program options that seek to reduce all behaviors that lead to violence, whether defined as criminal or not.

Table 5.3. *Examples of Crime versus Violence*

Behavior	Legal Definition	
	Criminal Act	Noncriminal Act
Violent	Armed robbery	Domestic violence[a]
	Assault	Marital rape[a]
	Stranger rape	Corporal punishment
	Murder	
Nonviolent	Burglary	—
	Prostitution	
	Bribery and corruption	

[a]In some countries.

Types of Violence

The phenomenon of violence is highly complex and multifaceted. One of the most challenging tasks is to distinguish different forms of violence and better understand their characteristics, risk factors, and consequences.[9] Violence can be categorized according to different variables: the individuals who suffer the violence (e.g., females, children, young males, the elderly, or the disabled), the agents of violence (gangs, drug lords, youth, or crowds), the nature of the aggression (psychological, physical, or sexual), the motive (political, racial, economic, instrumental, emotional, etc.), or the relationship between the person who suffers violence and the person who commits it (relatives, friends, acquaintances, or strangers).

In this chapter, for conceptual and policy reasons, we focus on this last categorization and group all violent acts into two broad types to discuss violence that takes place between people related to each other by blood, marriage, or common law[10]—referred to as *domestic violence*, and violence that occurs between individuals not so related—referred to as *social violence*. The former usually takes place within the confines of the household, whereas the latter usually takes place in the street or public places—and is consequently more visible.

The categorization into social and domestic violence is made here largely because of the links that bind the two. Violence is largely a learned behavior. The first opportunity for learning to behave violently is in the home, from one's parents, siblings, and other role models. Parental rewards for aggressive behavior, parental mistreatment of children, and violent parental role models are some of the mechanisms by which children learn violence early in life (Bandura 1973; Berkowitz 1993). Consistent evidence supports the claim that a child's exposure to violence in the home—either as a victim or witness—significantly increases the likelihood of that child committing domestic and social violence as an adult (Huesmann et al. 1984; American Psychological Association 1993; Dahlberg 1998).

In addition to highlighting that domestic violence is strongly linked and/or leads to social violence, other types of violence can be seen to have similar links: political violence (in the form of prolonged civil conflict), for example, has been shown to generate subsequent increases in the homicide rate as a result of the erosion of social norms against the use of violence. Two other considerations lie behind examining these links. First, domestic violence has long been a hidden form of violence. Cloaked in the "sanctity" of the home, it was considered a private rather than a public matter. A spate of recent research in different regions of the world, however, has shown the very real social effects of domestic violence.[11] Second, recognition of the link between domestic and social violence is a compelling reason to pursue policies to reduce domestic violence, even if the ultimate goal is to reduce social violence and improve citizen security.[12] In other words, an important new policy weapon in the fight against social violence is action designed to reduce domestic violence.

Domestic violence, which can be physical, psychological, or sexual, is commonly characterized according to the type of violence and the identity of its victim(s). Although males are occasionally the victims of domestic violence, the most common victims are females and children (there are, unfortunately, no reliable data on the elderly). Domestic violence can be physical, psychological, or sexual. *Physical violence*, the most obvious type, includes slapping, shoving, choking, kicking, hitting, arm-twisting, intentionally inflicting burns, holding someone against his or her will, or cutting someone with a knife or other object.

In the context of domestic violence against females, *psychological violence* is more common than physical violence; it occurs when an individual is a victim of frequent insults, is threatened, has personal belongings destroyed, or is subject to threats and yelling as a predominant means of seeking compliance or resolving conflicts. In the case of children, the opposite appears to be the case; they are subject to physical abuse much more often than to psychological abuse. *Sexual violence* occurs when a male household member (usually the partner) forces a female to engage in sexual activities against her will, or sexually abuses a minor.

Definitions of *social violence* often focus exclusively on physical force. The U.S. Centers for Disease Control and Prevention (1989), for example, define violence as "the use or threat of use of physical force, with the intention of causing harm to others or oneself." Although physical violence is the most important manifestation of social violence, psychological abuse (e.g., bullying) is also important in its own right and is a frequent antecedent to physical violence.

Social violence can be categorized by geographic locale (urban vs. rural), the motive (political, economic, social drug, or random), the agent (youth, gangs, police, or crowds), or the existing legal code (criminal vs. noncriminal violence). The last categorization, though perhaps appealing to those with a law enforcement focus, is not particularly useful in designing policies to curb social violence. First, as has already been mentioned, the same violent act may be illegal in some countries and quite legal in others. Second, there are frequently strong links between noncriminal violence and criminal violence. Children, for example, may begin to exhibit violent tendencies by mistreating or torturing animals; although not illegal in many countries, this behavior is a strong predictor of future interpersonal violence.

One distinction that *is* useful in thinking about whether to pursue preventive or punitive actions to address violence is that between *instrumental* and *emotional* violence. Instrumental violence is violence used as a means to obtain a goal. Politically motivated and drug-related violence are classic examples of activities in which violence is used, among other things, to intimidate or ensure obedience.[13] In emotional violence, the violent response is an end in itself. Domestic and social violence can be either instrumental or emotional. The distinction between the two is important because rational offender models of violent criminal behavior, much favored by economists who study crime, contribute to but cannot fully explain emotional violence.

These models posit that potential criminals examine the cost–benefit ratio of crime and decide to pursue criminal activities only if the expected benefits exceed the expected costs. Individuals who engage in emotional violence, however, do not carefully calculate the potential costs and benefits of violent behavior before engaging in it. As a consequence, standard punitive anticrime measures—increasing the probability of being caught through increased police presence, increasing the probability of conviction if caught through improved detective work and judicial efficiency, or increasing the severity of the penalty if convicted of a violent offense—will not wholly deter individuals who engage in emotional violence. If one's goal is to reduce emotional violence, in which psychosocial and cultural variables tend to prevail over rational ones, prevention, along with apprehension and punishment, should be pursued. In fact, as will be argued in the concluding section, prevention is an efficient, underutilized strategy for dealing with almost all types of violence.

The Multicausal Nature of Violence

There is no single factor that can adequately account for the high levels of violence in Latin America and the Caribbean; many risk factors are at work. In discussing the factors that contribute to or inhibit violent behavior—that is, in discussing risk and protective factors—it is useful to distinguish among factors operating at the levels of community and society, the household, and the individual. Figure 5.4 identifies some of the more important factors operating at these different levels. They are described below. It is also useful to take into account social and situational antecedents of violence—those features in the social and physical environment that promote or dissuade individuals from behaving violently.

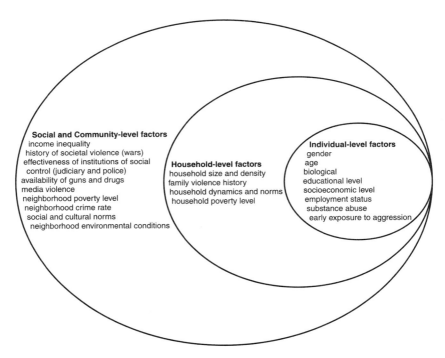

Figure 5.4. *Community and Social, Household, and Individual Determinants of Violence*

Community and Societal Factors

The most salient societal factors include income inequality; media violence; the availability of guns; postwar effects; weak institutional controls (particularly the frailty of police and judicial systems); cultural norms; and, possibly, neighborhood poverty levels and violence history.[14] A recent cross-regional study on the correlates of violence carried out by the World Bank bears out the strength of the relationship between high income inequality and violent behavior (Fajnzylber et al. 1997). More so than in the case of poverty, income inequality increases notions of deprivation and frustration, which can be powerful antecedents of violent behavior. The underlying conditions of inequality can become an even more serious contributing factor to social and domestic violence because of the role of the media in popularizing the consumption patterns of the wealthy and thus heightening poor people's sense of deprivation.

The media also influence the level of violence by providing often prized models of violent behavior that viewers learn and emulate; these, in turn, tend to stimulate and fuel aggressive behavior. Repeated exposure to rewarded violence in the media is consistently associated with increased incidence of aggression, especially in children (Huesmann and Eron 1986). Media violence is a situational trigger for aggressive behavior; other situational triggers include the easy availability of guns, as well as environmental conditions that facilitate crime, such as a lack of privacy in homes or the absence of streetlights.

Societies that have recently emerged from civil conflicts are particularly vulnerable to sustained outbreaks of violence. A comparison of homicide rates in a large number of countries before and after they had participated in wars found a significant increase in homicide rates, regardless of whether nations were victorious or not, and whether their postwar economies improved or worsened (Archer and Gartner 1984). In addition, though it is hard to derive precise measures of institutional performance, it is clear that the effectiveness of police and judicial systems may be especially compromised in post-conflict societies, which in turn influences the incentives and anticipated costs of engaging in violence.

Social and cultural norms are also an important determinant of behavior. Violence is woven into the cultural fabric of many societies and becomes a part of a set of norms that guides behavior and helps shape group identities. Thus, for example, hitting children is often culturally accepted and frequently inculcates in these same children the belief that violence is an acceptable way of resolving conflicts. Gender stereotypes reinforce the notion of the "right" of a husband to control his partner's behavior, and such control may be exercised via the use of domestic violence. At the community level, norms regarding participation in community organizations and mutual self-help have an impact on cohesiveness and consequently the level of violence as well. The existence of social and cultural determinants of violence has important implications for violence prevention and intervention programs. In particular, violence prevention initiatives that do not address cultural norms are at greater risk of not achieving their stated goals.

Although neighborhood poverty levels seem to be associated with greater violence, for domestic violence there is empirical evidence on this score only from the United States (O'Campo et al. 1995). However, poverty may trigger social violence, especially when associated with high income inequality, high unemployment, and low education among youth (PAHO 1998). Poverty may also be the result of violence, which diminishes human, physical, and social capital (see the discussion below on the economic multiplier costs of violence). A high crime rate in a neighborhood may itself engender violence. Violent crime lowers inhibitions against violent conduct, both via a demonstration effect (criminals provide an example for those so inclined to emulate their behavior) and the erosion of social norms that regulate interpersonal relations (Fajnzylber et al. 1997). Neighborhood environmental conditions, such as population density and the availability of streetlights, matter as well.

The existence of risk factors at different levels of aggregation does not imply a lack of interaction between factors at different levels. For example, at the individual level factors such as biological and physiological dysfunctions and experience with physical abuse can predispose an individual to behave violently. Low incomes and high density levels in households and communities are more likely to aggravate such a predisposition to violence by increasing frustration and stress levels. Conversely, high incomes and low density levels would diminish the likelihood that an individual's predispositions would lead to violent behavior. In other words, particular situational stimuli trigger social or domestic violence, activating such individual factors as previous experience with physical abuse.

The key question, of course, is which of these social- or community-level factors are responsible for the surge in violence seen in Latin America during the past 10 years. The data on income inequality are too scanty to make any definitive statements; for the small number of countries with data for both the late 1980s and mid-1990s, there is no simple relationship between trends in income inequality and violence, at least measured by homicide rates. Several countries have witnessed an increase in inequality accompanied by increased violence, as might be expected; but several (Brazil and Venezuela) have seen declining inequality accompanied by rising violence, and some have had decreasing violence accompanied by increasing inequality (Costa Rica and Mexico).

The availability of guns and postwar effects seem to be particularly appropriate explanations for increases in violence in the region. The Arms Control and Disarmament Agency has estimated that the value of all arms transfers to Latin America between 1991 and 1993 was $2.5 billion, with small arms and ammunition representing about 13 percent of the transfers. Thus, approximately $170 million worth of small arms entered the region in this short period, leading one publication to assert that many Latin American countries are "awash" in light weapons (Klare and Anderson 1996). Societies that have recently emerged from conflicts (such as El Salvador and Guatemala) have homicide rates far in excess of the regional average; so also, of course, does Colombia, where the internal conflict is ongoing. A reasonable hypothesis is that the widespread availability of weapons and attenuation of inhibitions against the use of violence in these societies exacerbate such already powerful contributing factors to violence as inequality, the negative role of the media, and high levels of poverty.

Household Factors

Contributing factors at the household level are similarly relevant to a comprehensive analysis of social and domestic violence. The most central factors are size and density, family violence history, dynamics and norms (especially whether the prevailing norms are more authoritarian than egalitarian or democratic), and per capita income. Chilean fathers with four or more children were three times more violent toward their children than similar fathers with one child (Larraín et al. 1997). A possible explanation for this finding is the crowding experienced by large families, which leads to frustration and is conducive to violent conduct. In this same study, children with parents who were violent to one another also suffered significantly more physical abuse than children with nonviolent parents. Violent families tend to perpetuate themselves.

Other dysfunctional behaviors in the dynamics of families and households, such as ineffective parenting skills, including poor monitoring and supervision of children, are linked with antisocial, aggressive, and delinquent behavior (Dahlberg 1998; Farrington 1991). A cross-cultural study of ninety societies showed that those with high levels of domestic violence were also ones with authoritarian household norms, where males are dominant and where there is social acceptance of the use of physical violence (Levinson 1989). Feminist writers and activists have also emphasized unequal gender relations as a central factor in explaining domestic violence against females. [15]

Gonzáles and Gavilano (1999), in a study of domestic violence against females in Lima, Peru, found that household poverty increased the likelihood of psychological and overall levels of violence, but not of physical and sexual violence. The finding that—holding other factors constant—domestic violence against females is more likely to occur in poorer households suggests two possible explanations. The first is that poverty itself is a risk factor for violence. The second is that poverty (or low socioeconomic level) is not itself a direct cause of violent behavior, but instead is associated with greater stress caused by uncertainty, precarious economic conditions, and overcrowding. Stress, in turn, is more likely to result in violence for those people with a predisposition to behave aggressively (either because of nature or nurture) than for those without this predisposition. Frustration and stress, in other words, are situational triggers for violence (Berkowitz 1993). But if poverty is associated with but not causally linked to violence, violence, as the previous section shows, impoverishes people and societies.

Individual Factors

The evidence suggests that a cluster of key factors at the individual level can shed significant light on patterns of both social and domestic violence. These factors are: gender; age; biological and physiological factors; educational level; socioeconomic level; employment status; substance abuse; and early exposure to aggressive stimuli, including the experience or witnessing of physical abuse. Each risk factor has its own marginal effect on the probability of an individual behaving violently. Males are more aggressive than females in all human societies for which evidence is available, and this is the only difference in behavior between the sexes that emerges before age two, indicating that there are biological roots to male aggression (Maccoby and Jacklin 1974).

Young males, individuals of relatively low socioeconomic level, the unemployed, the poorly educated, or those who abuse alcohol or drugs exhibit a greater propensity to engage in social and domestic violence. The risk of violent behavior is greater still if such a person has suffered from brain abnormalities or has a neurological dysfunction, both of which increase the risk of aggressive responses. Other dysfunctions with a physical origin include attention deficit hyperactivity disorder, learning disabilities, poor motor-skill development, prenatal and perinatal complications, minor physical anomalies, and head injury (Ospina 1998; Buka and Earls 1993). Policymakers often assume that biological and physiological factors are exogenously fixed and not amenable to policy interventions, but this is frequently not the case. Learning disabilities, for example, can be addressed via specialized educational programs, and prenatal and perinatal complications often can be avoided with appropriate maternal and child health interventions.

The Socioeconomic Costs of Violence

In her book on violence in Colombia, Moser (1999) distinguishes the impact of violence on four different types of capital: physical, human, social, and natural. The effect on *physical capital* captures the consequences of violence for firms' investment decisions: whether to invest domestically or abroad, whether to invest in productive assets or "nonproductive" security, and so on. Violence may also reduce domestic savings if people have less confidence in a country's future growth prospects. *Human capital* is involved because violence affects both access to education and its quality, and because violence limits individuals' ability to utilize their accumulated human capital in productive work. Social violence also reduces human capital formation by inducing some individuals to invest not in education but in the development of criminal skills. *Social capital* is diminished when violence reduces cooperation within formal and informal organizations, as well as among the members of these organizations. Finally, *natural capital* is attenuated by violence when civil conflict leads to the destruction of natural resources or environmental damage. With all these negative effects on capital formation, it is no surprise that social violence is a serious impediment to economic growth and development.

Domestic violence also damages prospects for economic development—not just the lives of its victims. Abuse affects children's performance in school and, therefore, their future productivity and the returns on national investments in schooling. Females who suffer from domestic violence are less productive in the workplace, and this lower productivity is a direct loss to national production. There are also important multiplier effects: Females who are less productive tend to earn lower incomes, and these lower incomes in turn imply less consumption spending and a consequent lower level of aggregate demand (Morrison and Orlando 1999). In addition, both domestic and social violence make claims on scarce societal resources—including expenditures on police, judicial systems, and the provision of social services—that otherwise could be used to meet different needs.

For analytical and illustrative purposes, the costs of domestic and social violence can be divided into four categories: direct costs, nonmonetary costs, economic multiplier effects, and social multiplier effects (table 5.4).

Table 5.4.   *The Socioeconomic Costs of Violence: A Typology*

Direct costs: value of goods and services used in treating or preventing violence
  —police
  —criminal justice system
  —medical
  —psychological counseling
  —housing
  —social services
Nonmonetary costs: pain and suffering[a]
  —increased morbidity
  —increased mortality via homicide and suicide
  —abuse of alcohol and drugs
  —depressive disorders
Economic multiplier effects: macroeconomic, labor market, intergenerational productivity effects
  —decreased labor market participation
  —reduced productivity on the job
  —lower earnings
  —increased absenteeism
  —intergenerational productivity impacts via grade repetition and lower educational attainment of children
  —decreased investment and saving
  —capital flight
Social multiplier effects: impact on interpersonal relations and quality of life
  —intergenerational transmission of violence
  —erosion of social capital
  —reduced quality of life
  —reduced participation in democratic process

[a]Some of these will be partially reflected in medical costs. However, if individuals do not seek medical treatment, the health effects were included in this category.

Direct Costs

Direct costs capture the value of goods and services used in attempting to prevent violence, offering treatment to its victims, and capturing and punishing its perpetrators. Thus, direct costs include expenditures on police; judiciary systems (prison and detention costs, as well as prosecution and other court costs); medical treatment (emergency room care, hospitalization, care at a clinic or a doctor's office, dental care, and the costs of treatment for sexually transmitted diseases); psychological counseling for victims and, in the case of domestic violence, sometimes also for abusers; housing (shelters and transitional housing for abused women and their children); and social services (job training; parole officers; domestic violence prevention and education; advocacy programs; and training for police, doctors, and others).

No estimates of the direct costs associated with domestic violence are available for any Latin American or Caribbean country, but the assumption is that they are significant, although somewhat lower than in industrial countries, where there is greater availability of services. The figures available for these latter countries are high; for instance, in Canada, Greaves (1995) estimates that violence against females (which includes domestic and stranger violence against women, but excludes violence against female children) imposes an annual cost of 684 million Canadian dollars on the criminal justice system and $187 million on police. The cost of counseling and training in response to violence against females is estimated to be approximately $294 million annually. Thus, the total direct costs exceed 1 billion Canadian dollars a year, a large figure even for an economy of the size of Canada.

In the case of social violence, data are available for several Latin American countries on the amount spent on public security and justice systems.[16] In Colombia, public spending on security and criminal justice was 5 percent of the country's gross domestic product (GDP) in 1996; private expenditures on security amounted to another 1.4 percent of GDP (CEDE-UNIANDES 1997, 23–25).[17] In El Salvador, expenditures on government institutions, legal costs, personal injuries, and prevention activities represented more than 6 percent of 1995 GDP (Cruz and Romano 1997, 32). In Venezuela, public expenditures on security were approximately 2.6 percent of 1995 GDP (IESA and LASCO 1997, 25–27).

The data from Mexico and Peru are not strictly comparable, because they refer to Mexico City and Lima, respectively, rather than the nations as a whole. In Mexico City, expenditures on public and private security measures summed to $181 million in 1995 (Fundación Mexicana para la Salud 1997); administration of justice and prisons accounted for an additional $128 million and $690 million, respectively. Public spending by the national government on police, courts, and prisons for Lima was approximately 1 percent of metropolitan Lima's regional product in 1997, whereas private spending on security measures accounted for another 0.41 percent of regional product (Instituto APOYO 1997, 26–28).

Nonmonetary Costs

Nonmonetary costs encapsulate health effects that do not necessarily generate a demand for services from medical providers, such as increased morbidity, increased mortality through homicide and suicide, abuse of alcohol and drugs, and depressive disorders.[18] If one calculates the impact of domestic violence on health, the results are sobering. The World Bank estimated that rape and domestic violence cause 9 million DALYs to be lost annually in the world, more than the total for all types of cancers affecting females, and more than double the total DALYs lost by females in motor vehicle accidents (World Bank 1993).[19] In a study calculating the burden of disease for females in Mexico City, Lozano (1999) found that violence against females was the third most important source of DALYs lost, after diabetes and complications from childbirth. Spousal and other forms of abuse against females was a more important source of lost DALYs than traffic accidents, congenital abnormalities, rheumatoid arthritis and osteoarthritis, cardiovascular diseases, cerebrovascular diseases, or pneumonia.

There are also estimates of DALYs lost to social violence. In El Salvador, 178,000 DALYs were lost in 1995 because of violent death (Cruz and Romano 1997, 30). The number was 60,792 in all of Peru (Instituto APOYO 1997, 16), 163,136 in Rio de Janeiro (ISER 1998, 42), and 57,673 in Mexico City (Fundación Mexicana para la Salud 1997, 14). In Caracas, disabilities were not included in the calculation (only death was); even so, 56,032 potential DALYs were lost in 1995 because of homicide (IESA and LASCO 1997, 31). Although the numbers are large, their real significance should be gauged in comparison with DALYs lost for other causes. Unfortunately, these comparisons are only available for Colombia. In Colombia, between 18 and 27 percent of all DALYs lost from 1989 to 1995 were due to homicide—well above the worldwide average of only 1.4 percent. DALYs lost due to homicide were three times greater than those due to infectious diseases, and two times greater than those caused by cardiovascular disease (CEDE-UNIANDES 1997, 12–16).

Economic Multiplier Effects

Economic multiplier effects of violence include decreased accumulation of human capital, lower rates of labor market participation, reduced productivity on the job, increased absenteeism, lower earnings, intergenerational productivity effects, and—at the macroeconomic level—lower levels of savings and investment. Studies in the United States and Canada show that females who suffer domestic violence are more likely to lose their jobs and have higher rates of absenteeism.[20] Unfortunately, there is no evidence on job loss and absenteeism for Latin American or Caribbean countries. However, with respect to females' earning power, evidence from a study by Morrison and Orlando (1999) indicates large differences in labor earnings between females who do and do not suffer severe domestic violence. In Managua, Nicaragua, females who suffered severe physical violence earned only 57 percent as much as their nonabused peers; in Santiago, Chile, this was 39 percent. In Chile, lost earnings for all females accounted for more than 2 percent of Chilean 1996 GDP, whereas in Nicaragua lost earnings accounted for approximately 1.6 percent of 1996 GDP.

It is worth emphasizing that these losses capture only the effects on female earnings; they do not include effects on labor force participation or absenteeism. The last type of economic multiplier effect of domestic violence is the intergenerational impact on children's economic future. Children who experience or witness domestic abuse are more likely to have disciplinary problems in school and may also be more likely to repeat grades (Morrison and Orlando 1999). In Chile, children who reported suffering serious abuse also did significantly worse in school than children who reported no physical abuse (Larraín et al. 1997). These effects suggest nothing less than a direct impact on these children's human capital and their future ability to obtain adequate employment at a decent wage.

Social violence also has important economic multiplier effects. The Inter-American Development Bank sponsored studies on the economic impact of urban criminal violence in six countries of the region: Brazil, Colombia, El Salvador, Mexico, Peru, and Venezuela. The studies disaggregate the costs of violence into four categories: health effects (expenditures on health services incurred as a result of the violence), material losses (private and public expenditures on police, security systems, and judicial

Table 5.5. *Economic Costs of Social Violence in Six Latin American Countries (percentage of 1997 gross domestic product)*

Cost	Brazil	Colombia	El Salvador	Mexico	Peru	Venezuela
Health losses	1.9	5.0	4.3	1.3	1.5	0.3
Material losses	3.6	8.4	5.1	4.9	2.0	9.0
Intangibles	3.4	6.9	11.5	3.3	1.0	2.2
Transfers	1.6	4.4	4.0	2.8	0.6	0.3

Source: Londoño 1998.

services), intangibles (the amount that citizens would be willing to pay to live without violence), and transfers (the value of goods lost in robberies, ransoms paid to kidnappers, and bribes paid as a result of extortion; see table 5.5). The estimates were then expressed as a percentage of 1997 GDP. Estimates of health losses from violence ranged from a low of 0.3 percent of GDP in Venezuela to a high of 5.0 percent in Colombia. For material losses, the range was from 2.0 percent (Peru) to 9.0 percent (Venezuela). The highest level of willingness to pay for a reduction in violence (intangibles) was in El Salvador, with 11.5 percent of GDP; the lowest willingness to pay was in Peru, with 1.0 percent of GDP. Finally, the value of stolen goods, bribes, and ransoms was highest in Colombia (4.4 percent) and lowest in Venezuela (0.3 percent). In all countries except for El Salvador, material losses were the most important cost resulting from violence.[21]

Social Multiplier Effects

Social multiplier effects include the intergenerational transmission of violence, erosion of social capital, reduced quality of life, and reduced participation in democratic processes. In the case of domestic violence, there is significant evidence documenting the link between a man's witnessing or experiencing abuse as a child and later behaving violently with his wife or partner;[22] some authors question the strength of this relationship, but not its existence (Stark and Flitcraft 1991). Other research in Canada and the United States shows that children exposed to domestic violence have inappropriate views on the acceptability and utility of violence as a means to resolve conflicts (Jaffe, Wilson, and Wolfe 1989) and are at increased risk of being both a victim and perpetrator of violence (Dahlberg 1998; Thornberry et al. 1995). The connection among domestic violence, poor parenting, and future violent behavior outside the home has yet to be examined empirically in the Latin American and Caribbean region, but it would be surprising were such a link not to emerge. Nor are the effects on children limited to their reproducing violent behaviors as adults. Children who are victims of or who witness abuse are more likely to have behavioral problems while still children. In the Chile study of child abuse already cited, children who said they were victims of serious physical violence also had poor interpersonal relationships, not only with their parents but also with other children (Larraín et al. 1997).

Of particular importance is the erosion of social capital that occurs because of the isolation experienced by victims of domestic violence. Domestic violence against females in many cases is instrumental in nature; that is, a male uses domestic violence as a means to an end—in this case, control of the woman and her contacts with the world outside the home. This simultaneously reduces a woman's quality of life and her ability to participate in activities outside the home, including income-earning and community activities. Social violence also has important social multiplier effects, even though they are extremely difficult to measure empirically. Moser and Holland (1997) note that community-level violence in Jamaica often translated into widespread fear and the absence of fundamental norms of cooperation and communication—in effect, destroying social capital. One crucial impact is the intergenerational transmission of violence. If children and youth are taught by adults, by the media, and by society at large that violence is a means to a quick accumulation of wealth, it is not surprising if young people—especially young males—adopt violent conduct.[23]

Social violence increasingly constitutes the most significant threat to fundamental liberties, the rule of law, and democratic consolidation for the region's human rights organizations (Frühling 1997; Instituto de Defensa Legal 1996; Gregori 1997). Structural violence, in which police forces and/or paramilitary groups become agents of violence perpetrated on certain groups, especially street children, both prejudices democracy and generates further violence. In addition, democratic institutions face new demands and challenges created by collective insecurity that not only affect economic development but also raise serious doubts about their ability to deal effectively with crime. As a result, the political impact of social violence is very large within a regional context characterized by a weak democratic culture (Frühling 1997).

Policy Recommendations

Policy responses should respond to the risk factors that are responsible for violence in a given location, and the impact of policy interventions should be carefully monitored. A four-step process, often called an "epidemiological focus," can help ensure that the proposed policy interventions are indeed effective in reducing violence. The four steps are:

1. Define the type of violence to be addressed and collect data on the magnitude of the problem.
2. Identify the risk factors for this type of violence.
3. Develop and test intervention(s).
4. Analyze the effectiveness of the intervention(s).

Although this epidemiological approach is easy to describe, it is less easy to implement. It requires a significant commitment to data gathering and analysis, as well as a commitment to measure the impact of program interventions; nonetheless, the payoffs in terms of violence reduction if this approach is followed—as well as the enormous risk of policy failure if it is not—make the epidemiological approach an essential component of any violence reduction program.

Precisely because the phenomenon of violence is multicausal, a combination of actions at different levels—individual, household, and community and societal—is generally necessary. This should not preclude the possibility that policy responses targeted at specific risk factors (e.g., initiatives to control illegal gun ownership or media campaigns against the abuse of alcohol or drugs) can by themselves prove effective; they are also far easier to implement successfully. Governments must carefully weigh the costs and benefits of *integrated* versus *targeted* programs.

Governments must also be cognizant of the fact that the most successful violence prevention programs will be local and not national in character, precisely because the factors generating violence are likely to vary from municipality to municipality in a given country. One-size-fits-all national policies—though better than nothing—that are not tailored to local conditions will not be as effective (Volokh and Snell 1997). Thus, municipalities are a promising setting for antiviolence action, especially for multisectoral activities that require coordination that can be accomplished more easily at municipal rather than national levels.

Policy choices can further be divided into *preventive policies* and what might be called *treatment or remedial measures*. Ideally, one would like to have data on the costs and benefits of integrated versus targeted programs, and of preventive versus remedial policies in different settings in order to choose the more cost-effective strategy. Unfortunately, in the region there is little or no information available on program costs even from a simple accounting perspective to evaluate program options, to say nothing of knowledge of the benefits generated by various types of programs.

Experts in industrial countries, where there is more evidence on program costs and benefits, agree that preventive strategies are generally more cost-effective than treatment strategies. A recent study by the RAND Corporation, for example, compared the cost effectiveness of California's "Three Strikes and You're Out" law to four preventive measures: high school graduation incentives; a training program for new parents teaching parenting skills; weekly home visits by a child care professional from the third trimester of pregnancy through age 2 years, plus day care and education from age 2 to 5; and intensive supervision and mentoring of young delinquents (Greenwood et al. 1998).[24]

The results of this study are remarkable. In general, prevention programs are more cost-effective in preventing crime than the three-strikes law. Per million dollars spent, graduation incentives prevent 258 serious crimes, parent training prevents 157 serious crimes, and delinquent supervision 72 prevents serious crimes. For each million dollars spent on building, equipping, and running prisons to enforce the three-strikes law, only 62.5 serious crimes are prevented. In fact, the three-strikes approach is only more cost-efficient than the home visits/child care intervention.

It is important to recognize that prevention and treatment are not either–or options; rather, they are located along a policy continuum. At the treatment end of the continuum are more conventional policies that typically involve the police, courts, and prison system. The explicit aim of these policies is to control the behavior of individuals who engage in violence (Frühling 1997). Moving along the continuum, there are secondary preventive measures that are targeted at particularly high-risk groups, such as young males who have witnessed or been victims of violence; these measures attempt to modify behaviors that put these individuals at risk to commit or be victimized by violence. At the other end of the continuum are primary prevention policies that attempt to change attitudes, social norms, and behavior in the general population; they often target more than one risk factor and attempt to influence the behavior of particular age groups or other classes of individuals, such as parents and young children.

At the prevention end of the treatment–prevention continuum, a useful distinction is between prevention focused on the situational antecedents of violent behavior and prevention focused on the social determinants of violence. The first is focused on potential victims and seeks to reduce the likelihood that violent behavior will take place (by making violent crime more difficult, more risky, or less rewarding), whereas the second targets potential aggressors and seeks to reduce the probability of producing violent individuals (by emphasizing good parenting and positive social learning interventions with young children and/or subgroups in the population at high risk of engaging in violent behavior).

The emphasis in the region has been to combat violence with punitive action through the police and the courts, and to provide some treatment to the victims of violence. Although effective punishment is a powerful crime deterrent, prevention measures of comparatively low cost and high potential returns have been woefully lacking. There are only a handful of prevention programs, many of them in Colombia, which has taken the lead in investing in antiviolence action.[25] Yet prevention measures can reduce risk factors for violence, increase protective factors, and address either situational or social determinants of crime and violence. Situational measures can increase the risks and reduce the benefits of violent behaviors as well as minimize environmental stimuli for aggressive actions. Prevention can be directed to the whole population (primary prevention) or can be targeted to high-risk groups, such as children who have experienced abuse, unemployed youth, or single-parent households (secondary prevention).

Strong child abuse prevention programs through community organizations (including local churches) as well as in primary and secondary schools could turn out to be among the more modest interventions with large dividends in terms of crime prevention. Other low-cost, high-productivity interventions include mother and child health; early childhood development; violence prevention curricula in elementary and secondary schools; alcohol and substance abuse prevention programs; and situational crime prevention measures, including gun control or exchange programs, street lighting and other public security measures, and restriction of alcohol sales during certain high-risk periods. Well-crafted and targeted media campaigns, including commercial media programming, can significantly help reinforce civic values, alter prevailing views of acceptable behavior between the genders, and aid in the prevention of domestic and social violence.

Antiviolence interventions, whether they are closer to the prevention or the treatment end of the policy continuum, need to have an identified target group (e.g., elementary school students or youth gang members), a setting in which the target group can be reached (e.g., schools or detention centers), and a method or strategy to accomplish violence reduction (e.g., instruction in nonviolent conflict resolution or vocational training; National Center for Injury Prevention and Control 1993).

Finally, antiviolence interventions need to give priority to poor neighborhoods, both because they tend to experience greater violence than more affluent ones and because the social capital of poor people is especially vulnerable to erosion by violence. Particularly important are investments in early childhood development and in economic opportunities for poor people, both women and young males, to prevent violence, reduce inequalities, and promote economic growth.

Notes

1. Data were provided by Rafael Lozano of the World Health Organization.

2. Data on Latin America and the Caribbean were provided by the Health Situation Analysis Program of the Division of Health and Human Development, Pan American Health Organization (PAHO). The figures are based on mortality by cause of death, supplied by PAHO member countries. These data are maintained in PAHO's Technical Information System database. The homicide rate for Latin America in 1994 was 53.1, whereas that for the Caribbean was 20.5.

3. Low-violence countries were those with both 1984 and 1994 homicide rates below 10 per 100,000 people. High-violence countries had homicide rates above 10 in one or both periods (in the countries in this high-violence subsample, all had both initial and terminal homicide rates above 10 per 100,000).

4. Data on Latin America and the Caribbean were provided by the Health Situation Analysis Program of the Division of Health and Human Development, Pan American Health Organization. The figures are based on mortality by cause of death, supplied by PAHO member countries. These data are maintained in PAHO's Technical Information System database. The homicide rate for Latin America in 1994 was 29.0, whereas that for the Caribbean was 11.8.

5. The countries included in the various regions are as follows: Western Europe (Austria, Belgium, England and Wales, Finland, France, Germany, Italy, Malta, Netherlands, Northern Ireland, Norway, Scotland, Spain, Sweden, and Switzerland); New World (Australia, Canada, New Zealand, United States); Central and Eastern Europe (Albania, Belarus, Bulgaria, Croatia, Czech Republic, Estonia, Georgia, Hungary, Kyrgyzstan, Latvia, Lithuania, Macedonia, Mongolia, Poland, Romania, Russia, Slovenia, Ukraine, and Yugoslavia); Asia (China, India, Indonesia, and Philippines); Africa (Egypt, South Africa, Tanzania, Tunisia, Uganda, Zimbabwe); and Latin America (Argentina, Bolivia, Brazil, Colombia, Costa Rica, and Paraguay).

6. The victimization rate of men ranges from a high of 8.4 percent in the New World, to a low of 2.4 percent in Asia. The victimization rate of women is highest in Latin America (14.3 percent) and lowest in Asia (4.8 percent). In three of the six world regions (Latin America, Asia, and Africa), women's victimization rates are signifi-

cantly higher than men, whereas in two regions (Central and Eastern Europe and the New World) women's victimization rates are slightly lower. In Western Europe, victimization rates are the same for the two sexes.

7. In the Global Burden of Disease study, causes of death and disability were grouped into three large categories: (1) communicable, maternal, perinatal, and nutritional conditions; (2) noncommunicable diseases; and (3) injuries. Injuries, in turn, are divided into unintentional and intentional injuries. Violence, in addition to self-inflicted injuries and war, is included in the intentional injuries category (see Murray and Lopez 1996).

8. Efforts to collect statistics on violence against women in the home are recent and as yet unable to support a comprehensive assessment of the magnitude of the problem in the region. Statistics on violence against children and the elderly are even more scant, but the little available evidence suggests that they too have serious problems, as would be expected given the high rates of domestic violence against women. Estimates place the number of children suffering severe abuse in the region, including abandonment, at 6 million and indicate that 80,000 children die each year as result of parental abuse. One of the few existing population-based surveys reveals the magnitude of the problem of domestic violence against children. A full 63 percent of Chilean children in eighth grade (drawn from a nationally representative sample of 1,533 children) reported that they had suffered physical violence in the home; 34 percent of them indicated having suffered severe physical abuse, suggesting that serious abuse against children is as great or greater than similar abuse against women (Larrain et al. 1997).

9. There are very few true causes of violence. The word "cause" implies a deterministic relationship; heat *causes* ice to melt, for example. Instead, we use the term "risk factors" for violence, that is, factors that make the commission of violence more likely. A good analogy is that of the relationship between smoking and cancer. Smoking is a risk factor for cancer. Not everyone who smokes will get cancer, but smoking does increase the probability of contracting cancer.

10. Violence between individuals who formerly belonged to the same household—especially between ex-spouses or ex-cohabitators—is also classified as domestic violence.

11. E.g., see Gonzales and Gavilano 1999.

12. This by no means is meant to imply that reduction of domestic violence is not a reasonable policy goal in and of itself.

13. At the same time, sustained use of instrumental violence may lead to increased emotional violence, as individuals become accustomed to solving problems violently.

14. It is likely that three other societal factors—the overall crime rate, the amount of social capital, and cultural values about the use of violence—are important, but their impact is very difficult to quantify.

15. E.g., in the United States, a national Family Violence Survey in 1975 found that violence against wives was most likely to occur when wives were both economically and psychologically dependent on dominant husbands (Berkowitz 1993).

16. Some extremely small percentages of national expenditures on security go toward providing police and judicial services for cases of domestic violence. Because this percentage is extremely low in all countries of the region, we treat police and judicial expenditures as if they were exclusively for the issue of social violence.

17. Counting all expenditures on law enforcement and criminal justice systems as "direct costs" of violence will overstate the true direct costs, because some of these ex-

penditures would exist even were there no violence. In addition, the very existence of law enforcement and criminal justice may prevent some (instrumental) violence.

18. Care must be exercised here to avoid double counting. If an episode of morbidity generates a demand for medical services, it is no longer considered a nonmonetary cost and should be included in the category of "direct costs."

19. DALYs capture not only the years lost due to premature mortality, but also the years affected by disability or sickness.

20. For the United States, Stanley (1992) reports that 30 percent of abused women lost their jobs as a direct result of the abuse. The U.S. Department of Justice reports that 94 percent of abused women lost at least one work day a year as a result of the abuse suffered, and 50 percent of abused women lost as much as 3 days a month. In Canada, 34 percent of battered women and 11 percent of sexual assault victims indicated that they could not work the day after the assault, leading to lost earnings in excess of 7 million Canadian dollars a year (Greaves 1995).

21. Note that these categories are neither exclusive (e.g., citizens may be revealing a willingness to pay for reductions in the impact of violence on health) nor exhaustive (e.g., they do not include explicitly the cost of lowered saving and investment).

22. Research by Strauss, Gelles, and Steinmetz (1980) in the United States documents that the rate of spousal abuse was ten times higher for men who came from violent childhoods compared to men who had nonviolent childhoods.

23. In Colombia, young people of 18 to 24 years of age were asked in a survey, "What groups do you think are doing well in Colombia?" (A quién cree Ud. que le va bien en Colombia?) The (non–mutually exclusive) responses were: politicians (41 percent); rich people (25 percent); opportunists/"vivos" (18 percent); dishonest people (17 percent); people with contacts (15 percent); lucky individuals (14 percent); those who work (13 percent); and those who study (13 percent). With study and work ranking last, it is no surprise that Colombian youth frequently resort to violence to achieve their goals. See Cuéllar de Martínez (1997) for the full results from this survey.

24. California's "Three Strikes and You're Out" law mandates life in prison for an individual convicted for a third offense, after two previous felony convictions.

25. Also see the descriptions of interesting prevention initiatives under way in other countries of the region in chapters 2 and 9 of this volume.

References

American Psychological Association. 1993. *Violence and Youth*, vol. 1. New York: American Psychological Association.

Archer, D., and R. Gartner. 1984. *Violence and Crime in Cross-National Perspective*. New Haven, Conn.: Yale University Press.

Bandura, A. 1973. *Aggression: A Social Learning Analysis*. Englewood Cliffs, N.J.: Prentice Hall.

Berkowitz, Leonard. 1993. *Aggression: Its Causes, Consequences, and Control*. New York: McGraw Hill.

Buka, S., and F. Earls. 1993. Early Determinants of Delinquency and Violence. *Health Affairs* 12(4): 46–64.

CEDE-UNIANDES (Centro de Estudios sobre Desarrollo Económico de la Universidad de los Andes). 1997. Violencia en Colombia: Dimensionamiento y políticas de control. Bogotá: Centro de Estudios sobre Desarrollo Económico de la Universidad de los Andes.

Centers for Disease Control and Prevention. 1989. *Injury Prevention: Meeting the Challenge. A Report of the National Committee for Injury Prevention and Control.* New York: Oxford University Press.

Centro Paraguayo de Estudios de Población, Centers for Disease Control and Prevention, and U.S. Agency for International Development. 1996. *Encuesta nacional de demografía y salud reproductiva, 1995–96.* Asunción: Centro Paraguayo de Estudios de Población.

Cruz, Jose Miguel, and Luis Ernesto Romano. 1997. La violencia en El Salvador en los noventa: Magnitud, costos y factores posibilitadores. San Salvador: Instituto Universitario de Opinión Pública, Universidad Centroamericana José Simeón Cañas.

Cuéllar de Martínez, María Mercedes. 1997. *Valores y capital social en Colombia.* Bogotá: Fundación Porvenir and Universidad Externado de Colombia.

Dahlberg, Lina. 1998. Youth Violence in the United States: Major Trends, Risk Factors and Prevention Approaches. *American Journal of Preventive Medicine* 14(4): 259–72.

Fajnzylber, Pablo, et al. 1997. What Causes Crime and Violence? Office of the Chief Economist Latin America and the Caribbean, World Bank, Washington, D.C.

Farrington, D. P. 1991. Childhood Aggression and Adult Violence: Early Precursors and Later-Life Outcomes. In *The Development and Treatment of Childhood Aggression,* ed. D. J. Pepler and K. H. Rubin. Hillsdale, N.J.: Lawrence Erlbaum.

Frühling, Hugo. 1995. Judicial Reform and Democratization in Latin America. Paper prepared for the conference Fault Lines of Democratic Governance in the Americas, North–South Center, University of Miami, May 4–6.

———. 1997. La prevención del crimen: Notas sobre la justicia penal y la reducción de oportunidades para la delincuencia. Paper presented at a conference on the challenge of urban criminal violence sponsored by the State of Rio de Janeiro and the Inter-American Development Bank, Rio de Janeiro, March 2–4.

Fundación Mexicana para la Salud. 1997. *La violencia en la Ciudad de México: Análisis de la magnitud y su repercusión económica.* Mexico City: Fundación Mexicana para la Salud, Centro de Economía y Salud.

Gonzáles de Olarte, Efraín, and Pilar Gavilano Llosa. 1999. Does Poverty Cause Domestic Violence? Some Answers from Lima. In *Too Close to Home: Domestic Violence in the Americas,* ed. Andrew R. Morrison and María Loreto Biehl. Washington, D.C.: Inter-American Development Bank.

Granado Shiroma, Marcela. 1995. La violencia doméstica en contra de la mujer. In *Foro estatal para el Programa Nacional de la Mujer: Memoria,* ed. Gobierno del Estado de Nuevo León, Desarrollo Integral de la Familia Nuevo León y El Consejo Estatal de Población de Nuevo León. Monterrey, Mexico: United Nations Population Fund (UNFPA).

Greaves, Lorraine. 1995. Selected Estimates of the Costs of Violence against Women. London, Ontario: Centre for Research on Violence against Women and Children.

Greenwood, Peter, et al. 1998. *Diverting Children from a Life of Crime: Measuring Costs and Benefits.* Santa Monica, Calif.: RAND Corporation.

Gregori, José. 1997. Crimes e direitos humanos. Paper presented at a conference on the challenge of urban criminal violence sponsored by the State of Rio de Janeiro and the Inter-American Development Bank, Rio de Janeiro, March 2–4.

Heise, Lori L., Jacqueline Pitanguy, and Adrienne Germain. 1994. Violence against Women: The Hidden Health Burden. World Bank Discussion Paper 255. Washington, D.C.: World Bank.

Huesmann, L. R., et al. 1984. The Stability of Aggression over Time and Generations. *Developmental Psychology* 20:1120–34.

Huesmann, L. R., and L. D. Eron, eds. 1986. *Television and the Aggressive Child: A Cross-National Comparison.* Hillsdale, N.J.: Erlbaum.

IESA and LASCO. 1997. La violencia en Venezuela: Dimensionamiento y políticas de control. Final Report, IESA y LACSO, Caracas.

Instituto APOYO. 1997. *La violencia intencional en Lima metropolitana; Magnitud, impacto económico y evaluación de políticas de control, 1985–1995.* Peru: Instituto APOYO.

Instituto de Defensa Legal. 1996. Calles peligrosas: Aparte del miedo, ¿qué hacer? Serie *Diálogo y Participación* (Lima), November, pp. 26–27.

ISER (Instituto de Estudos da Religião). 1998. Magnitude, Custos Económicos e Políticas de Controle da Violencia no Rio de Janeiro. Rio de Janeiro: Instituto de Estudos da Religião.

Jaffe, Peter G., S. K. Wilson, and D. Wolfe. 1989. Specific Assessment and Intervention Strategies for Children Exposed to Wife Battering: Preliminary Empirical Investigation. *Canadian Journal of Community Mental Health* 7: 157–63.

Klare, Michael, and David Andersen. 1996. *A Scourge of Guns: The Diffusion of Small Arms and Light Weapons in Latin America.* Washington, D.C.: Federation of American Scientists.

Larraín, Soledad. 1993. *Violencia puertas adentro: La mujer golpeada.* Santiago: Editorial Universitaria.

Larraín, Soledad, et al. 1997. *Relaciones familiares y maltrato infantil.* Santiago, Chile: UNICEF.

Levinson, D. 1989. *Violence in Cross-Cultural Perspective.* Newbury Park, Calif.: Sage Publishers.

Londoño, Juan Luis. 1998. Epidemiología de la violencia urbana. Slides from a presentation at the conference on promoting citizen coexistence sponsored by the Inter-American Development Bank, Cartagena, Colombia, March 14.

Lozano Ascencio, Rafael. 1999. The Health Impact of Domestic Violence: Mexico City. In *Too Close to Home: Domestic Violence in the Americas,* ed. Andrew R. Morrison and María Loreto Biehl. Washington, D.C.: Inter-American Development Bank.

Lopez, Alan, and Christopher Murray, eds. 1996. *The Global Burden of Disease: A Comprehensive Assessment of Mortality and Disability from Diseases, Injuries and Risk Factors in 1990 and Projected to 2020.* Cambridge, Mass.: Harvard School of Health.

Maccoby, E. E., and C. N. Jacklin. 1974. *The Psychology of Sex Differences.* Stanford, Calif.: Stanford University Press.

Morrison, Andrew R., and María Beatríz Orlando. 1999. Social and Economic Costs of Domestic Violence: Chile and Nicaragua. In *Too Close to Home: Domestic Violence in the Americas,* ed. Andrew R. Morrison and María Loreto Biehl,. Washington, D.C.: Inter-American Development Bank.

Moser, Caroline. 1999. La Violencia en Colombia: Cómo construir una paz sostenible y fortalecer el capital social. In *Ensayos sobre paz y desarrollo: El caso de Colombia y la experiencia internacional,* ed. Solimano et al. Washington, D.C.: World Bank.

Moser, Caroline, and Jeremy Holland. 1997. *Urban Poverty and Violence in Jamaica.* World Bank Latin American and Caribbean Studies Viewpoints. Washington, D.C.: World Bank.

Murray, Christopher, and Alan Lopez. 1996. Estimating Causes of Death: New Methods and Global and Regional Applications for 1990. In *The Global Burden of Disease: A Comprehensive Assessment of Mortality and Disability from Diseases, Injuries and Risk Factors in 1990 and Projected to 2020,* ed. Christopher Murray and Alan Lopez. Cambridge, Mass.: Harvard University School of Health.

National Center for Injury Prevention and Control. 1993. *The Prevention of Youth Violence: A Framework for Community Action.* Atlanta: Centers for Disease Control and Prevention.

O'Campo, Patricia, et al. 1995. Violence by Male Partners against Women during the Childbearing Years: A Contextual Analysis. *American Journal of Public Health* 85(8): 1092–97.

Ospina, Pamela. 1999. Who Is Violent? Factors Associated with Aggressive Behaviors in Latin America and Spain. In *Violence in the Americas: One New Challenge to Public Health.* Washington, D.C.: Pan American Health Organization.

PAHO (Pan American Health Organization). 1998. *Health in the Americas,* vol. 1. Washington, D.C.: Pan American Health Organization.

Quiróz, Edda, and Olga Barrantes. 1994. *Y vivieron felices para siempre?* San José, Costa Rica: Centro Nacional para el Desarrollo de la Mujer y la Familia.

Stanley, Connie. 1992. Domestic Violence: An Occupational Impact Study. Domestic Violence Intervention Services, Inc., Tulsa.

Stark, E., and Flitcraft, A. 1991. Spouse Abuse. In *Violence in America: A Public Health Approach,* ed. Mark L. Rosenberg and Mary Ann Fenley. New York: Oxford University Press.

Strauss, M. A., R. J. Gelles, and S. Steinmetz. 1980. *Behind Closed Doors.* New York: Doubleday.

Thornberry, T. P., et al. 1995. The Prevention of Serious Delinquency and Violence: Implications from the Program of Research on the Causes and Correlates of Delinquency. In *Sourcebook on Juvenile Offenders.* Washington, D.C.: U.S. Department of Justice.

United Nations. 1999. *Global Report on Crime and Justice.* Office for Drug Control and Crime Prevention, Center for International Crime Prevention. New York: Oxford University Press.

Volokh, Alexander, with Lisa Snell. 1997. *School Violence Prevention: Strategies to Keep Schools Safe.* Reason Public Policy Institute Policy Study 234. Los Angeles: Reason Public Policy Institute.

World Bank. 1993. *World Development Report 1993: Investing in Health.* New York: Oxford University Press.

Part II

Case Studies

6

Citizen Insecurity and Fear: Public and Private Responses in Argentina

Catalina Smulovitz

Even though Argentina is far below international statistical averages in crimes per capita, nonetheless there has been an increase in its crime rate. What is less widely known is that opinion polls show that the perception of insecurity is far higher than is warranted by actual crime statistics, and this perception has increased recently, independent of increases in crime. This disparity between perceived insecurity and crime rates is not a new phenomenon; hence, politicians have long been aware that in formulating public policy, they must take people's beliefs into account. An increase in perceived insecurity is significant not only because it will generate more policy demands but also because it highlights the need, in formulating responses, to distinguish between the perception and the reality of crime.

It should also be noted that increasing insecurity among large segments of the Argentine population is attributable to the activities of the very en-

The author acknowledges the collaboration of Hernán Lerena Ortiz, who assisted with data collection.

tities responsible for maintaining law and order. The population distrusts and fears the police as well as other government institutions responsible for guaranteeing citizen security, such as the judiciary (*La Nación*, September 9, 1998; Centro de Estudios Unión para la Nueva Mayoría 1998). There has been police involvement in selling protection for illicit economic activity; in illegal business activities; in fabricating and/or concealing evidence; in the indiscriminate and frequent abuse of power (as in the case of police edicts or background checks, which serve as grounds for preventive detention); and in the arbitrary and excessive use of force, as evidenced by the proportion of citizen deaths during "confrontations." That citizen insecurity may be the result of ineffective and/or criminal conduct on the part of state institutions responsible for ensuring security highlights the seriousness of the perceived insecurity, and several responses can be anticipated: There will be proposals to reform the structure and functioning of police institutions; institutional and societal mechanisms will be developed to monitor police activity; and parallel security systems, such as private security arrangements, will emerge and develop.

This chapter analyzes the different types of insecurity and the various public policy responses to them. However, any approach must take into account the scars and the lack of trust left over from the activities of government security forces during the periods of military government. These fears and the lessons of the past exert an influence on the formulation of current crime policy. Although some people believe that there is no longer any danger of government security forces gaining autonomy or engaging in the arbitrary use of power, others are more wary. Some segments of the population view the expansion of rights as part of the problem, whereas others see it as part of the solution. Each of these views has different implications for policy formation. Hence, the design of current policy and the attempt to define a public response to security issues depend both on an assessment of the causes of insecurity and on the importance assigned to past experiences.

Public Policy and the Increase in Crime

Police statistics from the past two decades reveal an increase in the number of crimes and in the crime rate in Argentina that is consistent with trends in industrial and developing countries (Dijk and Mayhew 1993). Police statistics (INDEC 1990), which were the only source of information on crime in Argentina until 1996, indicate the following trends for the period 1980–95:

1. There was an increase in both the crime rate (150.6 percent) and in the total number of crimes reported (212 percent). Several phases can be distinguished in the pattern of the increase in crime rate: (a) an increase between 1980 and 1989, with 1989 representing the peak—exceeded only in 1995; (b) a decline between 1989 and 1991, though this decline did not fall to the peak levels of the 1970s; and (c) an increase beginning in 1991, which does not yet appear to have peaked.
2. Property crimes, which increased 241 percent, accounted for at least 60 percent of all crime. In 1989, property crimes accounted for 74.7 percent of crimes reported, but beginning in 1990, they decreased as a proportion of the aggregate crimes rates.
3. Crimes against individual liberty showed a greater increase than any other category of crime (732 percent) and also had the highest increase as a proportion of the aggregate crime rates.
4. Second and third places, as a percentage of all crimes reported, went to crimes against persons involving criminal intent—a 201 percent increase—and crimes against persons involving culpable negligence—170 percent increase.
5. The number of homicides per 100,000 inhabitants grew 23 percent in the 1980s and 1990s. However, the current rate remains lower than those in Brazil, Colombia, Mexico, Venezuela, or the United States for the same years.
6. The geographical distribution of crime indicated a marked increase in crime rates in the nation's capital and in Mendoza, compared with increases in other parts of the country.

International crime policy experts agree that data collected by police sources have two important characteristics. First, there are virtually no controls to ensure that the data collection process is reliable. Second, because not all crime is reported, police data tend to underrepresent the dimensions of the problem. For precisely this reason, since 1989, the United Nations has promoted conducting surveys to ask whether people have been victims of crime and thus to measure the unreported crime rate. In 1996, the National Office of Crime Policy carried out the first such survey in the nation's capital and in Greater Buenos Aires (table 6.1).[1] In 1997, a second survey was conducted, which included the city of Rosario (table 6.2); and a third survey is in progress.[2]

A comparison of police statistics and victimization surveys indicates that the crime rate is much higher than reflected in the police data. According to

Table 6.1.   *Answers to the Survey Question "Were you the victim of one or more crimes during the year?" (percent)*

Answer	Capital, 1995	Greater Buenos Aires, 1996	Capital, 1997	Greater Buenos Aires, 1997	Rosario, 1997
Yes	35.7	51.8	42.0	44.1	50.3
No	64.3	48.2	58.0	55.9	49.7

Note: In the survey, crimes were defined as including residential theft, vehicle theft, theft of objects from vehicles, theft involving violence, and personal theft.
Source: Own elaboration with data from Ministry of Justice, National Office of Crime Policy and from the report "Hacia un plan nacional de política criminal," Ministry of Justice, National Office of Crime Policy, 1998.

Table 6.2.   *Ranking of Crimes: Comparison among the Cities of Rosario, Greater Buenos Aires (Northern and Western Sections), and the Capital (percent)*

Type of Crime	Capital, 1995	Greater Buenos Aires, 1996	Capital, 1997	Greater Buenos Aires, 1997	Rosario, 1997
Theft of objects from vehicle	6.9	16.8	14.3	16.2	22
Residential theft	4.5	14.9	5.9	9.5	11.5
Personal theft	8.7	9.7	12.9	7.5	10.7
Theft involving violence	4.5	9.4	8.6	9.8	7.4
Injuries	3.2	4.4	3.8	3.4	4.7
Auto theft	3.0	4.6	3.6	3.3	1.8
Motorcycle theft	n.a.	n.a.	0.9	1	1.5
Bicycle theft	n.a.	n.a.	2.9	6.1	6.4
Other[a]	16.4	16.5	1.8	1.4	2.8

Note: "n.a." means not available.
[a]In 1996, "other" included swindles and fraud, corruption, and sexual crimes. These categories were not disaggregated for the 1997 data.
Source: Ministry of Justice, National Office of Crime Policy (1998b).

the National Office of Crime Policy, 70 percent of crimes are not reported.[3] However, before conclusions can be drawn, certain methodological issues must be clarified. Unlike data from police sources, the determination by survey of whether a person has been the target of a crime is based on whether the victim perceives the event involved as a crime. Hence, the crimes accounted for in these surveys do not necessarily correspond to the legal definition of crimes. It should also be borne in mind that victimization surveys do not include as many types of crimes as do police statistics; homicides and crimes against national security or against the government are not included in the victimization surveys. Thus, although certain impressions can be created by comparing the two sources, the differences in defining which crimes are taken into account must be considered.

An explanation for the increase in crime depends, naturally, on the assessment of its causes. According to some, the increase is the result of social factors, and consequently the potential solution emphasizes implementing social policy to solve the problem. If, however, the problem is due to failures in crime control and systems of punishment, solutions will focus on improving the capacity of the police—whether through modernization and increasing material resources or by improving training and labor conditions for police forces. The latter view can be expected to involve proposals for increased police powers, as well as for more severe punishments.

Despite a lack of studies providing data to demonstrate convincingly the causes of the rise in crime rates, certain social and economic factors traditionally associated with crime are worth mentioning. Statistics show that between 1986 and 1996 the unemployment rate doubled in Greater Buenos Aires, with a fourfold increase among people 18 to 25 years of age (INDEC 1986, 1998). Data from the Secretariat of Economic Planning indicate that, between 1991 and 1996, 48 percent of youths between 14 and 19 years of age from low-income households dropped out of school (Marabotto 1999). Studies carried out by researchers at the Fundación Mediterránea (Navarro 1997) show that both income and employment are key factors in explaining crime rates.[4]

Although no single set of data explains the phenomenon, the overall statistics shed light on the social context in which the phenomenon is occurring.[5] The data also suggest that preventive policy should include social measures focused on such critical elements as unemployment and school dropout rates. It should be noted, however, that existing studies do not specifically address the socioeconomic characteristics of those committing crimes beyond a general examination of the relation between crime and employment and dropout rates.

Though there are some differences among the proposals advanced by national, provincial, and municipal officials, most authorities clearly attribute the increase in crime to ineffective punitive mechanisms. In November 1997, officials of the Interior Ministry announced that a commission would be formed to study penal code changes, with a view to increasing sentences for certain crimes. In February 1998, they proposed increasing the minimum sentence for certain crimes, increasing the time during which arrestees may be held incommunicado, making the system for repeat offenders more severe, eliminating parole for weapons possession offenses, increasing sentences for resisting arrest, granting the police authority to interrogate arrestees, and lowering the age of criminal liability (*Clarín,* February 12, 1998).

In September 1998, Argentine president Carlos Menem rejected the concept that unemployment and social exclusion are the cause of crime, suggesting instead that the solution is "a strong arm and zero tolerance." Two weeks later, the government proposed a new set of measures, including proposals for increasing sentences for repeat offenders, reducing the possibility of parole, and increasing police authority to counteract the effects of recently approved rights legislation.[6]

This set of initiatives was in some cases in opposition to, in some cases in competition with, or in some cases complementary to measures implemented or proposed by authorities of the autonomous governments of the city and province of Buenos Aires. In February 1998, the Buenos Aires municipal legislature approved the Código de Convivencia Urbana. The code, approved unanimously, set standards for the protection of citizens' rights and property. One of its innovations was to eliminate Federal Police authority to carry out detentions not strictly within their jurisdiction.[7] The approval of the code triggered intense debate, which was reflected—and at times stimulated—by the media, and stimulated participation by neighborhood residents as well as Federal Police officials and national and municipal officials. Most of those involved called for establishing more stringent standards than those approved by the Buenos Aires legislature.

Much of the controversy focused on abolishing the authority of the police to make discretionary arrests for misdemeanors. A series of dramatic and highly publicized crimes at the end of August 1998 lent weight to the argument made by the national government and, to a lesser extent, by the municipal government and by the Federal Police, that the new code left the police ill-equipped to prevent crime.[8] As a result of the reactions provoked by passage of the code, the municipal legislature introduced a series of modifications restricting the scope of the regulations it had approved. They drafted a bill to restore the ability of the police to carry out preventive detentions. Simultaneously, the national government drafted another series of bills, one of which would reinstate some of the powers of the police to detain suspects.

Public policy responses to security issues may tend to focus on punitive measures and neglect social aspects because public officials view the problem of insecurity primarily as a political demand that requires a quick response. Solutions based on social policy and social measures, which produce results over the long term, are seen as inadequate to meet the urgent political necessity involved. Thus, responses are likely to be based on measures with a high degree of public visibility and that can be implemented immediately—and punitive responses meet both of these requirements.

Punitive measures, however, can be implemented quickly and may appear to address the problem in an immediate way. But such policy has long-range ramifications. Although the political structure must prove its effectiveness in exercising the state's policing function, its ability to control the discretionary use of police powers and to reorganize the functioning of the police is limited. As a result, the police remain in a better situation to reverse or neutralize reforms that diminish their authority or prerogatives or make it possible to investigate or limit their activities.

The erratic course of this process highlights the degree of conflict that has come to surround these issues within government and in society as a whole. The controversy, and the presence of contradictory demands— some sectors demanding more rights, others demanding more punitive authority—result in a lack of coherence in formulating public policy. Though the growing perception of insecurity appears to be strengthening the push for more punitive solutions, it is clear that the debate over the best public policy approach is still in progress.

Insecurity and Fear: Public and Private Responses

Along with the increase in crime, opinion polls indicate changes in society's perception of the seriousness of the problem. Crime was not a priority issue in the public awareness between 1994 and mid-1997. During this period, surveys ranked crime fifth to eighth on a list of people's concerns, whereas unemployment, low salaries, and corruption were identified as the country's biggest problems.[9] Beginning in April 1997, however, a significant change occurred, with crime rising from sixth to second place and becoming one of the three main problems cited by respondents (Centro de Estudios Unión para la Nueva Mayoría 1998). Furthermore, though unemployment continued to be the leading concern of citizens in the province of Buenos Aires, the results of various surveys conducted in the capital in July 1998 confirmed that, in the opinion of those respondents, security was the biggest problem.

Although three out of ten individuals stated that they had been victims of crimes during the preceding year (27 percent), seven out of ten feared becoming the victim of a crime in the coming months (71.6 percent).[10] The most common fears were of a physical attack and robbery. For those living in the capital, the greater fear was of physical attack (52.5 percent), whereas among residents of Greater Buenos Aires, the greater fear was of robbery or theft (45.2 percent). People felt most unsafe in the street: 76.1 percent of those who were afraid of becoming the victim of a crime were afraid of this occurring in the street, with this fear being greater in the capital (80.6 percent) than in Greater Buenos Aires (73 percent).

An examination of the responses regarding the causes of increases in crime, and of what types of individuals were committing the crimes reflects certain prejudices, but also leads to some interesting insights. Unemployment and increased poverty were considered to be the main causes of growing crime rates by 64.7 percent of respondents. The other factors mentioned were increased drug use (11.7 percent), ineffectiveness of the police (6.4 percent), and overly lenient judges (4.1 percent).

Contrary to what might be assumed, and in contrast to the initial official responses to the problem, the population as a whole viewed deficiencies in the penal system as being of only secondary importance in explaining increased crime. Although 25.6 percent of the population believed that the poor were most likely to commit crimes, and 15.1 percent believed that those most often involved in crime were drug users, 18.5 percent believed that retired police and military personnel were the group that most frequently committed crimes, and 6.8 percent of the population believed that active police officers constituted the other major offending group.[11]

The study conducted by the Centro de Estudios Unión para la Nueva Mayoría also polled teenagers between 12 and 17 years of age, both in the capital and in Greater Buenos Aires. Not only did teenagers feel more unsafe than the overall population, they were also victims of crime more frequently than the general population; 80.1 percent feared that they would be victims of crime, whereas 32.5 percent stated that they had been actual victims of crime in the last year. As with the general population, the crimes most feared by teenagers were physical attack (38.3 percent) and theft of property (35.3 percent).

However, teenagers also had significant levels of fear of sexual assault (26.3 percent). As with the general population, the street was viewed as the most unsafe place (69.9 percent); and as was true of the rest of the public, they believed that increased unemployment and poverty were the main causes of crime (55 percent). The most striking differences between the general population and teenagers is whom they believed to be the most common perpetrators of criminal acts. Twenty percent of teenagers pointed to active police officers as the group most frequently involved in perpetrating crimes, and another 10 percent pointed to retired police and military personnel.

Few data are available on which to base an assessment of whether there is a relation between perceptions of insecurity and the social status of the respondents. Data from a survey conducted in September 1998, covering the capital and Greater Buenos Aires, show that the high-income segment of the population feels less unsafe than do low-income people. This is not surprising. As will be seen below, crime and perceived insecurity affect distinct social sectors differently, because those with greater resources are able to find ways to increase their security, with measures ranging from living in gated communities to employing private security services. Thus, the Centro de Estudios Unión para la Nueva Mayoría survey indicated that upper-middle-class individuals suffered fewer incidents of crime than did other segments of the population (table 6.3).

Three facts emerge from these data. First, there is a growing sense of in-security—that is, fear is increasing. Second, there is a significant discrepancy between actual victimization rates and sense of insecurity. Third, one of the sources of insecurity for significant segments of the population is the very entities responsible for ensuring that security. What is the significance of these facts, and why focus on them? The growing fear in society is significant, because the perception of crime is responsible for various behaviors that affect forms of social contact, relationships, urban structures, penal legislation, and the state's monopoly on the use of power. This fear generates demands for both public policy and governmental responses that tend to erode legislation protecting people's rights.

Thus, despite the fact that surveys consistently indicate that the majority of the population attribute increased insecurity to low wages and unemployment, 81 percent of the population in the capital and in Greater Buenos Aires supports establishing more severe sentences in the Penal Code, and 40 percent is willing to limit individual freedom in the interest

Table 6.3. *Answer to a Survey Question about Those Who Have Been Victims of a Crime in the Past 12 Months, by Socioeconomic Stratum (percent)*

Upper class, upper middle class, and self-employed professionals	12
Middle and lower middle class	28
Lower class and sectors with unsatisfied basic needs	40

Source: Centro de Estudios Unión para la Nueva Mayoría (1998, 36).

of providing for greater overall security (Centro de Estudios Unión para la Nueva Mayoría 1998, 56, 164). In other words, the demands resulting from increased fear have consequences not only for criminals but also for the entire population, which seems willing to sacrifice liberties for the sake of greater security.

How have the government and the public responded to this growing sense of insecurity? It has already been mentioned that the national government proposed legislation to increase sentences for repeat offenders, reduce the possibility of parole, restore the police's power to carry out preventive detentions, and change immigration law (*Clarín,* September 25, 1998). The government's response clearly suggests the assumption that crime is the principal cause of fear and perceived insecurity in the urban environment. Although these two phenomena are related, the discrepancy between the prevalence of socially perceived insecurity and the actual phenomenon of crime should raise questions about what other factors may be responsible for this sense of social alarm.

Fear has also brought about changes in people's habits and caused them to take private measures to protect themselves. In some cases, these responses are of a public, nongovernmental nature (as in the case of neighbors who meet to take preventive measures), whereas others involve individual self-defense measures. Thus, 58.7 percent of the population stated that their habits have changed; 36.9 percent said they go out less at night; 29.1 percent installed residential fences or alarms; 6.1 percent purchased weapons; and 2.2 percent engaged private security services (Centro de Estudios Unión para la Nueva Mayoría 1988, 45–46). A wide range of behaviors—from the 42 percent increase in the number of weapons permits granted between 1996 and 1997 (Registro Nacional de Armas 1998), to the increased number of agencies and personnel providing private security services,[12] to the move to gated communities—indicates that fear has introduced an element of suspicion and mistrust into interpersonal relations.[13]

What are the political and social consequences of the need to address demands arising from people's heightened sense of insecurity? In terms of its effects on public policy, the initial response has been to increase the state's authority to impose stiffer punishments and to increase the power of the police. As has been noted, this approach can have significant consequences for society as a whole. Although such measures allow the state to respond quickly and visibly to the problem, they may have no demonstrable ability to reduce crime. It has also been pointed out that the punitive approach diminishes the state's ability to impose restrictions on the police's discretionary use of power and hinders chances of implementing a functional reorganization of police institutions.

A social consequence of this fear is the use of private self-defense measures. It remains a question what effect the changes in living habits, referred to above, could have as they become incorporated into the life of society. One result of the trend to adopt self-defense strategies is that security is becoming privatized. The isolation of gated communities and the use of private security services have transformed security from a public good to something appropriated by the private sector. This has a variety of implications. First, because not all people are in a position to engage security services, it is evident that inequality in the provision and benefit of security has increased. This inequality in access to security is reflected in surveys showing that, according to respondents, persons with higher incomes have been victimized by crime less often than those belonging to lower-income strata.

The privatization of security has other consequences, as well. With the proliferation of private security agencies, the number of private security agents in the province of Buenos Aires, at present, is equivalent to the number of Buenos Aires police employees, after the personnel reductions that took place in the recent effort to reform the police. This parallel security system, and the possibility of private security agents using force, jeopardizes the state's monopoly on the use of force—a situation that has yet to be evaluated. However, there are inevitable risks involved in having a parallel group of the same size as the forces that are legally subordinate to the government. This is particularly problematic because these private forces have evolved in a legal framework with insufficient or antiquated government control and regulation.

The growth of the private security industry in recent years has provoked proposed legislation designed to impose regulations in this area (*La Nación*, October 30, 1998). There have been a number of confrontations involving theft in which private agents have injured, and in some cases killed, individuals who happened to be present at the time of these incidents. Various sources have stated that the personnel employed by these agencies have not necessarily been trained in weapons use, and in many cases they are individuals who have been barred from service in police agencies for bad conduct. Although these private organizations were originally created to fill the void resulting from deficiencies in government services, the fear of private agents simply compounds the existing fear of improper police behavior.

Finally, it should be emphasized that changes in habits, caused by fear, may have permanent and profound implications for the primary forms of social interaction within the community. In a social context in which differences in appearance can be a source of fear, it can be anticipated that different social groups will distance themselves from one another. A recent report by Nicolás Casullo stated that "Only those who are members of the 'tribe' are recognized—the tribe being the country club, the criminal group, the golf club or the gang" (*La Nación*, September 15, 1998). The need for added security within the group tends to limit community relations, excluding anyone who is unfamiliar; as a result, fear is likely to result in forms of social discrimination.

Furthermore, because relationships with unfamiliar individuals are perceived as potentially dangerous, it can be assumed that other forms of primary socialization will ultimately be affected. Given the prevailing fear, trust in personal relationships tends to be replaced by suspicion and caution. This creates a new set of guidelines—about whom children will relate to (or avoid) at school or whom youth or adults will interact with in the neighborhood; it also fosters anxiety about who really is one's neighbor.

These strategies are perceived as necessary for survival. However, rather than serving as strategies for relating to others, they become means of protecting oneself from unknown persons, because the unfamiliar is automatically suspect. The spread of such "preventive" behaviors in primary social interactions limits the development of relations based on cooperation and solidarity. Though the long-term implications of this growing mistrust are difficult to predict, such a situation can lead to a weakening of social links, an increasing reliance on the private realm, and political apathy—factors that in turn have an impact on democratic life. When fear isolates citizens, inserting a coercive element into their personal relations, they lose the capacity to act and to affect public affairs. Hence, in addition to the prejudices caused by fear and mistrust, potential social consequences must be dealt with.[14]

Police Abuse, Insecurity, and Police Reform

Extralegal police activity is not a new phenomenon in Argentina and has persisted despite changes in the political regime (see Elbert 1998; Dutil and Ragendorfer 1997; Zaffaroni 1982). Police use of illegal methods to enforce political and social repression during the most recent period of military dictatorship is widely known. Statistics also indicate that after the democratic transition began, there continued to be a high number of young people killed in supposed "confrontations" with police.[15] A number of cases of police violence in recent years have gained high public visibility, revealing not only police involvement in violent acts but also institutional attempts to conceal or falsify incriminating evidence related to these acts, police involvement in selling protection to those engaged in illicit economic activity, and direct participation in illicit business operations.

The survey conducted by the Centro de Estudios Unión para la Nueva Mayoría (1998, 47, 48) shows that 19.3 percent of the population in the capital and in Greater Buenos Aires fear the police more than they fear criminals, with 7 percent indicating that they had been victims of police abuse in the past year. These percentages are significantly higher among respondents between 12 and 17 years of age—37 and 15 percent, respectively (p. 161). According to this survey, 26 percent of the population and 30 percent of teenagers believe that military officers, retired police, and active police officers are among the groups most frequently involved in criminal acts.

Complaints that violence and police corruption are a source of insecurity, and the high public visibility of several cases in which there was confirmed police involvement, have made the topic of the police a potential election issue. Reforms of the police force have been formulated and implemented in a number of districts as one result of the increased public attention brought to the problem. These reforms have not been implemented in all cases and, as indicated by the following account, police reform is still an unfinished process.

One new aspect, however, is that the issue of police reform has become part of the political agenda and draws on the participation of a wide range of players. In addition to politicians and the police, experts from political parties, members of a variety of nongovernmental organizations, and citizens who have been victims of police violence have organized to influence the process. Unlike the past, the inclusion in the debate of such a wide range of participants has transformed police policy into an issue that can no longer be resolved in camera.

Police reform in the province of Santa Fe used, as a starting point, an evaluation that pointed to the following problems: growing mistrust of the police; an increased sense of insecurity; a high degree of militarization within the police organization; a process in which the police tend to be autonomous from the political structure; and increased anarchy within the organization, resulting in criminal acts and a lack of discipline (Rosúa 1998).

In response to these problems, the provincial administration, which came to power in 1995, developed a series of measures, such as neighborhood councils for community security, aimed at reestablishing trust between the police and the community; and improving the educational level of the police—involving changes in recruitment at both the command level and among officers—and modifications in the process of training future police personnel. In an attempt to reestablish internal discipline, an oversight mechanism (the Provincial Office of Internal Affairs) was established, headed by a political official whose functions include initiating investigative proceedings against police officers who have been involved in serious incidents and monitoring the management and functioning of certain police divisions.

In September 1998, the provincial government proposed legislation to change the organizational structure of the police.[16] According to Rosúa (1998, 43), "This reform attempts to establish rules governing a demilitarized, professional police force in which personnel are granted workers' rights; make merit a priority factor in promotion, and provide transparent operational regulations; increase the effectiveness of police, while observing respect for individual liberty and human rights; and make police accountable to the political structure in a democratic system." Although this description makes clear the political objective of the proposed changes, there is no way to predict the ultimate fate of these well-intentioned efforts.

The initiation of reform of the Buenos Aires police was sudden and dramatic. It began on December 19, 1997, with a decree by Governor Eduardo Duhalde, which provided for a 90-day intervention period to reorganize the police and dissolve the command and management structure. The reorganization was based on an assessment (Arslanián and Binder 1997) that, among other things, indicated a crisis in multiple areas: the system for investigating crimes, the autonomy of the private security system, the lack of measures and approaches to deal with crime prevention, security and criminal prosecution, the poor relationship between the police and the community, and the lack of adequate mechanisms for politically supervising the police.[17]

This assessment (Saín 1998, 72–75; and interview with the author) described the police organization as "unitary and vertical" and thus unable to deal internally with the organizational crisis. The assessment proposed replacing the organizational structure with a new system, which would include establishing an investigatory police force responsible for investigating crimes in collaboration with the Judicial Police; the strengthening of the Judicial Police through a transfer of technical personnel and experts from the existing police force; the creation of eighteen community security police units, one for each of the province's judicial districts, responsible for preventing crime and maintaining public security; the creation of a new organization responsible for the transport and custody of prisoners; and the creation of a new and autonomous traffic police force.

According to Saín (1998), the proposed reform sought to differentiate functions, divide the organization into separate sections, and decentralize the command. The reform plan also included the creation of a "new structure for political oversight of the security system," through a "Ministry of Security"; strengthening community participation in dealing with security issues; regulating the private security industry; and transferring criminal cases investigated by police officials to a judicial forum.

During the 3 months of intervention by the governor, changes were made in the management structure of the police, which included retiring more than 300 police superintendents and upper-level officers;[18] dissolving the regional units and instead creating 18 police divisions for the different judicial districts; initiating a process of transferring criminal proceedings and cases; and eliminating all of the investigative squads, forming instead 18 investigatory units for the individual judicial districts. Between March and June 1998, the provincial legislature studied and debated public security legislation,[19] as well as legislation on the organization of the provincial police,[20] which, after certain modifications (see Saín 1998), was passed on June 16.

In spite of the changes made to the original, the legislation that was passed did involve a change in the conception of public security. The functioning of the system is no longer the sole domain of the police, and now involves community participation; there have been changes in regulations regarding police performance, making it consistent with legislation already in effect; detention periods have been reduced; and internal mechanisms have been created to monitor corruption and the abuse of official powers—elements that were nonexistent in the now defunct Buenos Aires police.

Although these regulatory changes are significant, the process of implementing the reforms remains uncertain and still entails overcoming major obstacles. In addition to resistance within the police on the part of officers who, as a result of such reform, were removed from the force,[21] there was opposition from those remaining on the force, who saw their powers being restricted. There have also been complaints that some of the police captains dismissed for misconduct and corruption had been hired at some police stations as "security directors."[22] If this is true, another impediment to the success of the reforms could be the actions of municipal authorities, who do not seem to share the objectives or sense of urgency of provincial authorities.

Further, there is a lack of state resources and capacity to implement some of the measures called for in the new legislation. Thus, although the provincial bar association supported the transfer of investigative functions to prosecutors, it also complained of an inability to properly implement the regulations, due to insufficient personnel and lack of financial and material resources (*Clarín*, September 29, 1998).[23] The problem is compounded by the fact that the measure has two objectives: preventing police manipulation of investigations and ensuring that procedures are conducted properly and with greater accountability. This combination of problems suggests that some of the proposed objectives could ultimately be abandoned in the highly conflictive implementation process.[24]

Reform is also being undertaken within the Federal Police, which has been the subject of complaints of corrupt economic activities, with the population showing a high level of mistrust of this body. Here, an additional difficulty is causing delays in formulating the reform, namely, a dispute between the national government and the city of Buenos Aires regarding the conditions under which the Federal Police is to be granted municipal jurisdiction. In the city's view, the national government is attempting to shift responsibility for security to the municipality without giving it the necessary authority or funding (*La Nación* August 1, 1998). Until this conflict is resolved, reform is highly unlikely, because, in addition, the police force has its own preferences as to how to resolve the dispute over the transfer of authority.

A further consequence of the view that insecurity is caused by improper police activity is that various institutional and societal mechanisms to monitor police activity have emerged and developed. One common feature of proposals for reform, including those advanced by the police, is that they have included specific institutional entities to ensure community participation in formulating security policy. The Buenos Aires reform, for example, provides for neighborhood, municipal, and departmental participation, as well as for involvement by the Office of Municipal Security Advocacy.[25]

In the case of the Santa Fe reform, neighborhood boards for community security were formed to promote discussion between police and neighborhood members (Rosúa 1998). An article by the former head of the Federal Police, Pablo Baltazar García, states that to successfully deal with the causes of crime, people must support and cooperate in crime prevention and in maintaining security. García specifically proposes the creation of a precinct-based community crime prevention council to shift the task of crime prevention and conflict resolution from the exclusive domain of the police to a collaboration between the community and the police, "to establish and maintain social peace and tranquility" (García 1998). The government of the city of Buenos Aires, beginning in July 1997, promoted the creation of neighborhood-based councils to prevent crime and violence and to provide citizens with a forum for expressing their security demands and for working together in monitoring and implementing security measures.[26]

Nevertheless, despite these innovative efforts in which government institutions themselves implement mechanisms to channel participation and monitor police action, the most important aspect of the effort appears to have been the emergence of a number of civic associations and neighborhood groups, which include in their membership individuals who have been directly affected by crime. In May 1987, a group of police fired shots at three young people who were drinking beverages on a street corner in the working-class Buenos Aires neighborhood known as Ingeniero Budge.[27] This case, which the police categorized as "injuries, serious threats, resistance to and attacks on the police, illegal use of weapons and triple homicide in the course of a fight," triggered a social protest criticizing the police's actions and demanding justice.

The Ingeniero Budge case was followed systematically by the media. From that point on, coverage of the subject of the police's propensity to shoot—known as being *gatillo fácil* ("trigger-happy"), migrated from the police columns of the country's newspapers to the section covering political news. The social reaction and demonstrations also had an important effect: Although police violence, which certainly existed before the Ingeniero Budge case, continued, many of the new cases following this incident were met with demonstrations and protests criticizing the police and demanding justice.

The Ingeniero Budge case not only inspired those personally affected by particular cases to organize; it also led to the creation of national organizations such as the Committee of Families of Innocent Victims (COFAVI) and the Coordinating Group Against Police and Institutional Repression (CORREPI), designed to report repressive police activity and demand justice, a task these groups have undertaken in cases where police violence has been confirmed.[28] Over time, this work has led to the establishment of a mechanism to monitor police activity, a task carried out by citizen volunteers. Various neighborhood organizations—self-created in some cases, and with the support of public officials in others—have emerged that are dedicated to designing and carrying out crime prevention measures (Ministry of Justice and the Government of the City of Buenos Aires 1999; Martínez et al. 1998).

The high visibility of demonstrations provoked by individual cases and the emergence of these organizations, and their success in achieving their objectives of identifying and punishing the perpetrators, reflect the increasing use of alternative methods of ensuring accountability for specific public policies (Smulovitz and Peruzzoti 2000). In general, studies examining accountability have concentrated on the vertical (Przeworski, Manin, and Stokes 1999) and horizontal (O'Donnell 1998) dimensions of monitoring governmental activity—that is, elections and the system of checks and balances.

Recent experience in the new democracies, however, and particularly in Argentina, reveal the emergence and growth of a number of vertical procedures and activities to monitor government activity that go beyond the limits of traditional electoral control. These involve actions by individual citizens and by networks of citizen groups and social organizations, and they include judicial demands, media reports, complaints about acts by government agents, and public demonstrations. Unlike traditional mechanisms, these alternative forms of citizen oversight do not depend on electoral mandates or calendars. They are triggered by demand or need and are capable of addressing any area of public policy.

It should also be noted that the resources for carrying out this type of oversight differ from those used to bring about change through voting or through the system of checks and balances. To be effective, people using traditional mechanisms of accountability must broaden the scope of their claims by demonstrating their ability to garner electoral support. The new methods, conversely, rely on the ability of societal mechanisms to demonstrate the vital importance of the demands and their ability to have an impact on the agenda of public discourse. However, legitimacy is based on a different principle: the right to petition for rights independent of the extent to which those rights are being demanded by the population at large.

Though societal oversight mechanisms have made it possible to provide scrutiny of policy and set the public agenda relatively effectively, these mechanisms have certain limitations. A detailed account of this issue, however, is not given here (see Smulovitz 1998); rather, it suffices to point out that the use of such mechanisms reflects the inequality of access that characterizes citizen participation in general. Such inequality not only limits the breadth of the use of these mechanisms but also affects the selection of issues to be considered. Furthermore, in light of experience with models of collective action, the mechanisms can be expected to face additional difficulties when the goods demanded are public in nature.

The groups and organizations that emerged to protest the cases of *gatillo fácil* exemplify the new forms that are evolving to influence and affect the content of and the approach to policy formulation in the post-transition democracies. These groups have succeeded in making police abuse an offense to be reported and dealt with (Felstiner, Abel, and Sarat 1980–81). In recent times, demonstrations have followed many new cases of police abuse, giving them public visibility, and it is common for many of these cases to gain media coverage and ultimately result in judicial action. CORREPI (n.d., b), for instance, specifically indicates that one of its tasks is to "provide legal aid to victims and family members, and represent them in court cases initiated against the perpetrators of repressive acts." [29]

Despite their limited oversight ability, social mechanisms are nonetheless playing an important role in establishing accountability for policy and in influencing the public agenda. As a result of the anxiety and commotion engendered by these complaints and practices, the questions of police abuse and the way the police carry out their functions have become part of the debate on solving problems of citizen insecurity. Thus, whereas past approaches to the problem of insecurity have increased the repressive authority of the police, the current debate can no longer ignore the question of institutional and societal oversight of police activity.

Conclusions

The discussion above makes clear some of the difficulties in defining the problem of citizen security or insecurity in Argentina and highlights the sometimes contradictory nature of the answers that have emerged from different assessments of the problem. Some believe that citizen insecurity is caused by the increase in crime, which they attribute principally to deficiencies in the police and in the effectiveness of the judiciary. Those favoring this view maintain that public policy should concentrate on improving the material resources of the police, increasing their powers of detention, and making criminal sentences more severe.

Others point to data indicating that the increased perception of crime is far greater than the actual increase in crime rates. They maintain, on the basis of this finding, that public policy must differentiate between solutions designed to address the problem of increased crime and those designed to deal with the perception of it. They also warn that public policy must take into account the various ways in which increased fear has an impact on the possibility of peaceful coexistence within society—emphasizing the increasing mistrust, the growing recourse to self-defense tactics, and the rise in intolerance. Finally, large segments of the population attribute increased insecurity to the activity of the police themselves. Those who view the problems in this way believe that public policy should concentrate on reforming the structure and functioning of the police, and on developing the institutional and social mechanisms needed to adequately monitor police activity.

What have been the consequences of these differing assessments, and in what way has citizen security or insecurity affected public and private responses to the problem? The recent literature has placed particular emphasis on a broad redefinition of the concept of security. Unlike the past, when the primary concerns were the defense of territorial integrity or the repression of an "internal enemy," the concept today refers rather to "the needs of individuals to live in peace and have the economic, political, and environmental means to live with dignity" (Ramírez Ocampo 1998, 5). According to this view, citizen security is associated with the "absence of physical threats or risks, and with income, housing, health, education and other conditions" (p. 5). This broad redefinition of the concept appears to have two objectives: first, to underscore the role of social policy in achieving these goals; and second, to warn that security is more than the customarily cited relationship between deviant behavior (insecurity) and the suppression of such behavior.

The coexistence of these two concepts of security—one based on suppressing deviant behavior, the other based on bringing about the welfare of individuals—highlights the difficulties and the range of questions posed by the current problem. This complexity has been reflected, to some extent, in the different sections of this chapter. Some government officials and certain segments of the population view the cause of the problem as the inefficiency of government entities in suppressing deviant behavior, whereas others attribute the problem to the effect of economic policy, the consequences of such policy on personal life and liberty, and the increasing discretionary power of the state. The difference between these two views is more than academic, and involves more than simply a matter of definition, because they lead to varying, and at times incompatible, policy approaches. Thus, measures to increase the punitive and discretionary powers of the police are perceived by some as promoting security, whereas others see it as a threat to security. The difference in these views also explains the erratic and contradictory nature of some recent policies and suggests why this can be expected to continue.

Other developments also must be taken into account. Some relate to the functioning of the police in the new democracies, particularly with regard to the supervision and monitoring of police activity. Others involve the appearance of certain social phenomena connected with the "privatization" of violence.

Whether due to actual increases in crime, increased perception of insecurity, or because recent history has made the qualities of security forces a topic of public debate, the issue of citizen security and of how to ensure it has become a topic of public discussion. Because of the public visibility that the issue has gained and the divergent interpretations of its scope that have been put forward, it can no longer be "resolved" in camera by a few government officials, who decide on a course of action without further examination—a practice common in the past. Today, both the design and the implementation of policy to address the problem must to some degree incorporate the preferences of a wide variety of social sectors and players.

Discussion about and reexamination of the powers and functioning of the police have been another result of the growing insecurity. The initial approach to solving the problem was to institute measures to increase the material resources of the police by providing more police officers, more funds, and more training. However, when it became evident that the activities of the police themselves—in economic corruption, protection of criminal activities, and police abuse—were an intrinsic part of the problem, reforms inevitably began to incorporate plans to restructure the police organization. Proposed reforms have included provisions for external oversight, and although the ultimate success or failure of these measures is uncertain, they are an indication of the problems at hand. Because of the public visibility of the insecurity problem, there has been extensive discussion and review of the scope and powers of the police. In some cases, this has involved questioning age-old procedures that gave the police a high degree of autonomy and discretion in carrying out preventive detentions.

The other phenomenon indicating that much of the current discussion of citizen security concerns the debate on how force is used, and on mechanisms to monitor the use of force, is the emergence of groups to protest and demand justice for cases of police violence. The emergence of organizations such as CORREPI and COFAVI and of institutional entities to process citizen complaints about the improper use of police power are another illustration of this development. Such public accountability mechanisms show that oversight of public policy, especially as it is concerned with the use of force by the state, depends not only on institutional structures but also on the complaints and actions of an autonomous citizenry.

The exercise of this kind of oversight may be considered complementary to the institutional mechanisms provided for in the above-mentioned reforms. It should be borne in mind that these organizations are self-created and based on volunteers. However, their appearance suggests that, although there may be efforts to restrict the effectiveness of such institutional structures, accountability has become a permanent fixture of the social landscape.

There are, however, some negative elements in the current situation. In addition to demands for greater punitive capacity by governmental agencies, Argentina, like other Latin American countries, has seen a privatization of the use of violence (UNDP 1998, 133n). To supplement inadequate services by government agencies, a parallel security system is being built, consisting of private agencies; and individual self-defense behaviors are emerging: the purchase of weapons, the installation of alarm systems, people moving to gated communities, and the organizing of neighborhood watches.

In principle, providing security through a private, parallel system has two major drawbacks. First, the rapid growth and scant regulation of these private security forces could pose a future challenge to the state's monopoly on the use of force. Because agents operating under such a parallel system are not subject to public accountability, the overall population and its representatives are limited in their ability to monitor their actions (Diamint 1998). Second, the private provision of security services magnifies social inequities. It creates differences between those who can and cannot enjoy what by nature is a public good, namely, security; and those who are able to "buy" security and thus compensate for the state's inability in this area have far less incentive to pressure the government to remedy the overall problem, thus accentuating the differences in the quality of security services supplied to different segments of the population.

Increased fear has had specific, tangible effects on individual behavior: again, increased arms purchases for self-defense, installation of alarms, moving to gated communities, and the organizing of neighborhood security operations. In addition to the risks to individual security involved in some of these behaviors,[30] there is another problem. It is an established fact that increasing mistrust can result in greater intolerance and in discriminatory behavior, with "difference" being perceived as threatening. This increase in fear not only reveals but promotes a weakening of social ties within communities. When fear and mistrust affect the majority of social relationships, individuals refrain from participating in public activities and retreat into their own private lives.

The political science literature shows that the formation of institutions and the scope of democratic regimes depend on the type and extent of participation that they can generate and promote. Hence, it can be assumed that the increasing abandonment of public forms of social intercourse may, in the medium term, affect the quality of democratic institutions. Machiavelli, Hobbes, and Montesquieu warned long ago that subjects who are in fear tend to consider restrictions on their liberty preferable to threats of insecurity. In this sense, the most worrisome aspect of the current situation is not the danger that dictatorial regimes will reappear—for this seems unlikely in the present political context—but that the sacrifice of individual liberties will become, for some segments of the population, an attractive option for dealing with fear and insecurity.

Notes

1. Although Buenos Aires is the federal capital, the name of the city is often used to refer to the metropolitan area of Buenos Aires, which includes the capital and the densely populated areas surrounding it. Buenos Aires is also a province. To avoid confusion, this chapter refers to Buenos Aires, the federal capital, as "the capital" and the metropolitan area of Buenos Aires as "Greater Buenos Aires."

2. See Ministry of Justice, National Office of Crime Policy (1998a, 99; 1998b, 77).

3. See Ministry of Justice, National Office of Crime Policy (1998a, 99; 1998b, 77).

4. They also show that the "severity" of the law, measured by the lag variable, "probability of conviction," has a highly significant negative correlation with the number of crimes (see the data below). Similar results can be seen in studies relating unemployment to the number of crimes in different provinces (*Novedades Económicas* 1996).

A regression analysis of the extent of crime—with the variable defined as the number of crimes during the period 1971–94—is as follows. For the variable C, a constant, the coefficient is 3.90, the t-statistic is 1.07, and the probability is 0.29. For the variable $LPOB$ (–2), population, the coefficient is –0.37, the t-statistic is –4.70, and the probability is 0.00. For the variable LU, unemployment rate, the coefficient is 0.39, the t-statistic is 5.31, and the probability is 0.00. For the variable $LPBIPC$, per capita GDP, the coefficient is –0.75, the t-statistic is –1.96, and the probability is 0.06.

The logarithmic estimates were done by two-stage least squares. Instrumental variables: *LURB* (–2), *LPOB* (–2), *LPJOVEN* (–2), *LDELIT* (–1), *LPBIPC* (–1), *LU* (–1). *C*, constant; *LPROB*, probability of conviction; *LU*, unemployment rate; *LPBIPC*, per capita GDP; *LURB*, relation between urban population and total population; *LPOB*, population; and *LPJOVEN*, population between 15 and 29 years of age in relation to total population. Negative numbers in parentheses indicate number of lags in the variable. Adjusted R^2: 0.884253. Source: Navarro (1997).

5. Kessler (1999) states that recent research has shown differing results in regard to the usual association between unemployment and property crimes, and that the two variables are only associated based on a series of intervening variables. Thus, the relationship would be of the following type: One of the consequences of unemployment is the weakening of local social capital, which limits opportunities, works against mechanisms that generate and maintain social norms, and encourages alternative ones that facilitate illegal activities. Kessler adds: "The current consensus is that economic deprivation along with other local problems encourages the development of a social environment in which crime increases, without its being in any way the individual experience of economic deprivation that leads to criminal behavior."

6. The package also proposed changing the immigration law, specifying that foreigners with judicial proceedings in progress would be deported, providing punishments for using illegal documentation and sanctions for businesses hiring undocumented or illegal foreign workers. The package also included measures to punish possession and use of illegal civilian arms, as well as modifications to laws on soccer violence and measures to regulate private security operations (*Clarín*, September 24, 1998).

7. Until the approval of the Código de Convivencia Urbana, police edicts authorized the Federal Police to "make findings on and dispose of cases of those arrested for misdemeanors." In practice, this gave the police wide latitude in making arrests. The procedure authorized the police to make arrests, collect evidence, and pass judgment. The arrestee had no right to a defense, nor were minimum due process provisions guaranteed. The system resulted in massive and arbitrary arrests, in which the police themselves defined what made an individual a suspect. This became the principal tool of the police in crime prevention. One indication of the extent of this phenomenon is the number of arrests made under this procedure. For example, while there were 37,484 arrests for common crimes in 1994, there were 135,038 arrests for misdemeanors. In 1995, there were 150,830 arrests for misdemeanors, with a comparable figure reported for 1996 (see Garrido, Fabricio, and Palmieri 1997).

8. The division head of Metropolitan Security, for example, stated that "The Código de Convivencia is not effective, because it does not allow for prevention. It does not have the necessary provisions" (quoted in Chillier 1998, 22).

9. The data below come from research by the Centro de Estudios Unión para la Nueva Mayoría (1998). The survey was carried out in the capital and in Greater Buenos Aires in April 1998.

10. Data from the National Office of Crime Policy also show this gap; although 51.8 percent of the population were victims of crime in 1996 in Greater Buenos Aires, 82.5 percent were in fear of being victimized. The gap between the current victimization rate (35.7 percent) and those who fear becoming victims (87.7 percent) is even greater in the capital (Ministry of Justice, National Office of Crime Policy 1998b).

11. The question of the perception of insecurity caused by police activity will be discussed in greater detail below.

12. "The most recent data from CAESI (the Argentine Chamber of Security and Investigation Firms) indicate that in the capital and Greater Buenos Aires alone, more than 40,000 private security agents are employed, i.e., as many as are in the police force of the province of Buenos Aires" (*La Nación*, May 14, 1998). An item published in *La Nación* on August 24, 1998, mentions that there are estimated to be 100,000 private security agents throughout the country, and that in the province of Buenos Aires alone there are 683 authorized private security agencies. Yet another article in *La Nación*, published November 6, 1994, estimated that there were 8,000 security agents at work in 1984 (quoted in Maier, Abregú, and Tiscornia 1996, 181).

13. "More than a million and a half Argentines live in the almost 300 gated communities built in recent years in Greater Buenos Aires" (*Clarín,* September 6, 1998).

14. Many authors in recent years have dealt with the impact of trust and mistrust on political and social ties. These include Hardin (1996), Levi (1996), and Fukuyama (1995). Also, in relation to Latin America, the following are of note: Corradi (1992) and UNDP (1998).

15. Research based on information from the newspapers found the following figures on the number of civilians and police killed in confrontations in the capital and in Greater Buenos Aires: in 1983, 88 civilians and 7 police; in 1984, 130 civilians and 13 police; in 1985, 251 civilians and 20 police; in 1986, 155 civilians and 8 police; and in 1987, 127 civilians and 14 police (see Olivera and Tiscornia 1997). CORREPI (n.d., a) contained 329 cases of victims of police repression.

16. The bill states that activity by employees of public security organizations must respect the National Constitution, human rights, the principle of nondiscrimination, the prohibition on torture, and the stipulation that the claim of "obeying orders" cannot serve as a justification for criminal acts. The new organizational structure proposed in the bill places responsibility for the design of security policy in the political branch of government. It also provides for the creation of seven provincial security divisions headed by political officials, and places police departments under the authority of the Under-Secretariat of Public Security.

17. The document includes the assessment and plan of action that served as a foundation for the initial efforts at police reform that the governor of the province of Buenos Aires proposed. Saín (1998) analyzes the various alterations made to the original proposal.

18. Resolutions 209, 210, and 211, signed in May 1998, declared 296 police captains dispensable; in addition, 4,000 police officers were removed as of November 1996.

19. Provincial Law 12,154.

20. Provincial Law 12,155.

21. The police who were barred from service by the reform have formed a movement called Los Sin Gorra, claiming that they were removed from the force despite "impeccable records," and that they have not received the compensation they are owed (*La Nación*, August 2, 1998).

22. *Revista Viva de Clarín*, October 1998, "Manual Arslanián del Buen Policía."

23. According to *Clarín*, internal Buenos Aires Supreme Court sources said that haste in implementing the reform means that operational problems can be expected.

24. On August 6, 1999, in the midst of reviewing the text Leon Arslanián, the minister of security and justice of the province of Buenos Aires, resigned. The day before,

the vice president of the nation and candidate for governor of the province of Buenos
Aires, Carlos Ruckauf stated, "I want to see the murderers dead." Arslanián was replaced by a judge, Osvaldo Lorenzo, who announced changes in the security policy that
indicate a return to the use of repressive mechanisms, signaling his intention to reverse
the process of police reform that was begun in the province (*La Nación,* August 6,
1999). One of the announced measures is the review of procedures to deal with police
involved in misconduct that were in effect during Arslanián's term—a measure inter-
preted as an attempt to revert to the previous, highly questionable structure of the
Buenos Aires police. Before the appointment, six judges from the Cámara Federal of
San Martín had lodged charges in the Council of Magistrates against the new minister
for violation of individual rights committed during the time he served as a judge
(*Clarín,* August 22, 1999).
  25. See articles 11 and 12 of the Provincial Law on Public Security.
  26. A study of the functioning of these centers appears in Martínez et al. 1998.
  27. For a detailed analysis of the social consequences of the case, see the various
studies published since 1991 by Laura Gingold, especially Gingold 1997; also see Jelin
1996.
  28. There are significant differences in how these two organizations interpret their
missions, but such an analysis falls outside the scope of this chapter.
  29. These organizations and neighborhood groups have had varying results. In some
cases, as in the Ingeniero Budge case, the police were sentenced to 11 years in prison,
following a protracted judicial process; in others, the legal proceedings are still in
progress. CORREPI's document, "Alternatives for Legal Action," states that in 1997
the organization was involved in eleven court cases; of these, five culminated in convictions of the police officers involved, four are currently being prosecuted, one was
dismissed and the case has been appealed, and the other is still in the investigation
phase.
  30. Various studies have shown that the number of homicides is directly related to
the extent of weapons possession in a society.

References

Arslanián, León, and Alberto Binder. 1997. Plan de reorganización general del Sistema
    Integral de Seguridad e investigación de los delitos de la Provincia de Buenos
    Aires. Government of the Province of Buenos Aires, Buenos Aires.
Centro de Estudios Unión para la Nueva Mayoría. 1998. *La seguridad pública.* Buenos
    Aires: Editorial Centro de Estudios Unión para la Nueva Mayoría.
Chillier, Gastón. 1998. La sanción de un codigo de convivencia urbana: Causas y efec-
    tos de la eliminación de las detenciones arbitrarias por parte de la policía federal.
    In Documento de Trabajo del Seminario "Las reformas policiales en la Ar-
    gentina." Centro de Estudios Legales y Sociales, Buenos Aires.
Corradi, Juan, ed. 1992. *Fear at the Edge. Terror and Resistance in Latin America.*
    Berkeley: University of California Press.
CORREPI (Coordinating Group Against Police and Institutional Repression). No date,
    a. Archivo de casos de represión policial e institucional 1983/1997. CORREPI,
    Buenos Aires.
———. No date, b. Que hacemos en el ámbito judicial. CORREPI, Buenos Aires.

Diamint, Rut. 1998. Orden global, mercado y privatización de la seguridad. Paper presented at Canadian Foundation for the Americas Conference on the Privatization of Security, Ottawa. October.

Dijk, Jan, and Patricia. Mayhew. 1993. Criminal Victimisation in the Industrialised World: Key Findings of the 1989 and 1992 International Crime Surveys. In *Understanding Crime. Experiences of Crime and Crime Control*. Acts of the International Conference, Publication 49, Rome: United Nations Interregional Crime and Justice Institute.

Dutil, Carlos, and Ricardo Ragendorfer. 1997. *La bonaerense. Historia criminal de la policía de la Provincia de Buenos Aires*. Buenos Aires: Planeta.

Elbert, Carlos Alberto. 1998. Ideología, corrupción y excesos policiales. *Pena y Estado. Revista Latinoamericana de Política Criminal* 3(3): 63–80.

Felstiner, William, Richard Abel, and Austin Sarat. 1980–81. The Emergence and Transformation of Disputes: Naming, Blaming and Claiming. *Law and Society Review* 15(3/4): 631–54.

Fukuyama, Francis. 1995. *Trust*. New York: Basic Books.

García, Pablo Baltazar. 1998. La Policía Federal y la comunidad. *La Nación*, November 12.

Garrido, Manuel, Guariglia Fabricio, and Gustavo Palmieri. 1997. Control judicial de las actividades preventivas y de investigación policiales en el ámbito de la justicia nacional y local. In *Control democrático de los organismos de seguridad interior de la República Argentina*. Buenos Aires: Centro de Estudios Legales y Sociales.

Gingold, Laura. 1997. *Memoria, moral y derecho. El caso de Ingeniero Budge (1987–1994)*. Mexico City: Facultad Latinoamericana de Ciencias Sociales and Juan Pablos Editores.

Hardin, Russell. 1996. Trustworthiness. *Ethics* 107 (October): 26–42.

INDEC (Instituto Nacional de Estadística y Censos). 1986. *Encuesta permanente de hogares*. Buenos Aires: INDEC.

———. 1990. *Anuario estadístico de la República Argentina*. Buenos Aires: INDEC.

———. 1998. *Encuesta permanente de hogares*. Buenos Aires: INDEC.

Jelin, Elizabeth, et al. 1996. *Vida cotidiana y control institucional en la Argentina de los 90*. Buenos Aires: Grupo Editor Latinoamericano.

Kessler, Gabriel. 1999. El impacto social del desarollo. Unpublished.

Levi, Margaret. 1996. A State of Trust. Working Paper 96/23. European University Institute, Florence.

Maier, Julio, Martín Abregú, and Sofía Tiscornia. 1996. El papel de la policía en la Argentina y su situación actual. In *Justicia en la calle: Ensayos sobre la policía en América Latina*, ed. by Peter Waldmann. Medellín: Biblioteca Jurídica Diké.

Marabotto, Eva. 1999. La pobreza no va a clase. *Clarín*, Suplemento Zona, May 2.

Martínez, Josefina, Mariana Croccia, Lucia Eilbaum, and Vanina Lekerman. 1998. Consejos de seguridad barriales y participación ciudadana: los Miedos y las libertades. Centro de Estudios Legales y Sociales, Buenos Aires.

Ministry of Justice and the Government of the City of Buenos Aires. 1999 . Plan Piloto sobre prevención de la violencia en el barrio de Saavedra. *Bulletin no. 1*.

Ministry of Justice, National Office of Crime Policy. 1998a. *El delito urbano en la Argentina*. Buenos Aires: Ministry of Justice, National Office of Crime Policy.

———. 1998b. *Hacia un plan nacional de política criminal II*. Buenos Aires: Ministry of Justice, National Office of Crime Policy.

Navarro, Lucas. 1997. En Argentina el crimen paga. *Novedades Económicas* 19(196): 17–28. (Cordoba, Argentina: IERAL de Fundación Mediterranea.) *Novedades Económicas*. 1996. 19(167).

O'Donnell, Guillermo. 1998. Horizontal Accountability. *Agora. Cuadernos de Estudios Políticos* 8: 5–34.

Olivera, Alicia, and Sofía Tiscornia. 1997. La construcción social de imágenes de guerra. Centro de Estudios Legales y Sociales, Buenos Aires.

Przeworski, Adam, Bernard Manin, and Susan Stokes. 1999. *Democracy, Accountability and Representation*. New York: Cambridge University Press.

Ramírez Ocampo, Augusto. 1998. La seguridad hemísferica a puertas del nuevo milenio. In *Seguridad ciudadana y gobernabilidad en la región andina*, ed. Comisión Andina de Juristas. Lima: Comisión Andina de Juristas.

Registro Nacional de Armas. 1998. *Reseña estadística*, October: 6–10.

Rosúa, Fernando. 1998. La reforma policial en la Provincia de Santa Fe. In Documento de Trabajo del Seminario "Las reformas policiales en la Argentina." Centro de Estudios Legales y Sociales, Buenos Aires.

Saín, Marcelo. 1998. Democracia, seguridad pública y policía: La reforma del sistema de seguridad y policial en la Provincia de Buenos Aires. In Documento de Trabajo del Seminario "Las reformas policiales en la Argentina." Centro de Estudios Legales y Sociales, Buenos Aires.

Smulovitz, Catalina. 1998. Acciones judiciales y fiscalización de la política pública. Consejo de Investigaciones Científicas (CONICET), Buenos Aires.

Smulovitz, Catalina, and Enrique Peruzzoti. 2000. Societal Accountability in Latin America. *Journal of Democracy* 11(4): 147–58.

UNDP (United Nations Development Program). 1998. *Las paradojas de la modernización. Informe sobre el desarrollo humano en Chile*. Santiago: UNDP.

Zaffaroni, Eugenio. 1982. *Política criminal latinoamericana*. Buenos Aires: Hammurabi.

7

The Militarization of Public Security in Peru

Carlos Basombrío

"Momón" was a Problem, but not *the* Problem

On Wednesday October 14, 1998, all of the Peruvian newspapers had jubilant accounts of the fact that "Momón"—the confessed leader of a brutal band of criminals that had murdered ten poor street money changers,[1] as well as one of the country's most important businessmen—had been sentenced to life in prison by the Army's War Tribunal. The event was of great importance, because it was precisely the horrendous crimes of this criminal group that had created both a political and a psychological climate for further militarization of public security in Peru.

When news of the sentence was released, a sense of relief could be felt throughout the Peruvian population. Now that some time has passed, it is clear that people were blinded by a dual optical illusion. First, this was not a new solution. Frequent heavy sentences had been dealt out to similar criminal groups in the preceding years by ordinary courts. Second—and more serious—although it was important and healthy to punish these particular

153

criminals, there was no reason to suppose that Peru's crime and insecurity problems would be solved by doing so.

As many analysts publicly predicted at the time, the mere fact that judges turned in their robes for military uniforms, that trials were conducted without due process, or that the armed forces took a further step in the direction of controlling Peruvian society would not bring an end to violent crime.[2] This is not clearly reflected, however, in public opinion. Of all problems that plague modern society, (in)security is, perhaps, the most universal. Cutting across class lines, it is, by its very nature, an issue that easily inflames emotions and leaves reason by the wayside. One cannot exhort a father—whose daughter has been seized, raped, and murdered by juvenile delinquents—to understand the profound social and cultural reasons behind such actions. And it is almost equally difficult to induce parents, who fear that the same fate may strike their own daughters, to think about and examine the roots of the problem.

None of this, of course, is unique to Peru. Thus, this chapter's particular contribution to this book is to examine and analyze the results of a unique set of circumstances: when crime and insecurity (as well as efforts to confront the problem) follow in the wake of extended periods of violence. During such periods of violence, Peru militarized both its society and its state as a means of dealing with the war taking place within its borders, creating acute differences between the urban and rural environments. Furthermore, the problem must be addressed in the context of a political and social reality that is extremely tenuous, one in which democratic guarantees and institutional mechanisms to protect citizens' rights are uncertain, and where there are temptations to use the situation—and to take actions in responding to the problem of insecurity—to give legitimacy to an authoritarian regime and enhance its prospects for the future.

Peru's Unique Situation

To understand the public security problem in Peru today and, more particularly, to understand the way in which it is being addressed, it is necessary to appreciate the context of recent Peruvian history. Like the majority of Latin American countries, Peru made a transition from a military regime to a civilian, democratic regime in the 1980s. All the other countries in the region, despite their widely recognized problems, have managed to maintain democratic regimes.[3] In 1992, however, a coup d'état occurred in Peru; though many democratic structures have since been restored, the country was governed by a clearly authoritarian regime until President Alberto Fujimori fled the country in November 2000.

This situation has been examined and commented upon extensively in a variety of writings.[4] With the return of democracy, a highly fanatical armed group began a "people's war" against the state. The historical fractures in the structure of Peruvian society, along with the incredible number of errors that were committed in confronting them, transformed what was merely a peripheral problem into an extended wave of violence and human rights violations that shook the country to its very foundations in the late 1980s. At the same time, and only partially as a consequence of this situation, the country suffered an economic collapse, with Peru's recessionary indicators being the worst in Latin America. The inability of civilian governments to deal with violence and economic collapse, widespread corruption, inefficiency, and irresponsible behavior on the part of authorities, along with a state of panic in the face of uncertainty and despair, spelled an end to Peru's democratic transition.

August 1992 saw Fujimori's intragovernmental coup, which occurred with the enthusiastic support of a majority of the country's population, and shortly thereafter (for reasons not necessarily connected with the coup), the violence began to cease. This, combined with a significant economic recovery and general improvement in living conditions, gave legitimacy to the logic of authoritarian rule in the country. Only intense international pressure, led by the United States, brought the return of electoral activity and some democratic structures.

Nevertheless, the climate for democratic development remained inhospitable. The country's institutions were in a state of ruin. This was true both for institutions that had developed from the ground up (particularly political parties, which had virtually disappeared) and those that were necessary for a democratic state based on the rule of law. The judiciary and the Congress—two key elements of democratic functioning—suffered a complete lack of respect in the society and, in terms of decision making, were mere appendages to the executive.

Even the executive branch lost its institutional integrity. The country was, in reality, governed largely by an alliance between President Fujimori and the commanding officers of the armed forces, which in turn were in large measure controlled by the National Intelligence Service. Vladimiro Montesinos, the de facto head of the National Intelligence Service, was viewed as the second most powerful man in the Peru.[5]

Though the political situation was highly unstable and began to raise questions, it continued to account for the prerogatives enjoyed by the armed forces. These included, among other things, special immunity from judicial sanctions, the authority to try civilians, and a lack of institutional mechanisms to monitor their functioning (including promotions and budget).[6] Of further note, and of particular relevance here, is the fact that the armed forces were assigned a key role in maintaining public order.

The Subordinate Role of the Police to the Armed Forces

Given the role that the armed forces have come to play in the life of the country, it is not surprising that public security, despite its crucial importance, has been dealt with almost exclusively through repressive, military means. It should be noted that the armed forces' involvement in this area is not new. In particular, their relationship with the police, and the subordinate position to which they have succeeded in relegating them, are of long standing.

As in most Latin American countries, the concept of the police is based on a military rationale. The police view their mission in society as a military one; their hierarchical structure is almost identical to military hierarchies, and they enjoy immunity from prosecution for "offenses committed in the line of duty." As a result, the police view themselves as a fourth branch of the armed forces, with the armed forces regarding the police as a junior branch of the military. Thus, relations and, at times, tensions between the military and the police have centered not on their divergent approaches to fighting crime but rather on resentment by the police that they are regarded with contempt—particularly by the army—as the "lesser" branch of the army.

During the period of military rule from 1968 to 1980, this tension had concrete consequences. Inspired by the role of the *carabineros* during Chile's Augusto Pinochet dictatorship, the Peruvian police demanded to be part of the military government of the 1970s. They achieved this, at least symbolically, when General Juan Velasco Alvarado agreed, after a series of internal conflicts, that the "revolutionary government of the armed forces" would tentatively be called the "revolutionary government of the armed forces and the police."

This illusory equality was short lived. The problems facing Peru in the 1980s accentuated the decline of the police and the ascendancy of the armed forces. The rise of the Shining Path guerrilla group, and the inability of the police to preserve order in areas where the conflict was occurring, led to a gradual shift, in which the armed forces assumed responsibility for maintaining domestic order.[7]

During the Alan García government (1985–90), despite the fact that this situation remained unchanged, the police were unified into a single body and were renamed the National Police of Peru. This did not signal any change in police functions, and the police continued to operate on the same military concepts as before. García's decision to make this change was simply a pragmatic response to problems of rivalry and confrontation among the various existing police groups—the Civil Guard, the Republican Guard, and the Investigatory Police—whose disputes all too often ended in public armed clashes, to the alarm of a panicked citizenry.

Some sectors of the armed forces believed, on the basis of Peru's political history, that this unification of the police constituted a threat to their dominance. They saw it as a sort of "militarized force serving the APRA [Alianza Popular Revolucionaria Americana] Party."[8] With Fujimori's ascendance to power, any such fears on the part of the military were put to rest, with the police placed definitively in a position subordinate to the armed forces. Seven interrelated facts help shed light on this situation. First, when the new president was inaugurated, nine of the National Police's ten lieutenant generals were retired from service. The tenth, who was originally from the Republican Guard—the police unit closest to the army—assumed leadership of the institution.

Second, since 1990, the Ministry of the Interior, to which the police force answers and which is generally responsible for maintaining public order, has been commanded by an active army general. The post of minister of the interior has, in practice, become one of the most important offices to which an army officer can aspire, and it is but one step below the general command of the army. Under President Fujimori, the post was held by General César Saúcedo Sánchez, formerly commander general of the Army and also the former minister of defense. Fernando Ropigliosi currently serves as President Alejandro Toledo's minister of the interior.

Third, the police's role in the country's legal and institutional security structure has been diminished. Specifically, the police have been marginalized in their role within the national defense system, which was reformed in 1991. The police now serve only as an "instrument" in that system; they have no decision-making power or institutional rights with regard to issues of defense on the domestic front.[9]

Fourth, there has been an effort to minimize the significant successes of the police, which might have led to efforts to reorganize the police force and give it greater legitimacy. The best-known example of such success is the National Anti-Terrorism Division (DINCOTE), the police unit responsible for capturing the main commanders of the Movimiento Revolucionario Túpac Amaru (MRTA) and of the Shining Path, including Abimael Guzmán, himself.

The capture of "Presidente Guzmáris Gonzalo, nom de guerre,"[10] was pivotal in altering the national course of events in the past decade. The capture was executed under the command of General Antonio Ketín Vidal. It was professional in its design, and was executed with proper respect for human rights. From the very moment of the capture, it was evident that the president of the Republic was uncomfortable that he had not been informed of the operation beforehand.[11] In the following months and years, there were many periods of tension between the government and General Vidal. The members of the professional team of police organized by the Peruvian government's National Counter-Terrorism Division (DINCOTE) were dispersed and posted to minor duties, and many of the functions, as well as much of the information that had been concentrated in DINCOTE, were transferred to the National Intelligence Service.

Fifth, the police were found to have been solely responsible for a number of important intelligence failures that led to serious public security problems. The most notorious example was the negligence that allowed MRTA to take hostages at the Japanese Embassy and hold them for almost 5 months, from December 1996 to April 1997. These events clearly reflected an intelligence failure. The police were blamed, and even some high-ranking police officials who were held as hostages at the embassy were dismissed and court-martialed. The National Intelligence Service, which bore principal responsibility for the intelligence mistakes, was not only absolved of all blame, but the president of the Republic stated that much of the credit for the subsequent reoccupation of the embassy (which was an action only indirectly related to intelligence functions) belonged to Montesinos, the de facto head of that service.

Sixth, as an aggregate result, the Peruvian population on the whole has a negative perception of the police. In every public opinion poll, the police are one of the most criticized institutions. The main reasons given are inefficiency, corruption, and abuses against the people. In 1995, the present author commissioned a survey from Apoyo, Mercadeo y Comercialización S.A.[12] The results showed that 67 percent of the population regarded the management of the National Police as average, 19 percent as poor or very poor, and 13 percent as good or very good. In 1998, the Metropolitan Lima Victim Survey, which will be considered below, showed that 86.4 percent believed that the police functioned ineffectively.

Seventh, despite the institution's lack of credibility with the people, the government has shown no desire to reform it. Unlike other Latin American countries (e.g., Argentina, Colombia, and El Salvador, to mention three cases in which there have been important changes or where major changes are in progress), police reform is simply not a part of the government's agenda. This inaction is particularly revealing, for although the government can be criticized in many different areas, one thing is clear: When it is genuinely committed to dealing with a problem, it does so vigorously, without regard to how the results will ultimately be judged.

One indication of the government's lack of interest can be seen in the fact that, since 1994, many different versions of a new statutory law for the police have been debated in the Congress by the Committee on Domestic Order and Defense. The committee unanimously approved a final draft of the legislation on June 13, 1997, but it then languished, waiting to be taken up by the full Congress.[13]

It should be noted that a final resolution of the bill did not require major reforms, nor was it deleterious to the privileges of the armed forces. On the contrary, the proposed changes involved professionalization, organization, regulating relationships with private security organizations, and similar matters. As Gino Costa, now the deputy minister of the interior for President Toledo, stated, these are "matters of corporate interest" and "do not constitute an adequate approach to overcoming the problems of the National Police."[14]

Militarizing Public Security in the Countryside

Another important aspect of the militarization of public security in Peru is related to the situation in large rural areas that were subject to political violence and where drug trafficking occurs—primarily in rural areas of the Ayacucho, Apurímac, Huancavelica, Huánuco, and Junín Departments. To a lesser extent, this can also be found in the rural regions of many other departments, such as Ancash, Cajamarca, Cerro de Pasco, La Libertad, Lima, Piura, Puno, San Martín, and Ucayali.

Though the magnitude of the phenomenon varied, all of the areas saw a gradual withdrawal of the police between 1981 and 1986—retreating first from the countryside to small rural towns and later, when the violence became more extensive, from these towns to the departmental or large provincial capitals. The remaining rural areas subject to political or drug-related violence were largely left—and remain, today—without a police presence.

For a number of years, all public security problems in Peru's rural provinces were considered products of the political violence. Initially, the armed forces replaced the police, but they were no more successful in ending the violence. In the case of the military, failure was represented not by retreat (the size and strength of the military were sufficient to remain in place), but rather was the result of a strategic failure to regard the local population as a potential ally in combating the armed groups. The armed forces were unfamiliar with the terrain, lacked an understanding of the problem, did not have the political support of civilian authorities necessary to carry our broader operations, and were terrorized by constant provocations and acts of cruelty against their members and the civilian population. Instead of enlisting the cooperation of the local population to overcome these obstacles, their reaction was to institute indiscriminate repression.

Elsewhere, an account is given of the widespread incidents in five rural provinces in northern Ayacucho, where the problem was most severe as a result of military intervention. According to statistical information reconstructed by various Peruvian institutions, there were 5,645 deaths in the provinces of Cangallo, Huamanga, Huanta, La Mar, and Victor Fajardo in the first 2 years of the military's presence in Ayacucho (1983–84), representing 46 percent of all deaths that occurred in Ayacucho in the 14 years of violence. Perhaps more revealing is that this represented 20.5 percent of all deaths in Peru throughout the entire period of conflict. Also indicative of the level of violence concentrated in this area is the fact that "if there had been a proportionate number of victims in Lima as there were, for example, in Huanta, the figure, instead of being 2,014, would have been 213,453, and if the national rate had been the same as the Huanta rate, the national death toll would have been 816,540, rather than 24,117."[15]

This notion of intervention had a strong effect on the general course of the internal war in Peru, but that issue is not central to the focus of this chapter. It is, however, important to point out that these populations faced a serious public security dilemma. The Shining Path was a threat, not only because of the foreign, incompatible social model imposed by the group,[16] but also because its presence led to deadly repression by the state, which regarded the population as the social foundation on which the insurgency was constructed.

As a result, the vast majority of rural residents chose to flee from the countryside (between 600,000 and 1 million persons are estimated to have been displaced by the violence in Peru). Those who remained attempted to rebuild a rudimentary system of public order, to somehow establish the minimum conditions necessary for preserving life.

Hence, rural associations, also known as civil defense committees, were formed in many rural areas in the south-central mountain region. These groups were organized in military fashion, and included all adults in the rural areas involved, on a rotating basis. Their mission was to prevent the Shining Path from entering their areas, to drive guerrillas from the areas, and when necessary, to confront them physically.

This organizational model was quickly embraced by the military as an extremely valuable tool for confronting subversion in the countryside. Although the organization of these committees was encouraged by the military, however, and later legally regulated to bring them under the effective control and planning of the armed forces (limiting their operations and their arms, through Executive Orders 740 and 741), the situation was different from what occurred in Guatemala or Colombia.[17] The existence of these committees—their formation and the widespread participation they enjoyed—must be understood as the expression of a massive, autonomous decision on the part of the rural population.

This experiment was not the first attempt by Peru's rural population to take direct control of public order. In the 1970s, mainly in the northern provinces of Cajamarca and Piura, rural associations were formed in response to the inability of the police to the prevent the theft of cattle by cattle rustlers. The associations—based on a rotating system of direct territorial control by the community—were extraordinarily successful in their initial goal. This gave them further legitimacy, causing them eventually to become a key institution in these areas, not only providing security but also assisting in conflict resolution and the administration of justice. These groups have continued during the past two decades, subject to the fluctuations characteristic of many grassroots organizations. Today, they are recognized by the national constitution (article 141) and by Law 24,571.[18]

The associations and civil defense committees have become the most massive social organization in rural areas. According to the National Defense Research Institute,[19] as of 1994, there were 1,655 civil defense committees in Ayacucho and Huancavelica alone, with a total of 66,200 individual members and armaments, including 6,060 shotguns provided by the government. It is widely known that the arms provided by the government are the least effective and least suitable for the purposes of the local population.[20] The local groups have managed, via the black market, to acquire far more modern arms, which they hide when the military authorities conduct their inspections.

Despite the difficulty of determining national figures, Diez Hurtado reviewed a range of work on the subject and stated that in 1991 there were already 34,380 associations and 1,020 civil defense committees in the country. Many more committees were formed in the following years, reaching approximately 4,500. When the violence ended, there was only a slight reduction in this number, with approximately 4,200 active committees still functioning as of 1997.[21]

This massive organization of the rural population is recognized as a vital force in defeating the Shining Path in the Peruvian countryside. Even in the north, the Shining Path never managed to significantly penetrate the association-controlled areas. The most interesting point, however, is that they are still in existence several years after the virtual disappearance of the Shining Path, the very force that led to the development of the associations. Certainly, the primary reason for their continued existence is the belief that they are necessary to prevent a return of the Shining Path.

At the same time, these groups have become a widespread alternative to the government for maintaining rural security and public order. In much of rural Peru, security issues are largely overseen by the population itself; as a consequence, the government has been forced to relinquish its monopoly on the use of force—a characteristic feature of a modern state.

The situation is complex. On one hand, the participation of the rural population has enormous potential for the development of the citizenry in rural areas. For example, these committees could be a basis for a new and effective experiment in establishing rural police forces.

On the other hand, the situation brings with it both real and potential problems, the first of which is the question of the type of relationship that the armed forces establish with members of the associations. As Starn explains,[22] "In fact, military power takes a variety of forms in the everyday operations of the associations, from obligatory meetings at headquarters to requirements that soldiers be housed overnight. Within this relationship, there are instances of corruption, such as the sale of arms which, in principle, are to be provided free of charge by the government. Furthermore, though many association members do not resist following orders from the military, the very existence of the associations entails exploitation in enlisting unpaid workers from the community in order to guarantee public security, a responsibility previously assumed by the state."

In addition, it should be noted that the threat of "disarming" the committees—which the military has indicated as part of a medium-term agenda—could lead to violence. Considering the recent history of these areas, the importance of these associations to the rural population, the possibility that violent adherents of the Shining Path or drug-trafficking groups could seek to exploit such a situation, and the potential for poor management, it is clear that such a military decision could provoke a new and tragic wave of violence in the Peruvian countryside.

This anomalous and highly unstable situation exists throughout the rural areas of the country. As a direct legacy of the internal armed conflict, the armed forces are the de facto political authority responsible for public order. However, at the same time, it is understood that the practical task of protecting the public has been taken up by local community organizations, which have replaced not only the police but also the armed forces as part of a political process that has many unresolved conflicts.

Crime and Delinquency in the Urban Environment

We now turn to an examination of the urban environment, where conditions, which are similar to conditions in other countries in the region, differ considerably from the rural situation. An increase in common crime was a problem common to all of Latin America throughout the 1990s. El Salvador, with the world's highest murder rate, and Colombia, with 30,000 murders in 1997 alone,[23] headed the list. This growth in crime also poses the problem of how it can be addressed within the framework of the law and respect for the rights of citizens. Many commentators have observed that the vital importance of crime and how it is addressed will be one of the most crucial tests of democracy in Latin America during the coming years.

In Peru, as in a number of Central American countries that have also experienced political violence (El Salvador, Guatemala, Nicaragua), the problem became more visible with the end of domestic armed conflict, though it should be noted that the situations in these countries differed significantly from that of Peru.

Since the wars in some of these other countries, there have been consistent attempts to demilitarize public security. In the El Salvador peace agreements, for example, public security was defined as being "founded on unlimited respect for the individual and the social rights of the individual." It was also clearly established that public security was to be a civilian matter, and it was agreed that there was a need to clearly separate external security activities and responsibilities from domestic security issues. Thus, a civilian police force was created, as a practical expression of this approach—one that has been severely tested (as has been true in many other Latin American countries) by the extent of crime and the population's demands for immediate solutions.

Another major difference with Central American countries is that Peru's crime increase, covering the same years, has been less severe. In Guatemala, in 1996, there were eight to ten murders a day, in addition to about twenty automobile thefts, three kidnappings, and innumerable robberies and assaults.[24]

El Salvador, as has been indicated, presents a more complex situation. According to the National Public Security council, crime in El Salvador increased 20 percent between 1995 and 1996, with an increase of 8 percent between 1996 and 1997. In 1995, 47,273 crimes were reported, as compared with 59,252 in 1996 and 63,917 in 1997. These include an average of 7,211 murders a year between 1995 and 1997—at 120 per 100,000 inhabitants, the highest murder rate in the world.[25]

Though it hardly rivals the magnitude of the Central American problem, the end of political violence in Peru has also brought an increase in common crime and, perhaps more important, in the citizenry's perception of the seriousness of the problem. However, given the political situation in Peru (which will be discussed in more detail below), it is essential to clarify the actual dimensions of the problem. One way of doing this is by making a comparison with the prevailing situation in the region as a whole. In this sense, Peru occupies a middle ground. Its situation is certainly far less serious than that of Colombia, El Salvador, or Guatemala, and is less acute than that faced by Brazil, Mexico, or Venezuela. Conversely, Peru is not like Argentina, Chile, and Uruguay, where the problem is considerably less severe.[26]

A second indicator that reinforces the above conclusions is the assessment of the U.S. Department of State, which classifies the level of problems in various cities around the world as critical, high, or low with regard to citizen security. Although Lima is in the high category, it should be noted that Guatemala City, Kingston, Mexico City, Port au Prince, Rio de Janeiro, São Paulo, and San Salvador and are all in the even more extreme critical group.[27]

A third, similar indicator is the 1997 United Nations *Human Development Report*, which goes further and claims that the insecurity rate for Peru has actually improved, with a decline from the 1991 figure of 42 percent to 28 percent in 1995 (UNDP 1997). Although this is perplexing, it is supported by statistics and arguments that are difficult to ignore. The United Nations has measured insecurity by weighting three factors that are either elements in, or causes of insecurity: the number of violent incidents perpetrated by armed groups, the number of reports of human rights violations, and crime rates. Though crime rates have risen, the former two categories have shown significant improvement.

An examination of Peru's crime figures clearly indicates a change for the worse. The crime rate rose from 14.9 reported crimes and offenses per 1,000 inhabitants in 1991 to 15.3 in 1995. The figures for homicides have not shown an increase but rather a fluctuation. The statistics division of Peru's National Police recorded 3,223 homicides (of which 2,294 were in Lima) in 1994; this number dropped to 2,946 (1,778 in Lima) in 1995, it rose again to 2,904 (1,862 in Lima) in 1996, and it once again decreased to 2,506 (1,501 in Lima) in 1997.

There has been a continuing increase in property crimes. Police statistics showed a total of 118,199 (63,586 in Lima) for 1994, 109,112 (56,152 in Lima) for 1995, 110,698 (57,536 in Lima) for 1996, and 184,142 (84,060 in Lima) for 1997.

It should be noted that police statistics are not highly reliable, for three reasons. First, people consider it to be of little use to report crimes. Second, there are technical problems associated with properly recording the data. Third, there is the possibility of statistics being manipulated for political or other reasons.

Thus, the first household survey on victims in metropolitan Lima, conducted in February 1998 by the National Statistics and Information Technology Institute, is of great interest. It was the first of its type in the country and provides data that are extremely valuable in gaining an understanding of the true nature of the problem the country faces.[28]

According to the survey, 66 percent of crimes committed in Lima in 1997 were robbery or attempted robbery of individuals, 16 percent were residential thefts or attempted thefts, and 9.6 percent were vehicle or auto parts thefts. At the other extreme, only 0.4 percent were kidnappings or attempted kidnappings.

In terms of the social sectors most affected by the major crimes, the distribution is as follows: 60.2 percent of robberies of individuals occur in low-income and mid-low-income sectors, 17.1 percent in middle-income sectors, and 22.7 percent in mid-high-income and high-income sectors. A total of 60.7 percent of residential thefts are of low-income and mid-low-income sectors, 15.9 percent of middle-income sectors, and 23.4 percent of mid-high-income and high-income sectors. Overall, 33.4 percent of vehicle and auto parts thefts affect low- and mid-low-income sectors, 19.0 percent middle-income sectors, and 55.8 percent mid-high- and high-income sectors.

Assaults affected low- and mid-low-income sectors in 75.8 percent of cases, middle-income sectors in 14.0 percent of cases, and high- and mid-high-income sectors in 10.1 percent of cases. Vandalism affected low- and mid-low-income sectors in 64.2 percent of cases, middle-income sectors in 12.8 percent of cases, and high- and mid-high-income sectors in 22.9 percent of cases.

In terms of which security problems most affect people in their own neighborhoods, 58.1 percent of respondents point to muggings. Yet responses also describe problems that are not strictly crimes but rather are severe social problems. A total of 52.5 percent of respondents point to drug use, 42 percent to alcoholism, 45.5 percent to gang warfare, and 7.5 percent to prostitution. In terms of the respondents' own neighborhoods, 6.9 percent of those responding describe their neighborhoods as very safe, 51.4 percent as moderately safe, 26.0 percent as unsafe, and 15.7 percent as very unsafe.

In terms of the ages of victims of crimes directed against individuals (robbery, assault, and vandalism), 45.4 percent are under 29 years of age, 20.8 percent are between 30 and 39 years of age, and the remaining 33.8 percent are above 39 years of age. As regards the age of perpetrators, 24.4 percent are between 12 and 17 years of age, 39.6 percent are between 18 and 24 years of age, 17 percent are between 25 and 29 years of age, and 19 percent are adults above 30 years of age.

In terms of the number of perpetrators of incidents of robbery, 35.6 percent of such incidents were perpetrated by single individuals, 27.9 percent by two, and 22.6 percent by three or four. As regards the type of weapons used, 45.6 percent of incidents were perpetrated without arms, 16.4 percent involved knives, and 3.7 percent involved firearms.

Of considerable note is the fact that 90.6 percent of respondents stated that they had not reported the robbery or attempted robbery; only 8.9 percent placed a report with the police, whereas 0.3 percent reported the crime to private guards. A total of 93.1 percent of victims stated that they had not recovered any of the property stolen, whereas only 2.2 percent stated that they had recovered all of the property stolen.

These figures provide ample material for analysis and discussion. Briefly, it can be stated that the survey indicates that the population's perception of insecurity is high but not at the "desperate" level, and that much of the perception concerns police ineffectiveness; that the most significant factors contributing to the disruption of public peace are social problems that place many individuals in the area of borderline crime; that crime is primarily perpetrated by and on young people; that crime is most prevalent among poor people and generally does not involve sophisticated weapons; and last, that taking into consideration actual statistics (rather than at the psychosocial effects that result), it is evident that gang crime and major crime play a relatively insignificant role, from a numerical standpoint.

Political Manipulation of Fear

In terms of collective fears, fear of crime and violence in the streets—because it has the potential to affect all people, without regard to social class or age—is perhaps the most universal and most difficult to deal with. Thus, the perception of insecurity constructed in the collective imagination is as important as, or more important than, the actual threat. There is no direct correlation between crime levels and perception of risk in the society. Furthermore, in countries where the problem is still in its early stages, the sense of vulnerability may actually be greater than in cases where the crime wave is extensive and of long standing.

Because of this, it is even more difficult than in other areas to construct a balanced and reasonable collective concept of the measures and solutions to be adopted. Furthermore, it is a problem that is consistently subject to exploitation by political campaigns of different persuasions; in some cases, the people's fear is even manipulated for purposes quite distinct from any objective of actually solving the problem.

Peru is no exception. Given the country's political realities, the issue tends to be manipulated, on the one hand, to reinforce a power structure in which the armed forces dominate civil institutions and, on the other, to obtain the support of the population for a third presidential term of office.

An analysis of the media's methods for reporting crime in 1998 suggests that there was, indeed, manipulation of public opinion. The work of Helena Pinilla, director of the Association of Communicators of Calandria, is most useful here. She provides highly revealing conclusions through a study of daily news reporting.[29]

Examining media coverage in the first half of 1998, Pinilla notes that "the events reported begin to 'increase in caliber'. News and features on gangs, kidnappings, and 'drive-by' murders multiply in number and intensity. The sense of insecurity increases and the coverage moves from the police section of the newspaper to the political pages and front page headlines. Citizen insecurity becomes a leading topic and, with its newfound prominence, finds its way into the political agenda and political discourse, insinuating itself into a wide range of areas."

Pinilla adds that "the 'image' of city violence constructed by the media differs in two aspects from a realistic assessment of the situation. First, the media give priority coverage to the most 'spectacular,' violent incidents, which are generally the most unusual. One such example is kidnappings: although, according to the victim survey, they constitute a mere 0.2 percent of crimes committed, they received prominent press coverage in the first half of the year. Second, the profile of the typical perpetrator, as portrayed by the media, is that of a seasoned criminal who is highly 'professional' and carries sophisticated weaponry, a stereotype contradicted by the study, which shows that the majority of violent offenders are, on the contrary, young, relatively inexperienced criminals who do not carry weapons."

As will be seen in the following section, it was at the peak of such coverage that the government decided to promote a so-called national security package of legislative measures. "We never imagined," says Pinilla, "how rapid and effective they would prove to be. . . . Within a short time, we decided to do a new study of the news. With surprising results! We found an unanticipated significant drop in the percentage of news items devoted to incidents of crime. . . . Were newspaper headlines and television screens somehow 'cooled off' by these measures? Did crime rates decline? Did muggers, murderers and kidnappers flee in fear of cameras and microphones?. . . The decline in the statistics was not the only curious fact. We also found changes in the type of violence reported. While, a few months earlier, the entree on the media menu was cruel murders, kidnappings, and assaults, there was now a surprising 14.7 percent reference to 'successful police actions to combat crime.'"

Pinilla's study focuses exclusively on the role of the media, and though the paragraphs quoted subtly suggest a relationship between political power and the media, the study does not deal with this issue. However, on the basis of the conclusions of the study, it can be stated that there is a high probability that the type of crime coverage analyzed in the study was "suggested" by the government and accepted by the media. In Peru, it is widely known that the government exerts pressure on the media in a variety of ways, particularly targeting the most influential television channels in an attempt to get them to report or not report certain types of news.[30] The size and type of media involved lends additional support to the hypothesis that this case may involve something more than a spontaneous reaction and may be more the result of a "psychosocial operation" initiated by intelligence entities.

Common Crime and National Security

Government officials in Peru have not wished—and the political opposition has not known how—to turn the fight against crime and insecurity into a political debate on finding comprehensive measures to deal with the problem. Approaches to the problem have been dominated by a military perspective.

Since May 1998, along with the wave of media coverage discussed above, the government has begun to speak of the need to adopt the same approach in combating crime as the one that was, in the past, "successful in the fight against the Shining Path." The rationale is based on an incorrect assumption—namely, that the dictatorial and repressive measures taken were, indeed, the key factor in putting an end to political violence.[31] Despite the inaccuracy of this view, it remains widely accepted in Peruvian society, and the Fujimori government was therefore successful in obtaining authority from the Congress (through Law 26,955) to create specific laws to deal with the issue.

The set of regulations that were passed has five main features. [32] First, the definition of crime was changed; it was classified as a "national security" problem, with the current situation defined as an "emergency." The purpose of doing this was to legitimize the use of the armed forces in areas clearly beyond their normal functions. Two reports raise questions about this—the report of the Office of the People's Advocate ("It would have been more appropriate to use the concept of citizen security set forth in article 195 of the Constitution as the basis for joint authority by the National Police and the municipalities") and the report of the National Human Rights Commission ("Policy based on this understanding of national security has been extremely deleterious to the basic rights and freedoms established in the Constitution and in international human rights provisions").

Second, certain offenses—such as the use of weapons by gangs—are defined as "aggravated terrorism" (article 1, Executive Order 895[33]). The double purpose of this is to give the police a 15-day pre-judicial investigatory period (in place of the 24 hours allotted by the Constitution) and provide military courts the authority to try civilians for common crimes. [34]

Third, an opening is provided for the possibility of trying drug-trafficking offenses in military courts. Because it is widely perceived that many military personnel are involved in drug trafficking, this measure has been provided for in an almost secret manner, through nonspecific legal provisions. "Crimes committed by gangs using military types of arms" are mentioned as a basis for military trial, as well as "other crimes against persons, life, or health." [35]

Fourth, sanctions and procedures are stiffened, while defendants' rights are restricted, leaving citizens more vulnerable to abuses. Sentences are increased for all types of crime. Summary judgment is provided for, and the right to a defense is restricted. A military prosecutor directs the police investigation in cases of "aggravated terrorism," and for other crimes the police may assume prosecutorial authority. Affidavits assume probatory value. The use of habeas corpus and preventive injunction is restricted. Crimes are defined imprecisely and generically, leaving judges free to exercise their own interpretations. The police are authorized to detain a suspect for 15 days, if they consider it necessary, to investigate the individual. Criminal accountability for minors is increased. Bail and prison benefits are restricted, and the prison system is made more rigid.

Fifth, the authority of the National Intelligence Service is increased. It is allowed to intervene in the area of common crimes, for which purpose a National Intelligence Division for the Protection of Social Peace has been created. In addition, the police are instructed to coordinate their investigations with this office.

In an article published immediately after the approval of these measures, [36] the present author made, and considers still valid, six general criticisms of the security package. *First, it lacks imagination and creativity.* There is a total lack of innovative thinking. These measures are a nearly verbatim repetition of the measures taken against the Shining Path, with no critical assessment of the successes and horrors involved therein. In fact, the present measures entail even greater violations of human rights and of basic individual guarantees than in the previous case. [37]

Second, it does not take account of the nature of the problem. All surveys indicate that people know that the paramount causes of crime are, in order of importance, lack of jobs, poverty, breakdown of the family, and the values disseminated by the media, particularly by television. None of the measures deals with these areas. [38] Society's responsibility for the existence of the problem is ignored, and any rehabilitative effort on the part of government is abandoned, focusing exclusively on repressive action against criminals.

Third, it violates the Constitution and international treaties. This is true in respect to the procedures employed, because several of the regulations go beyond the delegated authority of the Congress. Even more important is the specific content of the provisions. A number of reports and analyses have pointed to the unconstitutionality of regulations restricting basic rights such as habeas corpus and preventive injunction, of the use of the legal concept of aggravated terrorism to justify the use of military courts, of prolonged police investigations, of sanctions against minors, and so on.

Fourth, though its stated purpose is effective action, it is ineffective. There are attempts to portray the previous legislation as soft, arguing that these measures finally provide stiff laws. Criminal punishment in Peru has always been severe and, for at least 3 years, it has been extremely severe. Many crimes were already subject to life imprisonment, and contrary to some claims, civilian judges have been sentencing criminal groups. Since March 1997, when the Supreme Court created the permanent and specialized criminal courts, 600 individuals have been handed down a variety of sentences.[39]

Fifth, it is counterproductive. It provides excessive punishment for minor crimes. [40] If punishments for robbery and murder are nearly equal, why risk leaving a live victim to tell the story?

Sixth, it aggravates the lack of controls on the regime. Of special concern here are the additional powers given to the already powerful National Intelligence Service[41] and new powers for the military, including the new spheres of authority of the military courts.[42]

One result of the executive orders is to give new roles to the National Intelligence Service—one of Peru's least controlled and most distrusted government entities. Already, through Executive Order 746, governing the National Intelligence System, that body and the National Intelligence Service were given extremely broad powers, including the authority to obtain any information whatsoever from public and private organizations, under penalty of criminal sanctions. The same order gave them budgetary secrecy. Intelligence entities subordinate to the national intelligence entities were created in ministries and other public agencies. After the coup, the government issued Executive Order 25,365, which reinstituted, with slight changes, the executive orders cited above, which had been rejected by the Congress as unacceptable.

The National Intelligence Service has evolved without any oversight, and it has assumed the role of a political police force with authority over even the armed forces while acting as a political tool for the regime and providing cover for illegal paramilitary operations. Its growth is closely associated with the role of the controversial secret presidential adviser, former captain Vladimiro Montesinos, who is known to have been the de facto head of the organization since 1991.[43]

Conclusions

As was stated at the beginning of the chapter, the particular characteristics of the Peruvian situation, in the extent of the problem of everyday violence and crime, are not unique. What is, however, distinctive, is the way in which the problem has been addressed, and the political and social consequences for the population. An examination of the Peruvian situation is also of great importance to other countries on the continent, for two reasons.

First, the militarization of public security that has occurred in Peru, though extreme in comparison with other countries, is hardly foreign to what is being done, or is being sought, in other Latin American countries. Second, there has been a loss of confidence in democratic institutions and in ways of dealing with a variety of problems in the present Latin American environment—particularly in the Andean countries and in Central America. Reference is too frequently made to the need to follow the "Peruvian example" of drastic, violent, authoritarian, and supposedly more effective solutions to these problems.

Thus, the case of Peru supports the concept suggested in the title of the chapter: that crime and citizen insecurity are a challenge of paramount importance in consolidating democracy in the region. Furthermore, it is evident that, in countries where democracy is weak, the fear of crime can easily be exploited to implement militaristic approaches to dealing with crime and public disturbances, to the detriment of the rights of citizens.

In summary, the package of "national security" executive orders—combined with the situation in rural areas, the country's fragile institutions, the situation of the National Police, and the military's role in the nation's life—attest to the militarization of public security in Peru. This militarization has not brought about positive changes with respect to the particular problems that were the object of the security measures. In fact, the contrary is true: The possibility of democratic governance that accords respect for human rights has been weakened. Even worse, there are indications that the "Peruvian example" could have a negative influence on nearby countries in the region that face similar situations.

Afterword: A Tale of Three Hats

In this afterword, the present author sheds some light on events that have occurred in Peru since this chapter was originally drafted in 1999. The underlying idea of the chapter is that in the context of an authoritarian government, the problem of citizen security was militarized and converted into one of the justifying elements of the continuing regime; as such, the fear of crime was used as a pretext for handing over extraordinary power to such sinister organizations as the National Intelligence Service. Throughout the chapter, this idea was resisted, and it was asserted that this was not the solution to the problem of citizen security; rather, it only worsened the problem. All of this quickly changed.

If I put on my social scientist's hat, I would have to say that what has happened in Peru is quite a shame. Reality does not allow us, as social scientists, to work sluggishly. In the time that it takes a chapter like this to be discussed, reworked, and converted into part of a book, reality can change in ways so dramatic that the entire body of the facts and processes described can have already changed radically.

However, if I put on my hat as an activist working for human rights and democracy, it could be said that fortunately, reality has found us to be correct sooner than we thought. The authoritarian regime collapsed, and a new opportunity has opened up to reconstruct Peru's institutions in ways that are more democratic.

Here is where I try on my third hat. As a footnote to my long life as an activist working in civil society, I now work for the government as a civil servant. More precisely, I am the vice minister of the Interior and the coordinator of the National Police Reform Commission. In other words, all the issues that I have explained as an analyst and denounced as an activist through the years are now the topics of my work, and I have the privilege of participating as a member of a team hoping to make big changes.

With regard to the specific issue dealt with here, the immense lines of reform that we promote coincide with the nature of the problems described in this chapter. The starting point is the need to demilitarize the police function. Separation is desired—from the actual Constitution to the training of new officers and even to all police activity—between what is the work of public order and citizen security and what is national defense. If the armed forces are defined as that which confronts external enemies, the police should be concerned with protecting the community, guaranteeing its safety and ensuring the free expression of its rights. This is the conceptual starting point for a reform that looks to bring the police closer to the community, create mechanisms of citizen participation and supervision that help to improve police efficiency, allow for the channeling of resources and contributions from the community to police work, and combat corruption in all its forms.

Today in Peru, although citizen security is an important source of concern, it is not first on the priority list of either the citizens or the state. It does create greater possibilities for the changes we propose. It is important not to forget that in many other Latin American countries, the lack of citizen security has historically been one of the largest and most important threats to democratic consolidation, encouraging the reappearance of authoritarian reflections deeply rooted in our societies and adding a factor of aggravation to the role that the armed forces must maintain in a democracy.

The project in which we find ourselves involved is not a simple one. Ultimately, government officials will be responsible. However, when the time comes, the social scientist must fairly analyze what has been accomplished and its inevitable limitations. Finally, the activist's role will be to continue the fight because, for the majority of Peruvians, democracy is no longer a meaningless word.

Notes

1. *Cambista* is the Peruvian term for a person who buys and sells dollars in the street for a living. Such people are unemployed individuals who earn a small amount on the difference between the two types of transactions but must have relatively large amounts of cash on their person and in sight. Thus, they are easy targets for all types of abuse and criminal activity.

2. The cruel return to reality was to come the following day, October 15, when the newspaper *Expreso* ran the headline: "Thugs Murder *Cambista* and Take Five Thousand Dollars." The following day's headline in *La República* confirmed this. "Lives of Ten *Cambistas* in Jeopardy" described the new wave of *cambista* murders and provided indications that new crimes against such individuals were planned. To complete the picture, *La República* reported, on October 20, the "fatal shooting of a businessman, with injury to two people accompanying him." This was an almost identical repetition of a crime that moved the country months earlier and led to changes in government strategy.

3. Unfortunately, this statement may cease to be true in the coming years, for several reasons: In Venezuela, President Hugo Chávez deliberately confuses popularity with democracy and is dismantling his country's institutions; in Colombia, the enormous problems in finding a peaceful solution to the armed conflict may pose insurmountable obstacles to democracy there; and in Ecuador, there are (though to a different degree) enormous problems in dealing with an economic crisis within a democratic framework, especially given the various signs of crisis in political institutions and the popularity that the military enjoys among the people.

4. E.g., see Basombrío 1996.

5. One example of the power of Montesinos: The U.S. government "drug czar," during his third and most recent visit to Peru, in August 1999, included, as the first item on his agenda, a one-to-one meeting with Montesinos. Only after this did he meet with President Fujimori and a number of ministers. It must be recalled that Montesinos, according to official information, does not hold any executive post in the Peruvian government.

6. In Basombrío 1998b, a comparison of the characteristics of that institution in different countries in the region shows that the state of democracy is most open to question in Peru.

7. E.g., see Degregori and Rivera 1993 and Pedraglio 1990.

8. See Rospigliosi 1999. To understand the military's apprehension concerning García's measures, it must be borne in mind that Peru's political history, from 1930 to the mid-1970s, was marked by open confrontation between the army and APRA and that this party was militaristic in both its organizational structure and its behavior.

9. See Alegría Varona 1998.

10. On the basis of this capture, the balance of the internal warfare changed, and there were a number of events that contributed to the defeat of Shining Path. On this subject, see Basombrío: 1999.

11. The direct participants in the incident have remained silent, but all analyses agree that Vidal intentionally kept the capture operation secret from Fujimori, the armed forces, and the National Intelligence Service. He apparently did so out of fear that the operation could fail if more than a minimal number of people knew about it, and/or because he believed that if others knew about the plan, they would not allow Guzmán to be captured alive and would instead kill him as an act of revenge. Such revenge would, of course, have been absurdly unwise and would have precluded the capitulation that occurred a year later, with its enormous benefits to the country.

12. This is found in *Ideel*, September 1995, p. 12.

13. Costa 1998, 121.

14. Costa 1998, 129.

15. Basombrío 1994.

16. Degregori 1996b.

17. This can be explained in part by the pattern of landownership—large holdings in the hands of large landholders in Colombia, and peasant landowners under various forms of ownership in Peru.

18. More can be learned on this subject in works such as López 1986, Starn 1991, Márquez 1994, and Giglitz 1998.

19. Degregori 1996a.

20. The author has also confirmed this from personal visits to mountain communities.

21. Diez Hurtado 1997.

22. Starn 1996.

23. "Colombia on the Brink," *Economist*, August 8, 1998.

24. *El País*, August 4, 1996.

25. Cuéllar 1997.

26. Basombrío 1997.

27. Peru Report 1998.

28. The survey was carried out in Lima in early 1998, at the request of the special commission investigating the causes and consequences of everyday violence in the Pe-

ruvian Congress. Manuel Piqueras, the commission's adviser, played an important role in promoting and shaping the survey. Many of the results are available in his recent book (Piqueras 1998).

29. Pinilla García 1998.

30. The issue of government pressuring the media has been prominent in public debate in Peru in recent years. To cite but two examples: Baruch Ivcher, owner of Channel 2, decided, in 1997, to distance himself from the government, which he had supported enthusiastically for some years, with the result that he lost both his citizenship and the channel. In November 1998, recorded conversations were disseminated (wiretapping of telephones is extensively practiced in Peru), between Vladimiro Montesinos and José Francisco Crouisillat, executive vice-president of Channel 4, the country's most important station, in which Montesinos gives the other man instructions on how to report on a given issue. In 1999, there was nearly total control over broadcast television, and this was a key element in the reelection effort.

31. The author's reasons for believing this assessment to be incorrect are dealt with in detail in Basombrío 1999.

32. This view is based on the most exhaustive studies of the executive orders available: Office of the People's Advocate 1998b; Coordinadora Nacional de Derechos Humanos 1998; and De la Jara 1998a.

33. "We maintain that the executive order was excessive in describing such criminal behavior as terrorism, distorting this concept to the detriment of the essential content of individual freedom and the natural right to trial" (Office of the People's Advocate 1998b, 7).

34. Contrary to the modern democratic tradition which, in this respect, prevails on the continent, Peru has lost jurisdictional unity and has broadened the authority of military courts, giving them the ability to act within a larger sphere. Though they have assumed authority for trying military personnel for all types of crimes, including drug trafficking, murder, and rape, the legislation allows civilians to be tried for what are considered the more serious crimes. This began with Executive Order 25,708, issued in August 1992, and continued with the approval of the 1993 Constitution, giving military courts the ability to try civilians for "treason" (the term that has been given to aggravated forms of terrorism).

35. De la Jara 1998a.

36. Basombrío 1998c.

37. De la Jara 1998b, 1998c.

38. In *Ideele*, June 1998. The Instituto de Defensa Legal published a memorandum with fifty suggestions for dealing with common violence.

39. "¿El fuero común habría absuelto a 'Momón' y su banda," *Ideele*, August 1998.

40. Ugaz 1998.

41. Basombrío 1998a; Rivera 1998.

42. See further writings on the subject in Lobatón 1998. The report is generally very critical of the militarization of the justice system in Peru. Office of the People's Advocate 1998a.

43. Including the armed forces, Montesinos is considered to have close to 15,000 men, and a budget fifty times larger than what he had in 1990. In addition to controlling the intelligence services of all branches of the armed services and of the police, he is known to have had, for several years, extensive influence and control in both the polit-

ical and the military branches of the government, through the National Intelligence Service. As a result of his presence at meetings with senior U.S. officials, it has also become known that he plays a key role in the fight against drug trafficking.

References

Alegría Varona, Ciro. 1998. Policía y sistema de defensa nacional. In *Control democrático en el mantenimiento de la seguridad interior*, ed. Hugo Frühling. Santiago: Centro de Estudios del Desarrollo y Ediciones Centenario.

Basombrío, Carlos. 1994. Para la historia de una guerra con nombre: ¡Ayacucho! *Ideele* 62 (April): 27.

———. 1996. *La paz: Valor y precio: Una visión comparativa para América Latina.* Lima: Instituto de Defensa Legal.

———. 1997. ¿Va a mejorar la situación de la seguridad pública en 1998? *Ideele* 103 (December): 66.

———. 1998a. Ayer inseguridad, Mañana *sin* seguridad. *Ideele* 107 (May): 10.

———. 1998b. *¿Están las fuerzas armadas subordinadas a la democracia en América Latina?* Lima : Instituto de Defensa Legal.

———. 1998c. Hacia un estado policiaco (. . . Pero a la peruana). *Ideele* 108 (June): 20.

———. 1999. Peace in Peru: An Unfinished Task. In *Comparative Peace Processes in Latin America.* Washington, D.C., and Stanford, Calif.: Woodrow Wilson Center Press and Stanford University Press.

Coordinadora Nacional de Derechos Humanos. 1998. *Informe sobre la legislación de seguridad ciudadana,* Lima: Coordinadora Nacional de Derechos Humanos.

Costa, Gino. 1998. La propuesta de nueva ley orgánica de la policía nacional: Novedades y limitaciones. In *Control democrático en el mantenimiento de la seguridad interior,* ed. Hugo Frühling. Santiago: Centro de Estudios del Desarrollo y Ediciones Centenario.

Cuéllar, Benjamín. 1997. Seguridad y derechos humanos. Presentation given at an international seminar-workshop on 50 years later . . . and now what, sponsored by Diakonía, Lima, November 6–8.

Degregori, Carlos Iván. 1996a. Ayacucho, después de la violencia. In *Las rondas campesinas y la derrota de Sendero Luminoso,* ed. Carlos Iván Degregori et al. Lima: Instituto de Estudios Peruanos and Universidad San Cristóbal de Huamanga.

———. 1996b. Cosechando tempestades. In *Las rondas campesinas y la derrota de Sendero Luminoso,* ed. Carlos Iván Degregori et al. Lima: Instituto de Estudios Peruanos and Universidad San Cristóbal de Huamanga.

Degregori Carlos Iván, and Carlos Rivera. 1993. *Fuerzas armadas, subversión y democracia 1980–1993.* Working Document 53. Lima: Instituto de Estudios Peruanos.

De La Jara, Ernesto. 1998a. Bombardeo contra la delincuencia común: Análisis de los decretos legislativos sobre seguridad nacional *Ideele* 108 (June): 1.

———. 1998b. Decretos legislativos sobre seguridad nacional: Segunda edición de la legislación antiterrorista, empeorada y agravada. *Ideele* 109 (July): 6.

———. 1998c. Todo depende del cristal con que se mire: De la violencia política a la violencia común. *Ideele* 107 (May): 64.

Diez Hurtado, Alejandro. 1997. Diversidades, alternativas y ambigüedades: Institu-
ciones, comportamientos y mentalidades en la sociedad rural. Paper presented at a
conference, SEPIA VII, Ponencias Centrales, Huancayo, August 27–29.

Giglitz, John. 1998. *Decadencia y supervivencia de las rondas campesinas del norte
del Perú.* Debate Agrario 28. Lima: Centro Peruano de Estudios Sociales
(CEPES).

Lobatón, David. 1998. ¿Quién es el juez militar en el Perú? *Ideele* 108 (June): 18.

López, Sinesio. 1986. Reflexiones sobre el autogobierno y la institucionalidad de las
rondas campesinas. ILLA, Lima.

Márquez, Jaime. 1994. *Ronderos: Ojos de la noche.* Lima: Instituto de Defensa Legal.

Office of the People's Advocate. 1998a. *Análisis de los decretos legislativos sobre seguridad nacional dictados al amparo de la Ley 26955.* Lima: Office of the People's Advocate.

———. 1998b. *Informe sobre la justicia militar en el Perú.* Lima: Office of the People's Advocate.

Pedraglio, Santiago. 1990. *Armas para la paz: Seguridad democrática integral.* Lima:
Instituto de Defensa Legal.

Peru Report. 1998. *Trend Report-Security.* Lima: Peru Report.

Pinilla García, Helena. 1998. Violencia en los medios: Imágenes peligrosas y crónicas
dependencias. *Ideele* 111 (September): 33.

Piqueras, Manuel. 1998. *Buen gobierno, seguridad pública y crimen violento.* Lima:
Instituto de Defensa Legal.

Rivera, Carlos. 1998. El Sin: La policía y la seguridad ciudadana. *Ideele* 107 (May): 14.

Rospigliosi, Fernando. 1999. Informe nacional: Carencia de control democrático sobre
las fuerzas de seguridad en el Perú. *Control democrático en el mantenimiento de
la seguridad interior,* ed. Hugo Frühling. Santiago: Centro de Estudios del Desarrollo y Ediciones Centenario.

Starn, Orin. 1991. *Con los llanques todo barro, Reflexiones sobre rondas campesinas,
protesta social y nuevos movimientos sociales.* Lima: Instituto de Estudios Peruanos.

———. 1996. Senderos inesperados: Las rondas campesinas de la Sierra Sur Central.
In *Las rondas campesinas y la derrota de Sendero Luminoso,* ed. Carlos Iván Degregori et al. Lima: Instituto de Estudios Peruanos and Universidad San Cristóbal
de Huamanga.

UNDP (United Nations Development Program). 1997. *Human Development Report.*
New York: Oxford University Press.

Ugaz, José. 1998. Fetichismo y seguridad ciudadana. *Ideele* 107 (May): 16.

8

Police-Community Partnerships in Brazil

Paulo de Mesquita Neto and Adriana Loche

This chapter examines the nature of community policing projects and the experiences of police-community partnerships in Brazil, focusing attention on the relations between the police, citizen groups, community associations and nongovernmental organizations and their cooperation to respond to the problem of crime and violence in the society in the 1990s. It is part of a collective project to comparatively analyze national approaches to citizen security and the implications of alternative responses to crime and violence in Latin America.

The main argument developed in this chapter is that community policing projects emerged in Brazil as a strategy to make the police not only more effective and efficient in crime control and order maintenance but also more accountable to the community and more responsive to the citizens. The success and sustainability of these projects depend, therefore,

Paulo de Mesquita Neto thanks the Center on Crime, Communities, and Culture at the Open Society Institute–New York for supporting much of the research included in this chapter.

not only on their impact on public security but also on their impact on the level of police respect for citizen rights and interests and the level of community trust in the police.

The first section analyzes the context and the pressures that led to the development of community policing in Brazil. The section provides information on the reality and the perception of crime and violence in Brazil, the effects of organized crime and the internationalization of crime and violence, the relations between national and local approaches to citizen security, the efforts to reform the police and government policies to respond to the growth of crime and violence.

The second section discusses the relations between the police and the community, analyzing the persistence of police brutality and abuse since the transition to democracy, the limited participation of citizens in the formulation and implementation of public security policies, and the limited accountability and responsiveness of the police to the public.

The third section analyzes experiences of community policing in different cities and states, focusing attention on the experiences of Rio de Janeiro, São Paulo, Rio Grande do Sul, Espírito Santo, Pernambuco, Amapá, and the Federal District. This section shows that community policing projects emerged in most cases as a democratically oriented strategy for crime control and order maintenance or as an alternative to authoritarian responses to the growth of crime and violence in the 1980s and 1990s.

The last section analyzes the differences between police–community partnerships and argues that the political orientation of the government and the nature and the level of organization and mobilization of the community are crucial factors in the determination of the democratic nature and the success and sustainability of community policing projects.

The National Context

The transition to democracy coincided with an increase of crime and violence in Brazil, as indicated by the number of homicides, which affected states with different government coalitions, public security policies, and levels of economic and social development (see table 8.1).

From 1980 to 1995, the number of homicides in Brazil increased from 13,910 to 37,129 (166.92 percent). In the states of São Paulo and Rio de Janeiro, which accounted for 53.25 percent of the homicides in Brazil in 1995, the homicide growth rate was higher than the national rate. In São Paulo, the number of homicides increased from 3,446 in 1980 to 11,555 in

Table 8.1. Comparison of Homicide Growth Rates in Brazil, 1980–95

State	Number of Homicides				Percentage Growth in Homicides				
	1980	1985	1990	1995	1980–95	1985–95	1980–85	1985–90	1990–95
Brazil, all	13,910	19,747	31,989	37,129	166.92	88.02	41.96	61.99	16.07
Rondônia	118	319	555	330	179.66	3.45	170.34	73.98	-40.54
Acre	26	51	64	103	296.15	101.96	96.15	25.49	60.94
Amazonas	138	184	367	424	207.25	130.43	33.33	99.46	15.53
Roraima	11	12	127	87	690.91	625.00	9.09	958.33	-31.50
Pará	304	507	748	700	130.26	38.07	66.78	47.53	-6.42
Amapá	7	34	45	124	1,671.43	264.71	385.71	32.35	175.56
Tocantins			54	77					42.59
Maranhão	108	162	442	385	256.48	137.65	50.00	172.84	-12.90
Piauí	50	76	109	114	128.00	50.00	52.00	43.42	4.59
Ceará	445	549	555	845	89.89	53.92	23.37	1.09	52.25
Rio Grande Norte	163	134	200	247	51.53	84.33	-17.79	49.25	23.50
Paraíba	302	380	440	457	51.32	20.26	25.83	15.79	3.86
Pernambuco	1,121	2,011	2,741	2,706	141.39	34.56	79.39	36.30	-1.28
Alagoas	280	512	719	737	163.21	43.95	82.86	40.43	2.50
Sergipe	82	64	151	255	210.98	298.44	-21.95	135.94	68.87
Bahia	319	540	867	1,536	381.50	184.44	69.28	60.56	77.16
Minas Gerais	1,164	1,028	1,177	1,214	4.30	18.09	-11.68	14.49	3.14
Espírito Santo	305	455	881	1,153	278.03	153.41	49.18	93.63	30.87
Rio de Janeiro	2,941	2,541	7,099	8,216	179.36	223.34	-13.60	179.38	15.73
São Paulo	3,446	7,027	9,503	11,555	235.32	64.44	103.92	35.24	21.59
Paraná	831	921	1,167	1,384	66.55	50.27	10.83	26.71	18.59
Santa Catarina	241	263	382	412	70.95	56.65	9.13	45.25	7.85
Rio Grande do Sul	633	681	1,689	1,437	127.01	111.01	7.58	148.02	-14.92
Mato Grosso do Sul	223	253	348	635	184.75	150.99	13.45	37.55	82.47
Mato Grosso	38	270	415	583	1,434.21	115.93	610.53	53.70	40.48
Goiás	469	523	681	784	67.16	49.90	11.51	30.21	15.12
Distrito Federal	145	250	463	629	333.79	151.60	72.41	85.20	35.85

Source: Ministry of Health data.

1995 (235.32 percent). In Rio de Janeiro, the number of homicides increased from 2,941 in 1980 to 8,216 in 1995 (179.36 percent). The states with the largest homicide growth rates in this period were Amapá (1,671.43 percent) and Mato Grosso (1,434.21 percent). The states with the lowest homicide growth rates were Minas Gerais (4.30 percent) and Paraíba (51.32 percent).

The largest growth in the number of homicides happened in the 1980s and particularly in the period 1985–90 (see table 8.1). The number of homicides grew 41.96 percent in the period 1980–85 and 61.99 percent in the period 1985–90. In the period 1990–95, the homicide growth rate declined to 16.07 percent. In the period 1980–85, the number of homicides increased in all states with the exception of Rio Grande do Norte (–17.79 percent), Sergipe (–21.95 percent), Minas Gerais (–11.68 percent), and Rio de Janeiro (–13.60 percent). In the period 1985–90, the number of homicides increased in all states. In the period 1990–95, the number of homicides declined in six states: Rondônia (–40.54 percent), Roraima (–31.50 percent), Pará (–6.42 percent), Maranhão (–12.90 percent), Pernambuco (–1.28 percent), and Rio Grande do Sul (–14.92 percent).

The growth of the number of homicides in Brazil affected especially the male population and the population of 15–24 years old (see tables 8.2 through 8.5). From 1980 to 1995, the number of male victims of homicides increased from 12,534 to 33,752 (169.28 percent) and the number of victims 15–24 years of age increased from 4,327 to 12,603 (191.26 percent). In both cases, the homicide growth rate was higher than the national rate. The homicide growth rates for the female population (145.75 percent) and the population 25–34 years of age (162.63 percent) were lower than the national rate.

There has been, however, a significant increase in the number of female victims of homicide (see tables 8.1, 8.2, and 8.3). In the period 1990–95, the female homicide growth rate (28.63 percent) was superior to the national rate (16.07 percent) and the male rate (14.93 percent).

Studies of the distribution of homicides in the cities of São Paulo, Rio de Janeiro, Salvador, and Curitiba show that the risk of homicide is higher in the poor areas in the periphery of these urban centers (CEDEC 1996a, 1996 b, 1997a, 1997b). In the city of São Paulo, for example, the homicide rate in 1995 reached 111.52 deaths per 100,000 inhabitants in the southern region of Jardim Ângela, but remained at 2.65 per 100,000 in the central region of Perdizes.

There is evidence that criminal organizations have developed national and international connections as well as connections within state institutions. The National Congress established a special parliamentary commis-

Table 8.2. Comparison of Homicide Growth Rates for Males in Brazil, 1980–95

	Number of Homicides				Percentage Growth in Homicides		
State	1980	1985	1990	1995	1980–95	1985–95	1990–95
Brazil, all	12,534	17,965	29,367	33,752	169.28	87.88	14.93
Rondônia	106	293	517	292	175.47	−0.34	−43.52
Acre	24	49	58	86	258.33	75.51	48.28
Amazonas	115	166	332	382	232.17	130.12	15.06
Roraima	9	10	107	79	777.78	690.00	−26.17
Pará	276	473	669	641	1,32.25	35.52	−4.19
Amapá	7	30	39	113	1,514.29	276.67	189.74
Tocantins			47	72			53.19
Maranhão	98	150	410	344	251.02	129.33	−16.10
Piauí	43	69	104	95	120.93	37.68	−8.65
Ceará	414	508	510	790	90.82	55.51	54.90
Rio Grande Norte	156	126	180	217	39.10	72.22	20.56
Paraíba	269	342	399	391	45.35	14.33	−2.01
Pernambuco	1,001	1,846	2,521	2,498	149.55	35.32	−0.91
Alagoas	250	454	663	676	170.40	48.90	1.96
Sergipe	70	52	138	227	224.29	336.54	64.49
Bahia	276	481	782	1,360	392.75	182.74	73.91
Minas Gerais	1,028	865	1,029	1,057	2.82	22.20	2.72
Espirito Santo	269	413	791	1,030	282.90	149.39	30.21
Rio de Janeiro	2,720	2,343	6,612	7,615	179.96	225.01	15.17
São Paulo	3,098	6,484	8,824	10,596	242.03	63.42	20.08
Paraná	744	817	1,041	1,220	63.98	49.33	17.20
Santa Catarina	218	222	1,533	364	66.97	63.96	−76.26
Rio Grande do Sul	574	608	336	1,286	124.04	111.51	282.74
Mato Grosso do Sul	200	235	306	581	190.50	147.23	89.87
Mato Grosso	34	246	376	516	1,417.65	109.76	37.23
Goiás	403	454	620	652	61.79	43.61	5.16
Distrito Federal	132	229	423	572	333.33	149.78	35.22

Source: Ministry of Health data.

sion to investigate the problem of drug trafficking, and the commission obtained evidence of the participation of elected officials and members of the judiciary and the police, from different states, in drug-traffic and extrajudicial executions.[1]

In the state of São Paulo, from 1996 to 1999, the police ombudsman received complaints against 481 police officers for participation in organized crime and particularly drug-traffic.[2] In the state of Rio de Janeiro, the ombudsman was created in 1999 and received 1,586 complaints against police officers in 9 months. The majority of complaints referred to extortion (19.8 percent) and excessive use of force (13.2 percent). The complaints resulted in the punishment of 117 police officers.[3]

Table 8.3.   *Comparison of Homicide Growth Rates for Females in Brazil,*
1980–95

	Number of Homicides				Percentage Growth in Homicides		
State	1980	1985	1990	1995	1980–95	1985–95	1990–95
Brazil, all	1,353	1,766	2,585	3,325	145.75	88.28	28.63
Rondônia	12	26	37	37	208.33	42.31	0.00
Acre	2	2	6	16	700.00	700.00	166.67
Amazonas	21	17	31	42	100.00	147.06	35.48
Roraima	2	2	20	8	300.00	300.00	−60.00
Pará	28	34	78	59	110.71	73.53	−24.36
Amapá		4	5	11		175.00	120.00
Tocantins			7	5			−28.57
Maranhão	10	12	32	40	300.00	233.33	25.00
Piauí	7	7	5	19	171.43	171.43	280.00
Ceará	31	41	45	55	77.42	34.15	22.22
Rio Grande Norte	7	8	20	30	328.57	275.00	50.00
Paraíba	33	38	41	66	100.00	73.68	60.98
Pernambuco	120	165	219	205	70.83	24.24	−6.39
Alagoas	30	58	55	61	103.33	5.17	10.91
Sergipe	12	12	13	27	125.00	125.00	107.69
Bahia	42	59	77	165	292.86	179.66	114.29
Minas Gerais	132	162	147	145	9.85	−10.49	−1.36
Espirito Santo	36	42	88	123	241.67	192.86	39.77
Rio de Janeiro	210	194	477	587	179.52	202.58	23.06
São Paulo	348	543	679	959	175.57	76.61	41.24
Paraná	87	103	125	163	87.36	58.25	30.40
Santa Catarina	23	35	45	48	108.70	37.14	6.67
Rio Grande do Sul	59	73	156	151	155.93	106.85	−3.21
Mato Grosso do Sul	18	17	40	51	183.33	200.00	27.50
Mato Grosso	4	24	39	66	1,550.00	175.00	69.23
Goiás	66	67	58	129	95.45	92.54	122.41
Distrito Federal	13	21	40	57	338.46	171.43	42.50

Source: Ministry of Health data.

In the state of Rio Grande do Sul, the secretary of justice and public security substituted the general-commissioner of the civilian police in the middle of political conflicts and accusations of police brutality, corruption and involvement in organized crime.[4]

Since the transition to democracy, politicians and elected officials at the federal, state, and municipal levels have focused attention on the problems of crime and violence, including the problems of police brutality and abuse. The 1988 Federal Constitution established the institutional basis for the organization of the democratic regime and the public security system and the limitation and control of the arbitrary use of force by the state. The Constitution established an ample bill of rights (articles 5–17) and the po-

Table 8.4.   *Comparison of Homicide Growth Rates for People 15–24 Years of Age in Brazil, 1980–95*

	Number of Homicides				Percentage Growth in Homicides		
State	1980	1985	1990	1995	1980–95	1985–95	1990–95
Brazil, all	4,327	6,482	10,954	12,603	191.26	94.43	15.05
Rondônia	24	59	140	93	287.50	57.63	−33.57
Acre	9	18	25	37	311.11	105.56	48.00
Amazonas	51	56	134	176	245.10	214.29	31.34
Roraima	3	2	39	30	900.00	1,400.00	−23.08
Pará	101	125	234	216	113.86	72.80	−7.69
Amapá	5	18	19	53	960.00	194.44	178.95
Tocantins			15	24			60.00
Maranhão	21	34	130	113	438.10	232.35	−13.08
Piauí	14	14	29	34	142.86	142.86	17.24
Ceará	128	162	158	268	109.38	65.43	69.62
Rio Grande Norte	46	47	54	63	36.96	34.04	16.67
Paraíba	76	113	109	167	119.74	47.79	53.21
Pernambuco	307	635	866	920	199.67	44.88	6.24
Alagoas	72	112	155	171	137.50	52.68	10.32
Sergipe	19	14	56	71	273.68	407.14	26.79
Bahia	80	142	299	540	575.00	280.28	80.60
Minas Gerais	305	244	293	367	20.33	50.41	25.26
Espirito Santo	74	115	234	385	420.27	234.78	64.53
Rio de Janeiro	1,070	846	2,530	2,880	169.16	240.43	13.83
São Paulo	1,282	2,895	3,875	4,219	229.10	45.73	8.88
Paraná	198	227	348	425	114.65	87.22	22.13
Santa Catarina	72	83	104	99	37.50	19.28	−4.81
Rio Grande do Sul	169	197	588	461	172.78	134.01	−21.60
Mato Grosso do Sul	48	59	90	196	308.33	232.20	117.78
Mato Grosso	5	45	82	119	2,280.00	164.44	45.12
Goiás	103	131	181	225	118.45	71.76	24.31
Distrito Federal	45	89	167	251	457.78	182.02	50.30

Source: Ministry of Health data.

lice obligation to follow the principles of legality, impartiality, morality, publicity, and efficiency (article 37).[5]

The police obligation to respect citizen rights was reinforced by the ratification of the International Covenant on Civil and Political Rights and the International Covenant on Economic, Social, and Cultural Rights in 1992; the Inter-American Convention on Human Rights in 1992; the Convention on the Rights of the Child in 1990; and the Convention against Torture and Other Cruel, Inhuman, or Degrading Treatment or Punishment and the Inter-American Convention to Prevent and Punish Torture in 1989.

Table 8.5. *Comparison of Homicide Growth Rates for People 25–34 Years of Age in Brazil, 1980–95*

State	Number of Homicides				Percentage Growth in Homicides		
	1980	1985	1990	1995	1980–95	1985–95	1990–95
Brazil, all	4,220	6,326	10,081	11,083	162.63	75.20	9.94
Rondônia	45	122	172	85	88.89	−30.33	−50.58
Acre	10	17	15	24	140.00	41.18	60.00
Amazonas	37	64	125	115	210.81	79.69	−8.00
Roraima	3	5	39	28	833.33	460.00	−28.21
Pará	91	180	239	197	116.48	9.44	−17.57
Amapá	1	2	11	29	2,800.00	1,350.00	163.64
Tocantins			13	20			53.85
Maranhão	36	43	132	108	200.00	151.16	−18.18
Piauí	18	26	35	37	105.56	42.31	5.71
Ceará	129	155	180	264	104.65	70.32	46.67
Rio Grande Norte	54	32	66	77	42.59	140.63	16.67
Paraíba	79	111	130	127	60.76	14.41	−2.31
Pernambuco	351	646	894	817	132.76	26.47	−8.61
Alagoas	101	192	226	228	125.74	18.75	0.88
Sergipe	26	22	51	83	219.23	277.27	62.75
Bahia	90	181	253	411	356.67	127.07	62.45
Minas Gerais	359	341	422	349	−2.79	2.35	−17.30
Espirito Santo	106	146	282	333	214.15	128.08	18.09
Rio de Janeiro	897	902	2,204	2,139	138.46	137.14	−2.95
São Paulo	1,006	2,150	3,029	3,869	284.59	79.95	27.73
Paraná	218	289	333	416	90.83	43.94	24.92
Santa Catarina	72	70	126	129	79.17	84.29	2.38
Rio Grande do Sul	203	209	510	416	104.93	99.04	−18.43
Mato Grosso do Sul	72	78	114	182	152.78	133.33	59.65
Mato Grosso	13	100	133	202	1,453.85	102.00	51.88
Goiás	152	162	219	234	53.95	44.44	6.85
Distrito Federal	51	81	128	164	221.57	102.47	28.13

Source: Ministry of Health data.

Brazil also recognized the competence of the Inter-American Court on Human Rights in 1998.

Contrary to what happened during the authoritarian regime, the police are subordinated to elected governments. The governor and the secretary of public security are responsible for the formulation and implementation of public security policies. The Legislative Assembly approves the police budget and, in many states, the Assembly has committees for public security and for human rights that focus attention on police priorities, objectives, and strategies and conduct hearings with government and police officials. The media and both national and international nongovernmental organizations regularly monitor police activities and expose cases of police violence, corruption, and deception.

In addition to the control of the police by elected officials, the 1988 Federal Constitution (article 129) attributed to the public prosecutors the responsibility of the external control of the police. The police, however, have systematically opposed the implementation of this external control. The military police have also systematically opposed the transference of the competence to judge police officers accused of crimes from the military courts to the civilian courts.

The police are no longer organized and prepared to repress the political opposition and social movements. The police generally respect the citizen's freedom of thought, freedom of opinion and expression, and freedom of peaceful assembly and association, even though there are frequent cases of excessive use of force against social movements. The police also respect the citizen's right to vote in free, fair, and periodic elections and to take part in the government directly or through elected representatives.

However, the transition to democracy did not automatically imply the limitation and control of the arbitrariness of state agents. Police violence was an institutionalized practice during the authoritarian regime and the change in political regime and legal norms was not enough to limit and control the illegal use of force by police officers.

During the transition to democracy, it became clear that the government and civil society groups had underestimated the authoritarian legacies and treated the police as neutral organizations capable of protecting the citizens under a democratic regime as well as the state or the government under an authoritarian regime (Pinheiro 1991; Pinheiro, Izumino, and Fernandes 1991). Years of authoritarian rule had weakened the police's accountability and responsiveness to the law and the citizens and rendered the police not only distant from citizens but also ill prepared to respond to the problems of crime and violence in a society respecting the constitutional principles of legality, morality, impartiality, publicity, and efficiency.

In addition, the coincidence of the transition to democracy, the growth of crime and violence, and the growth of fear and insecurity were exploited by conservative groups that associated the growth of crime and violence with the establishment of democratic practices and the efforts to protect and promote human rights. These conservative groups presented human rights as a "privilege of criminals" and opposed efforts to limit and control the arbitrary use of force by the police (T. Caldeira 1991).

The discussion of the problem of police violence and the means to limit and control police violence increased after the October 1992 massacre in the Caranidru Penitentiary in the city of São Paulo, in which the military police killed 111 prisoners during an operation to control a riot (C. Caldeira 1999).

After the Carandiru massacre, the military police organized a special course for police officers involved in shootings resulting in the deaths of civilians. The first course, for officers who had been involved in the massacre, lasted 1 month and included psychological assessment and the following topics: religion, human rights, public service, ethics, personal defense, music, and drawing. In 1993, the military police organized another course for police officers in ROTA (a special unit of the military police).

In 1995, the state of São Paulo established the PROAR (Programa de Assistência a Policias Envolvidos em Ocorrências de Alto Risco) for all police officers except those in ROTA participating in the courses established in 1993. In this special program, all police officers involved in shootings resulting in the death of civilians were suspended from patrol for 6 months and received psychological assistance and training during this period. After 6 months, the officers returned to patrol in the central area of the city, where the risk of confrontations and shootings is lower than on the periphery.

According to the military police, PROAR's objective was to prepare the police officer to act rationally and not emotionally, to detain and not kill those suspected of criminal activities. The program was considered successful and instrumental in reducing the number of civilians killed by the police in São Paulo. In 1997, ROTA was included in PROAR following an increase in the number of civilians killed by the police in the first month of the year.

Following the Carandiru massacre and the establishment of courses in São Paulo, military police officers began to have courses on human rights and professional ethics in other states as well. These courses were prepared not only by the police but also by Amnesty International and universities that established agreements to cooperate with the police in this area.

In 1998, with the support of the Ministry of Justice, the International Committee of the Red Cross developed a course on human rights and international humanitarian law for military police officers from all states of Brazil. The objective of the course is to ensure the respect for fundamental human rights by the police and reduce the risk of human rights violations in armed conflicts involving police officers.

The course is organized in six sessions that combine the theory of human rights and international humanitarian law to police practice (table

8.6). The International Committee of the Red Cross organized the first course, which lasted 12 days and included 21 police officers from different states. This group had the obligation to train 54 officers, 2 officers in each state and in the Federal District, which had the obligation to train new police officers.

In 1996, the National Congress approved federal law 9,299/96, which transferred from the military to the civilian courts the competence to judge the military police officers, but only in the case of crimes against life. In 1997, the National Congress approved federal law 9,455/97, which defined and punished severely the crime of torture, but few military officers have been prosecuted for this crime.

Five states have established a police ombudsman (*ouvidoria de polícia*) to receive complaints against the military police and the civilian police: São Paulo in 1995, Pará in 1997, Minas Gerais in 1998, and Rio de Janeiro and Rio Grande do Sul in 1999. The federal government proposed the creation of police ombudsmen in the states in the National Program for Human Rights (Programa Nacional de Direitos Humanos) in 1996 and supported the creation of the National Forum of Police Ombudsmen (Fórum Nacional de Ouvidores de Polícia) in 1998 with the objective of promoting the creation of the institution of police ombudsmen in all Brazilian states.

Table 8.6. *Human Rights Training of the International Committee of the Red Cross*

Session	Topics Covered
Law	Basic concepts in international law
	International law of human rights
	International humanitarian law
Basic Premises in Law Enforcement	Law enforcement in democratic states
	Ethic and legal conduct in law enforcement
Basic Responsibilities in Law Enforcement	Crime prevention and detection
	Order maintenance
Basic Powers in Law Enforcement	Apprehension
	Detention
	Use of force and fire arms
Law Enforcement and Vulnerable Groups	Women
	Children and Adolescents
	Victims of crime and abuse of power
	Refugees and displaced persons
Command and Management	Procedures of supervision and revision
	Investigation of human rights violations

Source: Rover 1998.

Since the Constituent Assembly in 1987–88, there have been several proposals for substantial change in the structure of the public security system and the structure of police organizations. The proposals include the civilianization of the military police, the fusion of the military and the civilian police, the transference of responsibilities from the military to the civilian police, and the creation of municipal police forces. However, these proposals depend on constitutional changes and have been systematically blocked in the National Congress. President Fernando Henrique Cardoso proposed a constitutional amendment to grant more autonomy to the states in the organization of the public security system in 1997, but the National Congress never voted on the proposal.

Since the late 1980s, state governments have expanded the size and modernized the equipment and armament of the military police and the civilian police, which are responsible respectively for order maintenance and criminal investigation in the states. Municipal governments have established municipal guards to protect municipal property.[6]

The federal government has expanded the size and modernized the equipment and armament of the federal police, who are responsible for border control and the prevention and repression of interstate and international crimes and particularly of drug traffic and smuggling. In 1998, the federal government established the National Anti-Drug Secretariat to coordinate preventive and repressive actions against drug trafficking.[7]

The federal government has also limited the participation of the armed forces in the area of public security to situations in which the military police and the civilian police are not capable of maintaining law and order.[8] However, the federal government still relies on the armed forces to maintain law and order, specially when the police become involved in illegal and/or disorderly actions. In 1997, the federal government employed the armed forces to contain police rebellions and strikes in seven states: Minas Gerais, Rio Grande do Sul, Pernambuco, Ceará, Alagoas, Paraíba, and Mato Grosso do Sul.

The Police and the Community

Despite all the measures adopted by the federal government and by state and municipal governments, the incidence of crime and violence continued to grow in the 1980s and 1990s and the quality of public security services became a major concern of the population. The effectiveness of governmental and police responses to the problem of crime and violence has been undermined by the persistence of police brutality and the low level of respect for and cooperation with the police and the criminal justice system on the part of the community. National and international human rights organizations have exposed the persistent problem of police violence after the transition to democracy and the ineffectiveness of instruments to limit and control police violence.[9]

Researchers have also developed studies showing the lack of trust of the population in the police and the judiciary and the persistence of authoritarian attitudes, norms, and values in society, the government, the police, and the judiciary that undermine efforts to limit and control police violence and improve the quality of police services.[10]

In the state of São Paulo, where statistical data on police violence have been available since 1983, military police officers killed 8,893 civilians and injured 9,100 from 1983 to 1998. Civilian police officers killed 247 civilians and injured 607 from 1990 to 1998. In 1992, the year in which the largest number of civilians was killed by police officers, there were 9,011 homicides in the state of São Paulo and police officers killed 1,458 civilians (16.2 percent of the total number of homicides). From 1996 to 1998, the police ombudsman received 10,238 complaints against police officers, including 1,476 complaints for the abuse of authority, 558 complaints for torture, 498 complaints for extortion, and 184 complaints for corruption.[11]

According to a survey realized in ten state capitals in Brazil in 1999, the performance of the civilian police was considered "good" and "very good" by 23 percent of the population, in contrast to 49 percent for the army and 40 percent for the federal police. The performance of the military police was considered "good" or "very good" by 21 percent of the population. The majority of the population considered the performance of the civilian police and the military police "average," "bad," or "very bad." Only 10 percent of the population believed that the police ensured the security of the citizens (Cardia 1999, 77–96).

According to a survey done in the city of Rio de Janeiro in 1997, police efficiency was considered unsatisfactory by 11.1 percent of the population and very unsatisfactory by 15.7 percent of the population (Briceño-Leon, Carneiro, and Cruz 1999, 125). Regarding the impartiality of law enforcement and criminal justice agencies, 95.7 percent of the population considered that the members of low-income groups would be treated more severely than the members of the high-income groups (Pandolfi 1999, 55–56). Another survey undertaken in the state of São Paulo in 1998 showed that 54.5 percent of the victims of robberies or thefts did not report the crime to the police (56.9 percent in the metropolitan region of São Paulo and 49.4 percent in the interior of the state).[12]

The majority of the citizens vote in elections for municipal, state, and federal governments and legislatures, which are responsible for the formulation and implementation of public security policies, but do not directly participate in the definition of police priorities, objectives, and strategies. Furthermore, the majority of the citizens, community associations, and nongovernmental organizations do not have information and have limited access to legal, political, and social instruments to ensure the accountability and responsiveness of the police to the law and the public (Mesquita Neto 1999).

There are also indications that a significant segment of the population tolerates or supports the illegal use of force by the police as an instrument for crime control and order maintenance. According to the survey in ten state capitals, 16 percent of the population "fully agree" that the police have the right to shoot armed suspects, 30 percent fully agree that the police have the right to search suspects based on their physical appearance, 6 percent fully agree that the police have the right to torture suspects to extract confessions, and 3 percent fully agree that the police have the right to search a house without a legal mandate (Cardia 1999, 89–96).

According to a survey in the city of Rio de Janeiro in 1997, 63.4 percent of the population believed that criminal offenders should not have their rights respected and 44.5 percent of the population believed that the police can always or sometimes use violence to extract a confession from criminals (Pandolfi 1999, 48–52). Furthermore, 14.8 percent of the population thought that the police have the right to search the house without a judicial order, 16.5 percent thought that the police had the right to stop young people based on their physical appearance, and 12.5 percent thought that the police had the right to use torture to extract information (Briceño-Leon, Carneiro, and Cruz 1997, 122).

The growth of private security services is one of the clearest expressions and responses to the crisis in the area of public security and declining confidence in the police. Since the 1980s, the population has increasingly turned to private security services as an alternative to or supplement for public security services.

According to the union representing private security employees, the number of private security employees increased from 80,000 in 1993 to 135,000 in 1996 (68.7 percent). Those employees were working legally in 286 companies. In addition, according to the two unions, there were about

100,000 private security employees working illegally in 500 companies. Since 1996, the number of employees in private security companies had grown continuously to reach one million.[13]

Police officers cannot legally have additional jobs. However, the government and the police authorities tolerate police officers having secondary employment. A large number of police officers have second jobs (known as "bico"), and many work formally or informally in private security. Despite recent increases in their salaries, police officers argue that they need the second job to complement their income. Police authorities accept the argument and argue that the tolerance of the second job is necessary to keep the officers in the police.

However, the illegal employment of police officers in private security services undermines and further aggravates the crisis in the military and the civilian police. In addition to weakening respect for law among the police and the credibility of the police with citizens, it undermines the security of police officers and the strength of the police. The majority of police officers killed every year are killed when they are off-duty, and many are killed working in private security. According to a report by the police ombudsman in São Paulo, 27 police officers were killed on duty and 110 off duty in the military police from December to June 1999. In the civilian police, 29 police officers were killed on duty and 25 off duty in the same period.[14]

Community Policing

Community policing was introduced in Brazil in the early 1990s. From the police perspective, community policing was primarily a strategy to bring the police and community closer and to promote the cooperation of the community with the police in crime control and order maintenance. From the community perspective, community policing was primarily a strategy to promote both the participation of citizens in the formulation and implementation of public security policies and also the police's accountability and responsiveness to citizens.

With different understandings of community policing, groups within the police and the community began to support community policing as a new approach to crime control and order maintenance. These groups saw community policing as a successful or at least promising policing strategy in Canada, Japan, the United Kingdom, and the United States,. They also considered possible the adoption of similar strategy in Brazil, despite the radical differences between the characteristics of the police and communities in Brazil and in the other countries.

In Brazil, community policing was perceived as an approach to crime control and a policing strategy that not only was more effective but also required the police to be more respectful of democratic institutions and human rights. It was an alternative to authoritarian approaches to crime control, which were increasingly in conflict with new democratic institutions and practices and undermined the legitimacy and the effectiveness of the police.

Conversely, community policing was an alternative to the growth of private security services. Private security services not only competed with but also weakened the police, who have the constitutional obligation to provide equal security services to all citizens. Furthermore, private security services were of more benefit to members of high-income groups that could afford better services than to members of low-income groups. In both ways, the growth of private security services increased the problem of unequal access to security services that weaken the democratic regime in Brazil. In the end, the development of community policing projects depended to a significant extent on the support and the coalition of actors in three spheres: the police, the government, and civil society.

Rio de Janeiro

In Rio de Janeiro, the Institute for Studies in Religion, Viva Rio, and the military police initiated a pilot project of community policing in the neighborhood of Copacabana in 1994, during the government of Nilo Batista (1991–94).[15] However, the government of Marcelo Alencar (1995–98) terminated the project in 1995. Following the development of Operation Rio (1994–95), in which the federal and state governments employed the armed forces to strengthen the police activities in crime control and order maintenance, the government adopted aggressive policing strategies focusing attention on serious crimes and particularly organized crime and drug trafficking.

The government of Anthony Garotinho (1999–2002) integrated the operational areas of the military police and the civilian police, creating community councils of public security to bring the police and community closer and reestablish community policing in some areas in the capital and other cities in the state. The military police organized a training program on community policing for all police officers. The program was initiated in 1999 and was expected to be completed in 2000. It lasted five days and included sessions on human rights, crime prevention, the use of force, racial violence, violence against homosexuals, domestic violence, inter-personal relationships, conflict management, service management, prob-lem-resolution, total quality management, community policing, and com-munity mobilization.

Rio Grande do Sul

In the state of Rio Grande do Sul, the government of Antônio Brito (1995–98) developed a program to foster cooperation between the police and the community called Segurança Cidadã. The government began to in-tegrate the operations of the military police and civilian police, flattened the command structure and the hierarchy of the military police, and pro-vided human rights training for police officers with the objective of pro-moting policing strategies and actions that would be not only more effec-tive but also more compatible with the rule of law and human rights.

The government of Olivio Dutra (1999–2002) extended to the state of Rio Grande do Sul and the area of public security the participatory budget system established in the capital city of Porto Alegre. According to this system, the state budget, including the budget for public security and the police, is debated in public forums, at the local and state level, before being submitted by the government to the Legislative Assembly.

Espírito Santo

Guaçuí, a city of 30,000 inhabitants, in the state of Espírito Santo in east-ern Brazil, in 1994 developed a citywide program to foster cooperation be-tween the police and community called "Interactive Police." The munici-pal government established an agreement with the state government and created the interactive public security council (*conselho interativo de se-gurança pública*). The council, formed by representatives from the com-munity and the government, including elected officials, civil servants, pub-lic prosecutors, and judges, promotes regular meetings with the police to discuss and define policing priorities.

In addition to the interactive council, the police established offices (*serviço de atendimento ao cidadão*) to receive complaints and informa-tion about crime and violence, which are answered in 48 hours. The of-fices, which are open from 8 a.m. to 10 p.m. and are staffed with specially trained police officers, also receive complaints and information about po-lice violence.

The experience of interactive police has been considered successful by the community and the police and has inspired similar experiences in other cities in Espírito Santo and in other states—including Pernambuco, Amapá, Pará, Sergipe, Goiás, and Santa Catarina—and the Federal District.

Federal District

In the Federal District, the government of Cristovão Buarque (1995–98) initiated a project of community policing in the city of Samambaia. However, Buarque lost the election to Joaquim Roriz. The government of Joaquim Roriz (1999–2002) initiated the program "Security without Tolerance," emphasizing the importance of aggressive policing strategies to maintain law and order over partnerships with the community.

Pernambuco

The city of Cabo de Santo Agostinho, in the metropolitan region of Recife, state of Pernambuco, northeastern Brazil, developed a community policing program called Polícia Amiga in 1997. The city registered homicide rates of 36 per 100,000 residents in 1996 and 56 per 100,000 in 1997. Concerned with the growth of violence, the municipal government established an agreement with the state government for the management of public security services in the city. According to this agreement, the state government provides the police officers and the municipal government provides the infrastructure for the development of a community policing program.

To implement the program, the municipal government created an interactive council, which is responsible for defining policing priorities and objectives. The council is composed of the mayor, the coordinator, a representative from the civilian police, a representative from the military police, a representative from the public prosecutors, a representative from the judiciary, a representative from the legislature, and—as observers—representatives from civil society groups. The responsibilities of the council include the formulation of public security policies, the promotion of new policing strategies, professional training, and studies and research on public security problems and services. The police officers received basic training for community policing before the implementation of the program and participated in seminars, with the participation of civilian professionals, focusing attention on the most frequent types of problems in the community.

Amapá

The state of Amapá, in northern Brazil, has been developing a community policing program called Polícia Cidadã since 1997. The objective of the program is to integrate the activities of the military police and the civilian police and promote policing strategies oriented toward the protection and promotion of human rights and the valorization of community participation in the resolution of public security problems.

With support from the federal government and Amnesty International, Amapá provided training for 632 police officers in 1997 and 1,276 in 1998, including sessions on the following themes: social integration, interpersonal relations, public security and citizenship, medical emergencies, interactive police, sustainable development, human rights, drug dependency, gender, and race.

São Paulo

Community policing became more prominent in Brazil in 1997, when the military police adopted community policing as an organizational philosophy and strategy in the state of São Paulo.[16] The government of São Paulo began to create community councils of public security in 1985. The military police had supported the development of community policing in the city of Ribeirão Preto since 1992. Following a series of highly publicized cases of police violence and divergence over public security policy, Governor Mário Covas substituted the general-commander of the military police in September 1997. The new general-commander established the Commission for the Implementation of Community Policing in October, and the military police initiated the implementation of community policing in 41 companies in December.

Despite the absence of any evaluation of the implementation and results of community policing in the first group of 41 companies, the military police decided to rapidly expand the number of companies implementing community policing. From December 1997 to September 1998, the number of companies implementing community policing increased to 205, divided into four groups:

- The first group has 41 companies (19 in the metropolitan region of São Paulo, 17 in the interior of the state, and 5 specialized companies).
- The second group has 59 companies (15 in the metropolitan region, 35 in the interior, and 9 specialized companies).

- The third group also has 59 companies (20 in the metropolitan region, 31 in the interior, and 8 specialized companies).
- The fourth group, established in September 1998, has 46 companies (19 in the metropolitan region, 26 in the interior, and 1 specialized company).

In August 1998, there were 4,922 community policing officers in three groups (1,576 in the metropolitan region and 3,346 in the interior). This number represented 6 percent of the personnel in the military police and 20 percent of the personnel in the companies with community policing projects.

The police argument in favor of the expansion was that the community policing project was being successfully implemented, and there were strong demands for the expansion of the project. It is also important to consider, however, that there were elections for the state government in October 1998. Governor Mário Covas and the police presented community policing as one of the main projects in the area of public security. The conservative candidate, Paulo Maluf, like Joaquim Roriz in the Federal District, emphasized the importance of aggressive order maintenance or zero tolerance policing strategies.

After the October 1998 election, the number of companies implementing community police stabilized. In November 1999, the general-commander of the military police declared that there were approximately 7,500 police officers implementing community policing in 221 areas in 192 cities in the metropolitan region and in the interior of the state. According to the commander-general, the military police had plans to establish 48 additional areas for the implementation of community policing.[17]

Jardim Ângela

The community policing program in the area of Jardim Ângela, in the southern area of the city of São Paulo, had a different origin. Rather than the result of a governmental or police initiative, the project was the result of the community mobilization.

Jardim Ângela has an area of 3,740 square kilometers, a population of 178,373 inhabitants, and is located in one of the areas of São Paulo affected by drug trafficking where there is a high risk of mortal violence. The homicide rate for the population 15 to 24 years of age reached 222 deaths per 100,000 inhabitants in 1994. The neighborhood was deprived of basic urban and public services, and police officers were afraid to patrol the area.

There are, however, many community associations and nongovernmental organizations in Jardim Ângela. Approximately 200 associations and organizations created a forum called Forum pela Vida e contra a Violência, which has monthly meetings to discuss the problems of the neighborhood and solutions, including the issues of housing, health, education, security, and justice.

Representatives from the government, including the commander of the military police and the commissary of the civilian police in the area, are invited to participate in the forum's meetings. Thus, rather than having community representatives participating in government forums, Jardim Ângela has government representatives participating in a community forum. Regarding the resolution of the problems of crime and violence in the region, the forum supports an approach that includes not only typical police actions but also the articulation of police actions in the areas of health, education, employment, and justice.

Jardim Ângela was not originally included in the community policing program developed by the military police. At the end of 1998, the forum sent a letter to the command of the military police complaining about the absence of the police in the region and the exclusion of the region from the community policing program. A month later, the military police established two community offices in the area and a training program for fifty police officers working in the area.

The community policing program allowed the police and the forum to expand their activities in the neighborhood, encouraged cooperation between the police and the community, and contributed to a reduction of violence in the area. According to the members of the forum, the community knows the police officers and can participate in the formulation and implementation of public security policies in the area. In addition, the incidence of crime and violence and the fear of crime and violence declined and the quality of police services improved. However, the problems of crime and violence were not resolved but displaced to adjacent areas without the same level of community organization and the same level of cooperation between the police and the community.

Community Policing Approaches and Perspectives

Despite the relatively simultaneous emergence of community policing projects in many states and cities in Brazil, there are significant differences in the characteristics of police–community partnerships and experiences.

There are community policing projects directed mainly or primarily by state governments, as in São Paulo, Rio de Janeiro, Rio Grande do Sul, and Amapá. In these states, the government and the police have developed statewide programs to encourage closeness between the police and the community and to promote the participation of the community in defining public security policies. In São Paulo, the government and the police promote the participation of the community through direct contacts with the police at the local level. In Rio Grande do Sul, the government has promoted the participation of the community through the discussion of the state budget and more specifically the public security budget. In Rio de Janeiro, after a localized experiment with limited success in Copacabana, the state government decided to develop a statewide community policing program.

There are also community policing projects directed mainly by municipal or local governments, as in Guaçui in Espírito Santo, Cabo de Santo Agostinho in Pernambuco, and Samambaia in the Federal District. The original aspect of these experiences is that local governments assumed the responsibility to bring the police and the community together and to develop community policing programs despite the fact that the police are subordinated to the state government.

Finally, there are community policing experiences directed not only or primarily by the government but also by community groups, as in Jardim Ângela in São Paulo and to a lesser extent Copacabana in Rio de Janeiro. The distinctive aspect of these experiences, particularly that of Jardim Ângela, is that the community had a high level of organization and mobilization to address the problems of public security before the development of the community policing. In Copacabana, the community policing program focused attention on the problem of order maintenance. In Jardim Ângela, the community policing program sustained an approach to crime control and order maintenance that relied not only on policing strategies and actions but also on strategies and actions to address structural problems in the areas of health, housing, education, employment, and justice that increase the risk of crime and violence in the region.

In most cases, community policing programs developed as a democratically oriented response to the growth of crime and violence. The development of community policing programs depended on the support of groups in the state and/or city government, the police, and the community. However, due to the history of police brutality and abuses, the development of community policing programs depended to a significant extent on the development of external and internal control mechanisms to increase the accountability and responsiveness of the police to the community, including the creation of public security councils with community participation, ombudsman offices, and the development of training programs on human rights for police officers.

The configuration of the community policing programs depended largely on the roles played by the state and municipal governments and by the community in their development. In most cases, despite significant participation by the community at the beginning of the program, community policing programs have been directed mainly by state or municipal governments. Community participation has been limited and dependent on government support. The programs have focused largely on policing strategies and actions for crime control and order maintenance and not so much on strategies to increase the accountability and responsiveness of the police to the community.

The experience of Jardim Ângela is to a certain extent exceptional due to the high level of community organization and mobilization and the adoption of a broader approach to crime control and order maintenance that integrates the police and different government organizations in the process of identifying and resolving public security problems. The high risk of crime and violence and the particular characteristics of the community policing project helped to direct attention to the experience of Jardim Ângela and promote a model of community policing in which community associations and nongovernmental organizations have an active and central role in the identification and resolution of public security problems. In this case, the accountability and responsiveness of the police to the community became a central component of the community policing project.

It is still too early to provide a general evaluation of the sustainability and results of community policing experiences in Brazil. But it is possible to say that the development and sustainability of these programs depends to a significant extent on the support of progressive governments. Some programs, such as those developed in Copacabana and Samambaia, were abandoned following the election of more conservative governments in Rio de Janeiro and the Federal District. In the states of São Paulo, Rio Grande do Sul, Amapá, Pernambuco, and Espírito Santo, progressive state and municipal governments have supported the development of community policing experiences.

Furthermore, particularly in areas with a high risk of crime and violence, such as Jardin Ângela, the development and sustainability of these programs depends to a significant extent on the level of community support. Community support may not be sufficient to sustain a community policing project if the government decides to withdraw support. However, community support, developed and sustained through practices that increase the accountability and responsiveness of the police to the citizens, contribute to the development and sustainability of community policing projects even in a situation of extremely high crime rates.

On the basis of preliminary assessments of community policing experiences, the federal government has decided to support the development not only of community policing programs but also of external and internal control mechanisms to increase the accountability and responsiveness of the police to citizens—particularly of human rights training programs for police officers, which are considered important components of the most promising police–community partnerships. Yet the impact of community policing programs is still limited, even in the states and cities where there is strong governmental and societal support for these programs, and their future is still uncertain. On the basis of current experiences, it seems clear that the sustainability of these experiences significantly depends on the joint commitment of progressive governments, progressive groups within the police, and civil society organizations not only to the objective of reducing crime and violence but also to that of increasing police accountability to the community and responsiveness to citizens.

Notes

1. See *Veja*, December 12, 1999, "Narcobrasil," and *Veja*, August 4, 1999, "Os Crimes da Polícia."

2. O Estado de São Paulo, December 10, 1999, "Ouvidoria apura denúnicas contra policiais." Statistical informational available at the website of the police ombudsman (www.ouvidoria-policia.sp.gov.br).

3. O Estado de São Paulo, December 22, 1999, "Ouvidoria recebe 1,586 denúncias no Rio."

4. Zero Hora, January 4, 2000, "Troca de comando na Polícia Civil."

5. Article 5, sections 3 and 43, prohibited the practice of torture and established that the persons that practice torture, the persons that order the practice of torture, and the persons that do not prevent the practice of torture are legally responsible for the practice.

6. The 1988 Federal Constitution authorized the establishment of municipal guards.

7. The federal government created the National Anti-Drug Secretariat through the provisory measure 1,689/98 and decrees 2,632/98 and 2,792/98.

8. Complementary laws 69 from July 23, 1991, and 97 from June 9, 1999, regulated the organization, preparation, and employment of the armed forces, including the employment of the armed forces in the maintenance of law and order.

9. See Núcleo de Estudos da Violência e Comissão Teotônio Vilela (1993, 1995), Americas Watch and Núcleo de Estudos da Violência (1993), Human Rights Watch/Americas (1997).

10. See Cardia 1999; Pandolfi et al. 1999.

11. Statistical informational are available at the website of the police ombudsman (www.ouvidoria-policia.sp.gov.br).

12. Fundação Seade, "Pesquisa de condições de vida 1998"; statistical data available from the foundation's website (www.seade.gov.br).

13. *Folha de São Paulo*, April 20, 1997, "Uso de segurança privada explode em SP"; *Jornal da Tarde*, September 9, 1996, "SP tem 500 empresas de segurança irregulares." The two unions are Federação dos Vigilantes de São Paulo and Sindicato das Empresas de Segurança Privada e Cursos de Segurança de São Paulo.

14. Ouvidoria da policia do Estado de São Paulo, *Relatório anual de prestaçôo de contas 1999*.

15. See Muniz et al. 1997; Musumeci et al. 1996.

16. On community policing in São Paulo, see Mesquita Neto (1999a, 1999b) and Mesquita Neto and Affonso (1998).

17. O Estado de São Paulo, November 4, 1999, "PM vai ampliar o policiamento comunitário."

References

Americas Watch and Núcleo de Estudos da Violência–Universidade de São Paulo. 1993. *Violência policial urbana no Brasil: Mortes e tortura pela polícia em São Paulo e no Rio de Janeiro.* São Paulo: Human Rights Watch / Núcleo de Estudios Violência–Universidade de São Paulo.

Briceño-Leon, Roberto, Leandro Piquet Carneiro, and José Miguel Cruz. 1999. O apoio dos cidadãos à ação extra-judicial da polícia no Brasil, em El Salvador e na Venezuela. In *Justiça, cidadania e violência*, ed. Pandolfi, Dulce, José Murilo de Carvalho, Leandro Piquet Carneiro, and Maurício Grynszpan. Rio de Janeiro: Fundação Getúlio Vargas.

Caldeira, César. 1999. Carandiru: Um estudo sócio-jurídico. *Revista Brasileira de Ciências Criminais* 29, 30.

Caldeira, Teresa. 1991. Direitos humanos ou privilégios de bandidos? *Novos Estudos Cebrap* 30: 162–74.

Cardia, Nancy. 1999. *Atitudes, normas culturais e valores em relação à violência em 10 capitais brasileiras.* Brasília: Ministério da Justiça, Secretaria Nacional de Direitos Humanos.

CEDEC (Centro de Estudos de Cultura Contemporanea). 1996a. Mapa de risco da violência—Cidade de Curitiba.

———. 1996b. Mapa de risco da violência—Cidade de São Paulo.

———. 1997a. Mapa de risco da violência—Cidade do Rio de Janeiro.

———. 1997b. Mapa de risco da violência—Cidade de Salvador.

Human Rights Watch/Americas. 1997. *Brutalidade policial urbana no Brasil.* Rio de Janeiro: Human Rights Watch/Americas.

Mesquita Neto, Paulo de. 1999a. Policiamento comunitário: A experiência em São Paulo. *Revista do Instituto Brasileiro de Ciências Criminais* 25: 281–92.

————. 1999b. Violência policial no Brasil: Abordagens teóricas e práticas de controle. In *Justiça, cidadania e violência*, ed. Pandolfi, Dulce, José Murilo de Carvalho, Leandro Piquet Carneiro, and Maurício Grynszpan. Rio de Janeiro: Fundação Getúlio Vargas.

Mesquita Neto, Paulo de, and Beatriz Affonso. 1998. *Policiamento comunitário: A experiência em São Paulo*. São Paulo: Núcleo de Estudos da Violência.

Muniz, Jaqueline, et al. 1997. Resistências e dificuldades de um programa de policiamento comunitário. *Tempo Social* 9(1): 197–213.

Musumeci, Leonarda, et al. 1996. *Segurança pública e cidadania: A experiência de policiamento comunitário em Copacabana (1994–1995)*. Final Report of the Qualitative Evaluation. Rio de Janeiro: Instituto de Estudos da Religião.

Núcleo de Estudos da Violência—Universidade de São Paulo and Comissão Teotônio Vilela. 1993. *Dossiê direitos humanos no Brasil 1*. São Paulo: Núcleo de Estudios Violência–Universidade de São Paulo.

————. 1995. *Dossiê direitos humanos no Brasil 2*. São Paulo: Núcleo de Estudios Violência–Universidade de São Paulo.

Pandolfi, Dulce. 1999. Percepção dos direitos e participação social. In *Justiça, cidadania e violência*, ed. Dulce Pandolfi, José Murilo de Carvalho, Leandro Piquet Carneiro, and Maurício Grynszpan. Rio de Janeiro: Fundação Getúlio Vargas.

Pandolfi, Dulce, José Murilo de Carvalho, Leandro Piquet Carneiro, and Maurício Grynszpan. 1999. *Justiça, cidadania e violência*. Rio de Janeiro: Fundação Getúlio Vargas.

Pinheiro, Paulo S. 1991. Autoritarismo e transição. *Revista Universidade de São Paulo* 9: 45–56.

Pinheiro, Paulo Sérgio, E. A. Izumino, and M. C. J. Fernandes. 1991. Violência fatal: Conflitos policiais em São Paulo (1981–1989). *Revista Universidade de São Paulo* 9: 95–112.

Rover, C. de. 1998. *Para servir e proteger: Direitos humanos e direito internacional humanitário para forças policiais e de segurança: Manual para instrutores*. Geneva: International Committee of the Red Cross.

9

Experiences with Citizen Participation in Crime Prevention in Central America

Laura Chinchilla

Violence in Central America, which for many years has plagued a major portion of the population, shows no immediate signs of abating. In previous decades, in countries such as Guatemala, El Salvador, and Nicaragua, this phenomenon took the form of armed conflict. Today, though the state of war has come to an end and peace agreements are in place throughout the region, the population is experiencing disturbing increases in violent crime. In some countries on the isthmus, rates for violent crime are among the highest in the world,[1] and according to available statistics, death rates from criminal activity are higher today than during the periods of armed conflict.[2]

This chapter addresses the problem of crime in Central America, focusing on responses that attempt to deal with the problem by encouraging citizen participation. The first section examines the main features of crime in the region and some of the associated factors. The second section provides a critical account of the main criminal justice and public security reforms that have been implemented in the region. The third section examines citizens' perceptions of crime and of government entities responsible for controlling crime. Finally, the last section describes a number of experiences with crime prevention and citizen security, in which organized sectors of society have played a dominant role, providing useful lessons for designing and implementing improved policies in this area.

Crime in Central America

It is difficult to analyze crime in the region using a historical and comparative approach, due to the lack of availability of reliable statistics and the nonuniformity of sources in the different countries.[3] For several reasons, largely as a result of the extended periods of armed conflict, it has been difficult to document crime developments in these countries during past years. Contributing to this difficulty have been the lack of attention devoted to the subject of crime (which was present prior to the conflicts) and to the social violence resulting from the conflicts; the absence of professional civilian police forces with the tools to properly record and analyze crime statistics; and the secret and restricted nature of information on security issues. However, by focusing on regional crime trends, rather than on a comparison between countries, the available information can be used to formulate a general description of the phenomenon of crime in the region.

Increases in Violent Crime

An examination of the region's crime problem in terms of victimization rates, which provide a more accurate indication than official statistics, shows that in 1997, three countries—Guatemala, El Salvador, and Nicaragua—had relatively high rates (greater than 29 percent), whereas three others—Costa Rica, Honduras, and Panama—had rates of 20 percent or below (see figure 9.1). Studies in the region indicate high numbers of assaults, battery, and other crimes, with Guatemala having the highest victimization rate, followed by El Salvador, Nicaragua, Costa Rica, Panama, and Honduras.

If this analysis is taken together with Central American crime statistics, it can be seen that along with a general rise in crime, the increase has been most acute in the case of violent crime,[4] a situation particularly evident in the countries with the oldest crime records, Costa Rica and Nicaragua. In

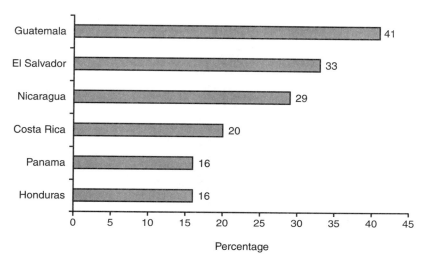

Figure 9.1. *Victimization Rates in Central American Countries, 1997*
Note: These numbers represent the percentage of people in each country that
have been victims of any crime. The figures result from national polls.
Source: UNDP 1997.

Costa Rica, for example, while the property crime rate grew 40.5 percent
between 1987 and 1997, the rate for crimes against individuals rose 79 percent during the same period—almost twice the rate of property crimes. In
Nicaragua, property crimes increased 39.7 percent between 1991 and
1997, while crimes against individuals grew 61.4 percent; and in Panama,
property crimes increased only 4.3 percent during the 1991–95 period,
while crimes against individuals increased 55.9 percent. Figure 9.2 shows
the contrast between the increase in general crime rates and the rise in
crimes against individuals in Costa Rica and Nicaragua (1991–97) and
Panama (1991–95).

A further disaggregation of the data indicates that in countries where
such records exist, the greatest increases have occurred in two areas:
crimes involving injury (with a 102 percent rise between 1991 and 1997 in
Nicaragua, and a 122 percent rise between 1994 and 1996 in El Salvador)
and robbery involving violence against individuals (with an increase of 88
percent between 1991 and 1997 in Nicaragua, and 72 percent in Costa Rica
for the same period).

Murder rates provide a good indicator of the level of violence in a society. From these figures, it can be seen that a number of Central American

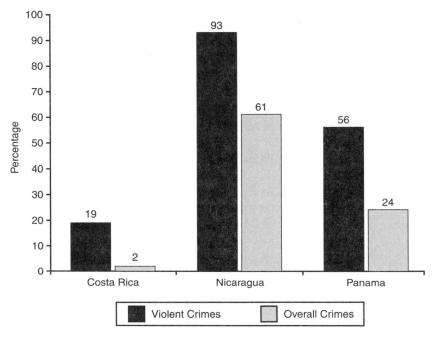

Figure 9.2. *Growth in Crime Rates in Central American Countries, 1991–1997 (percent)*
Note: Information in the case of Costa Rica and Nicaragua is for the period 1991–1997, and in the case of Panama is for the period 1991–1995.
Sources: Costa Rica: Judicial Branch (1991–1997); Nicaragua: Ministry of the Interior (1991–1997); Panama: National Police (1991–1995).

countries have levels above the average of 28.4 percent for Latin America and the Caribbean (PAHO 1999, 1). In table 9.1, El Salvador stands out, with one of the highest homicide rates in the world since 1994. Honduras and Guatemala also have high rates, and Panama had disturbing rates up until 1995. It should be noted that rates have been relatively low since 1994 in Costa Rica and Nicaragua.

Though there remains a lack of documentation for homicide rates for Central America, information available on some countries makes possible a more detailed analysis of those cases. In Honduras, for instance, factors contributing to deaths from homicide include fights under the influence of alcohol and drugs, and the carrying of firearms (Caldera 1998, 77). In Costa Rica, firearms play a major role in incidents of homicide; 33.7 per-

Table 9.1. *Homicide Rates in Central American Countries, 1994–97 (per 100,000 inhabitants)*

Country	1994	1995	1996	1997
Guatemala	31.4	34.4	30.0	n.a.
El Salvador	138.2	138.9	117.4	109.1
Honduras	30.3	40.9	n.a.	52.5
Nicaragua	9.9	9.5	8.8	9.2
Costa Rica	5.5	5.4	5.5	6.0
Panama	11.0	22.0	n.a.	n.a.

Note: "n.a." means not available.
Sources: Guatemala: United Nations, based on information from the National Police; El Salvador: Office of the National Prosecutor; Honduras: Public Security Force; Nicaragua: National Police; Costa Rica: Judicial Research Agency; Panama: National Police. Population data for all countries are from: Demographic Observer, Central American Population Program.

cent of victims were killed by firearms in 1990, and the percentage rose to 52.5 percent in 1997 (State of the Nation Project 1998, 229).

Likewise, in El Salvador, figures on violent death for metropolitan San Salvador, collected by the Institute of Forensic Medicine, indicate that most of these deaths are due to firearms—50.2 percent in 1995, 49.7 percent in 1996, and 55.2 percent in 1997 (Portillo 1998). As for motives, one study shows that homicides occur most frequently during the commission of a common crime, accounting for 26 percent of deaths (Cruz 1997, 986). In Guatemala, homicide tends to be the result of assaults or robbery, and fights involving political and personal conflicts; as in the other countries, most of these are committed with firearms (Marroquín 1997, 356).

Principal Factors Associated with Crime

Given the complexity involved in analyzing the genesis of criminal activity and the lack of field research on the subject in Central America, it would be difficult to make categorical statements as to direct relationships between specific factors and increased crime rates in the region. Nevertheless, certain elements are consistently associated with some of the violent forms of crime seen in these countries. The most common of these associated factors include deteriorating socioeconomic conditions, the aftereffects of armed conflict, and the growing presence of organized crime.

There is increasingly compelling evidence to support the thesis of a relation between deteriorating socioeconomic conditions among broad segments of the population in Central America and increasing criminal violence, particularly with regard to the phenomenon of juvenile delinquency.[5] It is estimated, for example, that 18.9 percent of children between 7 and 12 years of age in Central America, and 59.7 percent of children between 13 and 18 years of age received no schooling during 1997 (State of the Region Project 1999, 168), whereas the participation of young people in criminal gangs seems to be on the increase in all of the countries of the region. This is the case in El Salvador, where a recent study indicates that half of those involved in property crimes are minors (Universidad Centroamericana José Simeón Cañas 1997). Some authors have gone further still, citing a positive correlation between declining rates of consumption among the Central American population and increased property crimes (Carranza 1997, 23–49).

When the impact of armed conflict on current levels of violence is invoked, three circumstances are involved. First is the prevalence of patterns of behavior involving conflict and violence. One Salvadoran analyst, noting that patterns of violent behavior that contribute to the general problem of violence in the country are one of the legacies of the armed conflict, observes that "the civil war militarized the society, caused a deterioration in citizens' ability to live together peacefully, and trained people to use violence as a universal tool for dealing with disputes" (Cruz 1997, 980).

Second is the appearance of strategies to demobilize members of regular and irregular armed forces. The demobilization of armed groups that had participated in conflicts has received a great deal of attention in Guatemala, Nicaragua, and El Salvador. The deputy inspector of the National Civilian Police in El Salvador stated in 1995 that "most of the organized criminal groups operating in El Salvador are composed of former members of the armed forces or of the FMLN [Front for National Liberation]" (Alarcón 1997, 339).

Third is the extensive presence of firearms. As was indicated above, firearms are responsible for most of the homicides and injuries in the countries of the region, facilitated by the easy access of Central American citizens to a black market in arms, most of which come from the arsenals of groups that fought during the conflicts. There are estimated to be approximately 2 million firearms left over from the conflicts (International Peace Bureau 1998).

The link between criminal activity and organized crime tends to be primarily through drug trafficking and related activities. Clearly, the countries of Central America are located between the main drug-producing and drug-consuming countries, making the region the natural transit point for the transport of psychotropic substances. Recent estimates indicate that at least 50 metric tons of cocaine are transported through Central America by land each year (Joint Interagency Task Force East 1997). The rise in drug trafficking in the region is reflected in figures on confiscations of cocaine in the various countries, as is shown in figure 9.3. This statistic rose from 26,128 kilograms in 1994 to 46,534 in 1997, a 78 percent increase in 3 years.

The transit of drugs through the region has encouraged the development of local networks specializing in transport, warehousing, and packaging. The cash received from such activities has stimulated growing drug use within the countries of Central America and has encouraged the development of criminal organizations for selling drugs that employ violent methods.[6] For example, during the past 10 years, organized groups have emerged in Guatemala to provide local distribution of the drugs that remain in the country as a by-product of operations involving international drug shipments (Observatoire Géopolitique des Drogues 1997, 230).

Drug-related activity has also led to illicit activities, such as arms trafficking, auto theft, money laundering, producing criminal organizations

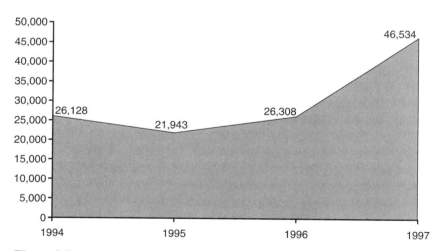

Figure 9.3. *Confiscation of Cocaine in Central America, 1994–1997 (kilograms)*
Note: The graph shows total confiscations reported for each year in the six countries analyzed (Costa Rica, Guatemala, El Salvador, Honduras, Nicaragua, and Panama).
Sources: CICAD 1998.

whose methods of operation tend to be violent and sophisticated. This can be seen, for example, on the Atlantic coast of Nicaragua, where major arms trafficking, in conjunction with the drug trade, has led to a barter system of arms for drugs (Observatoire Géopolitique des Drogues 1997, 232). In the Central American region in general, it is widely considered that a number of factors associated with increased drug use and distribution among the population, particularly among youth, are responsible for creating a new criminal "subculture" (IDEC 1998).

Institutional Responses to Crime

One additional factor that, in combination with the circumstances mentioned above, tends to aggravate violent crime in the region is the extremely limited effectiveness of institutions for social control. In most of the countries of Central America, the institutions responsible for preventing and dealing with criminal activity—in particular, the criminal justice system and the police—initiated major reforms during the 1980s, as part of a process of national reconciliation (Guatemala and El Salvador), in the context of the transition to a democratic government (Honduras and Nicaragua), and in relation to institutional modernization (Costa Rica and Panama). However, the absence of an institutional framework capable of articulating coherent, effective, and sustainable responses to the problem of violent crime has reduced the potential effectiveness of reforms.

Criminal Justice System Reform and Counterreform

Criminal justice system reforms have taken two approaches. The first emphasizes an integral approach to strengthen procedural guarantees, and provide nonprosecutorial alternatives for dealing with young offenders; the second focuses on reforming penal codes and providing more severe penalties. However, new regulations have been put forward that weaken recent procedural reforms and introduce, as part of the institutional response to crime, the concept of "danger to society."

On the procedural side, in line with changes occurring throughout Latin America, Central America initiated reforms, at the beginning of the present decade, to move the judicial system toward adopting an accusatory model.[7] This type of legal structure is currently in place in Costa Rica, Guatemala, El Salvador, and Nicaragua, whereas proposals for such reform are being discussed in Honduras. The most innovative aspect of these reforms is the introduction of live hearings, public access, and an adversarial process in all stages of the court procedure, strengthening the authority of the Public Prosecutor's Office in the criminal area, promoting greater respect for and effectiveness of procedural guarantees, and introducing alternatives to criminal prosecution.

Equally important reforms have been advanced in the area of juvenile justice. Such changes have involved moving beyond the "irregular situation" doctrine, which characterized traditional legislation and emphasized the state's custodial and protective role, adopting instead a doctrine of integral protection that seeks, for minors, the same regulations and rights, under criminal law, that apply to adults.[8] This change in the legal regime for minors has affected the legal systems in Costa Rica and El Salvador and is being debated in other countries of the region.

In addition to the legal reforms discussed above, other institutional measures have been implemented. These include strengthening the right to a defense, through creation of public defenders' offices in El Salvador, Guatemala, and Panama (Costa Rica has had such a system in place since 1966), programs to improve the management of the judiciary's offices, and extensive training programs for judges, prosecutors, and public defenders.

However, other changes have been promoted to increase penalties and limit the scope of some of the institutions supported by the new codes of criminal procedure and by legislation on minors, in particular in regard to nonprosecutorial, alternative procedures for dealing with offenders. Penalties have been increased in all the countries of the region, with a rise in maximum prison sentences or the imposition of more drastic sentencing. In Costa Rica, for example, maximum sentences for a number of crimes have increased from 25 to 50 years; in Honduras, the Congress recently approved instituting life imprisonment; in Guatemala, capital punishment has been introduced, through reforms made to the Penal Code in 1995;[9] and in El Salvador, the death penalty has already been approved by one of the two legislative bodies required to make it law.

In countries that have approved new regulations providing for changes in the codes of criminal procedure (Costa Rica, Guatemala, and El Salvador), what could be called "counterreform" movements have emerged. These are primarily the result of strong pressure from various segments of the public and from certain representatives of police institutions. Thus, in El Salvador, for example, after a general strike ordered by the business sectors of Usulután, one of the country's major departments, in March 1996, the government reacted almost immediately by promulgating the so-called Temporary Emergency Law against Criminal Activity and Organized Crime, and also

submitted to Congress a Social Defense Law. These laws were in violation
of various provisions of the Constitution and of international treaties signed
by El Salvador.[10] It should also be noted that, as a result of pressure from
the National Civilian Police and from a variety of social groups, El Salvador's Code of Criminal Procedure has been the object of various amendments designed, above all, to give the police more power in conducting
criminal investigations.

Public Security Reform: A Zigzag Process

Public security has undergone major changes, as reflected in the adoption of
a new security doctrine and reforms to police institutions. As is true in the
area of criminal justice, however, the reforms implemented to date have
been jeopardized by actions that run contrary to the spirit of the reforms.
These include the continuing participation of the army in activities related to
citizen security, the continuing use of massive detentions by the police, and
the formation of special brigades. In regard to doctrine, the countries of Central America have embraced a new concept that is based on constitutional reforms, new laws governing police activity, and—of particular note—the
Framework Treaty on Democratic Security in Central America, which was
signed in December 1995 by the presidents of the six countries.

In contrast to the old national security doctrine, the new public security
doctrine has four features. First, it sees security as a condition for development rather than as an end in itself. Second, it proposes a comprehensive
definition in which security consists of the conditions resulting from a set
of factors that foster human development, as opposed to a strictly militaristic definition. Third, it uses this expanded definition of security to explain
that security is the result of actions based on the peaceful, free interaction
between the government and the governed, rather than on actions the state
takes toward civil society to preserve the status quo at any cost. Fourth, it
differentiates citizen security from national security, thus drawing a sharp
distinction between social, judicial, and police institutions, on the one
hand, and military institutions, on the other. The treaty defines this new
doctrine in the following terms:

> The raison d'être of the Central American Model of Democratic Se-
> curity is founded on respect, promotion and protection of all human
> rights, with provisions designed to guarantee the security of the Cen-
> tral American states and of their inhabitants, by creating the condi-

tions that allow for their personal, family and social development in the context of peace, liberty, and democracy. (Central American Treaty on Democratic Security, 1995, article 1)

In addition to the adoption of this new public security doctrine, Central American police institutions have undergone major changes to demilitarize, depoliticize, and modernize their forces. Demilitarization is being carried out in all countries of the region, with efforts to separate the police from the military and instill in them a civilian orientation. Thus, in Panama, an Executive Decree in 1990 dismantled the Defense Force and organized the National Police under the Ministry of the Interior and Justice. In El Salvador, as part of the peace agreements, the National Civilian Police was created in 1992, through Executive Order.[11] In Guatemala, in 1997, the traditional security forces that had been under the control of the army were dismantled, and a new National Civilian Police was created. Last, in 1995, the Honduran Congress approved the separation of the Public Security Force from the armed forces, becoming effective in 1998 with the passage of the law establishing the force under the new conditions.[12]

Current efforts to provide Central American police forces with a civilian orientation is being reinforced by changes in police training, which now incorporates education on humanitarian issues, special emphasis on human rights, legal education, and training in techniques for controlling crime and maintaining public order. This new approach includes stricter emphasis on moderation in the use of force and the more extensive use of techniques to enhance communications and relations with the community.

Efforts are also under way to strengthen both internal and external monitoring of police behavior.[13] Recently approved laws establishing and regulating Central American police forces provide for internal investigation units; examples of this are the Inspector General's Office or Police Inspector's Office in Costa Rica, Guatemala, and Nicaragua, and El Salvador's Disciplinary Investigations Unit. At the same time, external mechanisms have been strengthened through the creation of governmental bodies—such as prosecutors' offices charged with protecting human rights in all the countries and constitutional courts—as well as through existing civil society institutions that promote security and human rights.[14]

As a result of these monitoring mechanisms, there has been a large number of complaints and sanctions, reflecting the still problematic performance of the region's police forces in observing citizens' rights. Thus, most of the 1997 complaints to the Office of the Human Rights Commissioner in El Salvador were against the National Civilian Police (2,498, or 53 percent of all complaints), with most relating to the violations of the physical integrity of individuals (IDHUCA 1998, 19). In Guatemala, in 1997, the first sentencing of high officials in the security force occurred, including that of a former minister and a former deputy minister of the Ministry of the Interior, as well as of a former head of the police and two agents responsible for the death of a student during the breakup of a demonstration.

To depoliticize the police forces, all the region's forces are subject to statutes that require certain minimum criteria for police personnel. The worst lag in this respect is in Costa Rica, where, despite reforms dating from 1994,[15] a large section of the Police Force is still excluded from attaining official status, and thus remains highly exposed to political influence.

The area that, perhaps, most requires attention in terms of reforms to Central American police forces involves modernization and technical advances. Organizational structures are highly centralized and hierarchical, and there is a lack of reliable components (e.g., crime statistics, institutional resources, and deployment of units and personnel) to carry out operations. Thus, strategic planning is almost nonexistent, and operational planning consists merely of applying established routines, whereas technology is of poor quality and of limited scope, particularly as it affects communications, patrolling, and investigations.

Finally, with the recognition that the crime problem has regional characteristics, a system of interagency police cooperation has been instituted, involving sharing information and experiences and establishing uniform procedures to deal with certain types of crime. Notable in this regard are the following initiatives: the formation of the Association of Chiefs of Police of Central America in July 1992; the Central American Security Commission, created at the International Conference on Peace and Development in Central America in October 1994, later institutionalized in the Framework Treaty on Democratic Security in Central America; the Permanent Central American Commission for the Eradication of the Production, Trafficking, Consumption, and Illicit Use of Drugs and Psychotropic Substances, which was also supported by the International Conference on Peace and Development in October 1994; and the Central American Institute for Advanced Police Studies (ICESPO), established through an agreement signed in July 1996.

As a result of the serious problem of crime and its consequent social pressures, and despite police reforms, governments in the region have been promoting and adopting other types of remedies that run contrary to the spirit of the reforms. The most common of these is the use of the military to carry out police functions—examples of this are the use of patrols, such as in the Guardian Plan conceived in El Salvador in 1995; the Cordillera Plan implemented in Guatemala in 1997;[16] and the joint patrols carried out in Honduras throughout 1998. The military also participates substantially in ongoing intelligence work and in combating certain types of crimes, such as drug trafficking.

The police are also resorting to "social cleanup" operations, including raids such as those carried out in Costa Rica,[17] as well as imposing curfews as a way of "neutralizing" juvenile gangs, as in the case of Honduras.[18] Extreme measures include extrajudicial executions of juvenile gang members, petty thieves, and street children in Guatemala, actions in which "self-defense" groups have been involved. According to reports by human rights organizations and accounts in the national press, these groups work in complicity with certain members of the security forces.[19]

Community Approaches to Dealing with Crime

An analysis of the attitudes of Central American citizens toward the problem of crime indicates three findings. First, the majority of the population experiences a high sense of insecurity, although the relative importance assigned to problems of insecurity, compared with other national issues, varies considerably from one country to another. Second, there is considered to be a lack of institutional response to the problem. Third, fundamentally repressive measures are being proposed to deal with insecurity.

According to various public opinion surveys carried out in the countries of the region, there is a high level of concern among citizens regarding the insecurity in which they consider themselves be living. One opinion poll, for example, showed that a broad majority of the population believed that national crime increased in recent years (76.7 percent in Guatemala, 88.3 percent in Honduras, 89 percent in El Salvador, 92.7 percent in Nicaragua, and 96.7 percent in Costa Rica). When asked how insecure the country was, the answers "insecure" or "very insecure" predominated (65.7 percent in Guatemala, 66.1 percent in Costa Rica, 72.1 percent in Honduras, 82.7 percent in El Salvador, and 86 percent in Nicaragua; IIDH 1998).

Despite the dominant sense of insecurity among the Central American population, however, there are differences from one country to another in the importance assigned to the problem of crime. In some countries, it is given a lower priority than unemployment, poverty, inflation, and so on. The most recent survey of the United Nations Development Program's

Barómetro Centroamericano showed that though Guatemalans and Sal-
vadorans felt that problems of insecurity (crime, violence, drugs, and drug
trafficking) were the most important for their country, these problems
ranked second in Panama, fourth in Honduras, fifth in Costa Rica, and
sixth in Nicaragua (see UNDP 1997). In countries where national surveys
on the subject have been conducted, this concern has been evident for a
number of years. This is true in Costa Rica, where citizens have been expressing this sentiment since 1986,[20] and in El Salvador, where, as of 1992,
citizens considered crime to be the second most important problem, moving in 1994 to first place, where it has remained (see IUDOP 1996, 1997).

In addition to the perception of insecurity among the people of Central
America, there is a troubling and continuing decline in the credibility of
government institutions responsible for controlling crime. Thus, in respect
to the criminal justice system, the *Barómetro Centroamericano* survey
showed that the population had a low level of confidence in the judicial
branch of government; in Panama, 60.3 percent of respondents stated that
they had no confidence in the judicial branch; in Guatemala, the figure was
50.6 percent; in Nicaragua, 50.5 percent; in Honduras, 50 percent; in El
Salvador, 31 percent; and in Costa Rica, 26.9 percent.

Criticism of the police was also widespread: in Guatemala, 59.5 percent
expressed "no confidence" in the police; in Honduras, 48.6 percent; in
Nicaragua, 45.9 percent; in Panama, 41.8 percent; in Costa Rica, 37.3 percent; and in El Salvador, 33 percent (UNDP 1997). As a result of this attitude,
people rarely turn to institutions to solve the problems. In a survey of six Central American cities, only a small percentage of persons who had been victims
of crime stated that they had reported the crime to some authority—12.3 percent in El Salvador, 10.3 percent in Guatemala, 4.9 percent in Costa Rica, 4.4
percent in Honduras, and 4.3 percent in Nicaragua (IIDH 1998).

Also significant are the prevailing types of social reactions to crime. One
feature apparent in all of the countries of the region is the tendency, on the
part of the population, to give legitimacy to fairly repressive measures,
adopted by institutions, to deal with crime. The same opinion polls show that
the solutions most commonly suggested by citizens are legal reforms to increase sentences or establish more severe penalties, including the death
penalty; enlarging prisons; strengthening police action; and even, in some
cases, employing the armed forces to combat crime (IIDH 1998). With regard
to nongovernmental actions, there appears to be a trend toward greater reliance on private security services, more purchasing of arms, and increased
spending on security measures, such as alarms, fences, and guards.

There is also an increasing trend toward employing citizens' organizations to address the crime problem. These groups have proliferated in recent years with little or no input from government authorities, and they have taken over functions previously carried out exclusively by government security forces—a situation that has led to involvement in serious abuses.[21] In light of this situation, there is an urgent need to design strategies that not only combat crime effectively, using methods appropriate to a government operating under the rule of law, but also effectively address the high levels of anxiety that people experience in relation to crime, to reverse the trends described above.

Despite the complexity of the issues regarding citizen security, promising efforts have been undertaken in the region to design and implement crime prevention and control programs that call on the involvement of organized sectors of society.[22] Three experiments, from three countries of the region, will be mentioned here: the pilot project for community security in Hatillo, Costa Rica; the firearms collection program in El Salvador; and the participation of grassroots organizations in formulating an agenda for police reform and public security in Honduras. Although these experiments differ in scope (local, in Costa Rica; national, in El Salvador and Honduras) and in the variables they attempt to influence (people's sense of insecurity and perception of crime in Costa Rica, the availability of firearms among the population in El Salvador, and police performance in Honduras), the fact that they share certain common features, as indicated below, make them appropriate to consider here.

All three involve sustained efforts over a specific period of time, differentiating them from other spontaneous or sporadic initiatives and immediate, short-term measures. All three have resulted from a convergence of efforts by civil society organizations and government institutions, working together in a complementary manner, rather than on a confrontational, competitive basis. And, unlike many other experiments, the results of these three can be evaluated, in terms of their effect on highly specific variables, as in Costa Rica; on citizen's attitudes concerning the problem, as in El Salvador; or on ongoing national processes, as in Honduras.

The Community Security Model in Costa Rica

The first community security experiment in Costa Rica began in 1996,[23] for which a district in the central canton of the province of San José (the country's capital) was selected. The district chosen was Hatillo, covering an area of 4.27 square kilometers, with approximately 80,000 inhabitants; at 16,031 inhabitants per square kilometer, it has one of the highest population densities in the country.

The perception of insecurity among the district's inhabitants had been high, suggesting that a new approach to citizen security was needed for the area. Hatillo also had a highly organized citizenry, as reflected in the existence of different types of participatory groups—religious, sporting, cultural, and so on. During the first year of operation, the following actions were carried out:

- *Selection and training of police personnel.* One hundred and twenty agents were carefully selected, based on redefined criteria for personnel assigned to the unit. Once selected, they received training in police techniques, and legal and humanitarian issues, with special emphasis on interpersonal relations and familiarity with the environment in which they would be working.
- *Installation of police units.* To decentralize the police presence in the area, eight neighborhood substations were established in different parts of the district, separate from the central headquarters. The local government contributed financially to this effort, as did the neighborhoods, which were organized into "development associations."
- *Installation of the Community Security and Safety Council.* This council, a permanent advisory body designed to plan and implement security-related activities and supervise and monitor police activity in the community, was composed of ten citizens representing various sectors of the community, such as the Catholic Church, the local government, the education and health sectors, and the principal citizens' associations. Only one police representative—the highest-ranking police official in the area—participated, serving as the chair of the group.
- *Adoption of new forms of patrolling.* Hatillo has both boulevards and narrow streets, and it is transected by one of the main metropolitan arteries. Hence, foot and motorcycle patrols were primarily planned, allowing greater versatility and access to the boulevards. Motorized radio patrol units were deployed as support and response units to patrol the major arteries.
- *Implementation of special programs.* In response to the assessment conducted at the beginning of the project, priority was given to establishing programs dealing with violence in the family, juvenile delinquency, alternative conflict resolution, and drug use prevention.

Because this was a pilot project, the first evaluation was conducted 1 year after implementation. The evaluation was based primarily on a detailed survey of a representative sample of the inhabitants of Hatillo before the onset of the project (May 1996), and a similar survey conducted 1 year after the start of the program (May 1997). The results of the evaluations, given below, consider three variables: sense of insecurity, victimization rates, and image of the police.[24]

The evaluation showed major improvement in sense of insecurity, as is reflected in table 9.2. Though the population continued to consider assaults one of the main problems in the area, fewer people felt that crime had increased during the previous 6 months. The increased sense of security applied both to homes and public spaces; for instance, in 1996, 36 percent "strongly agreed" with the statement "I feel unsafe, even in my house," whereas in 1997 that dropped to 19 percent. There was a similar change with regard to the statement "I feel unsafe when I walk in the neighborhood during the day"; whereas 28 percent strongly agreed with this statement in 1996, in 1997 only 12 percent did so. With respect to the statement "I avoid going out at night because I don't feel safe," there was a decline in strong agreement from 53 to 23 percent from 1996 to 1997.

The evaluation also showed positive results in terms of the population's image of the police in Hatillo. As can be seen in table 9.3, there was a significant drop in the degree to which people had a negative image of the police.

Crime is the variable on which the project showed the least impact, at least during its first year. Before the project, figures indicated a 36.3 percent victimization rate. One year later, the rate had fallen to 35.7 percent; considering the margin of error, this represents virtually no change. As can be seen in table 9.4, the results tended to vary according to the type of crime. Thus, though there was a decrease in street muggings (armed or

Table 9.2. *Results of a Survey Question Regarding the Perception of Insecurity by Residents of Hatillo, Costa Rica (percent)*

Respondents Who Strongly Agreed with the Statement:	Before	After
Assaults are the main problem in Hatillo	45	44
Crime increased during the last 6 months	65	38
I feel unsafe, even in my house	36	19
I am afraid of being robbed in my house	54	22
I feel unsafe when I walk in the neighborhood during the day	28	12
I avoid going out at night because I don't feel safe	53	23

Source: Ministry of Public Security data.

Table 9.3. *Results of a Survey Question Regarding the Image of the Police among Residents of Hatillo, Costa Rica (percent)*

Respondents Indicating a Negative Response as to Whether the Police Were:	Before	After
Efficient	47	27
Honest	39	22
Disciplined	42	18
Well trained	46	20
Trustworthy	49	29
Fair in their treatment	37	16

Source: Ministry of Public Security data.

unarmed), there was a slight increase in residential theft and theft of automobiles or other vehicles.

Although positive results can be seen, there are challenges that need to be overcome to ensure sustained improvement. Special attention should be devoted to controlling crime and to strengthening police action in dealing with the main crimes that affect the population. Though citizens' perceptions of the project have been highly positive, they will not remain so indefinitely unless crime rates improve. There must also be continued efforts to improve the human resources assigned to the project. Although there was a reduction in negative opinions of the police, the prevailing opinion, though less negative, could not be classified as positive.

Last, the project must overcome one of the major obstacles faced by public programs in these countries, namely, political sustainability. Considering the high degree to which the Costa Rican police are vulnerable to political and partisan influence, their performance could be affected by changes in the upper levels of the hierarchy.[25] Nevertheless, the program has served as an example, both within the country and abroad, and it has inspired international cooperation organizations to conduct pilot projects in all of the Central American countries, based on the Costa Rican experience.[26]

Table 9.4. *Results of a Survey Question Regarding Victimization Rates of Residents of Hatillo, Costa Rica (percent)*

Type of Crime	Before	After
Residential theft	13	14
Street muggings (involving weapons)	5	2
Street muggings (not involving weapons)	9	8
Auto theft or break-ins	4	5
Motorcycle or bicycle theft	3	6

Source: Ministry of Public Security data.

Arms Collection Program in El Salvador

One of the factors associated with violence and citizen insecurity in Central America is the wide availability of firearms, mostly leftovers from past armed conflicts. In El Salvador, the firearms problem and its possible effect on current crime levels has been one of the most hotly debated issues within the society. In a national survey conducted in 1996, 75 percent of the population believed that the free sale of firearms had a large effect on levels of crime in the country (IUDOP 1996). Another survey conducted the same year found that 20 percent of adults living in metropolitan San Salvador had been victims of armed assault during the previous year (IUDOP 1997), with death due to firearms constituting one of the main causes of violent death in the country (almost 57 percent in 1995). Official sources put the number of illegally circulating firearms close to the number of registered firearms (125,000), whereas other analysts believe that illegal firearms in the possession of civilians are double this figure. Calculations indicate that approximately 300,000 people (9 percent of the population) in El Salvador possess firearms (Portillo 1998).

A detailed analysis examining the problem of firearms possession in relation to the social context of the country emphasized the importance of the cultural element that underlies the problem. Thus, in attempting to link the country's "culture of violence" with firearms possession, surveys determined that individuals stating that they possessed firearms had more favorable views of actions related to violent behavior than individuals stating that they did not possess firearms; citizens stating that they had firearms were also more approving of illegal measures, such as citizens taking justice into their own hands, than those who did not have firearms (Portillo 1998).

In the midst of public debate on the subject, a nongovernmental organization called the Patriotic Movement Against Crime initiated a program providing incentives for civilians to turn in their firearms. During the nearly two years during which the operation was in place (1996 to 1998), there were 17 days devoted to firearms collection. With funding from the national government, from foreign cooperation organizations, and from private business, weapons were exchanged for various goods (food, clothing, medicine, etc.) that could be claimed by using coupons at supermarkets or other stores. During the operation, the program collected approximately 4,000 weapons of different types (rifles, shotguns, handguns, and even grenade launchers), as well as a variety of types of ammunition. The weaponry collected represented close to 3 percent of handguns registered in the same period, and 23 percent of long arms.

Though the program collected a relatively small percentage of the illegal weapons circulating in the country, as evident from the figures, the operation is instructive in three important respects. First, the initiative represents a postwar continuation of the efforts carried out by the special United Nations Mission in El Salvador (ONUSAL), during the negotiation and signing of the peace agreements, to collect war armaments. Thus, it fills an important need in an area that has repeatedly been linked with crime rates in El Salvador.

Second, the program constitutes a social response to the crime problem that contrasts with what have been the prevailing trends among the Salvadoran people, who in the past have opted for repressive measures, including the purchase and possession of firearms. The national press coverage given to the initiative reflects its potential widespread acceptance. Although the program has not yet succeeded in mobilizing massive support, and despite its modest statistical results, it sends a new message with the potential to counteract long-standing patterns of behavior.

Third, the program has served as an important example for other countries in the region, such as Costa Rica and Honduras,[27] that are seeking to replicate the Salvadoran experience. However, to ensure that the program will have a significant impact on people's attitudes, its focus on weapons collection must be part of a more comprehensive strategy—including, among other measures, more detailed studies on the relationship between firearms and crime, reforms to current firearms legislation, and national campaigns on the subject.

The Citizens' Forum and Public Security Policy in Honduras

Honduras has the lowest victimization rates in Central America. Like the other countries, however, it has experienced a deterioration in citizen security in recent years. One important aspect of the problem in Honduras derives from the very institutions responsible for social control, which not only lag behind other countries in the region in terms of reform, but have themselves been one of the causes of violence and insecurity. Currently, the essential challenge for Honduras, with regard to citizen security, is to reform the relevant institutions, particularly the police, and to formulate an effective strategy that is consistent with the goal of consolidating democratic institutions.[28]

The Citizens' Forum was organized in 1997 to address this concern and to deal with public security issues, particularly with regard to police reforms that were under way in the country. The forum brings together more than twenty-five organizations of different types, from government institutions such as the Human Rights Commission, to nongovernmental human rights organizations, labor unions, workers' associations, and *campesino* organizations.

The Citizens' Forum's first significant action was in early 1998, when the Honduran Congress was about to approve legislation establishing the new police. At that time, members of the forum argued that the law had not been sufficiently debated by the various sectors of society, and that such discussion was crucial, given the overarching importance of this law in the life of the nation. From that point on, the organization's activities intensified, mobilizing more than thirty organizations from civil society to discuss the legislative initiative. Various forms of social communication were used, including press conferences, public releases, letters to the public and to legislators, and public debates.

The Citizens' Forum was generally supportive of the reform proposed in the law establishing the new police force; this law established that the new institution would be civilian, apolitical, subordinate, respectful of human rights, and efficient. However, the forum also promoted the incorporation of certain guidelines, such as organizational separation between the police who deal with crime prevention and those who are in the investigative branches, the development of a comprehensive security policy, the participation of civil society groups in making decisions related to public security, and the strengthening of mechanisms to ensure the cleanup of the country's police forces. Almost all the forum's suggestions were incorporated into the text of the law, which was eventually approved, with the exception of the proposal to separate the two main police entities.[29]

Civil society participation was achieved through the creation, pursuant to legal mandate, of the Domestic Security Council, composed of eleven members, including five representatives of government (the minister of security, the minister of the interior, a Supreme Court magistrate, the attorney general, and the national human rights commissioner), a representative of the local governments, and five representatives of civil society (the Committee for the Defense of Human Rights and one representative from each of the following sectors: workers, *campesinos*, business, and women).

The Citizens' Forum played a major role in the cleanup of the new National Police, lobbying strongly for extending the time period for the so-called Board of Intervention, to ensure that the process of selecting members of the new police entity was completed.[30] The organization has also played a leading role in challenging key appointments to the principal posts in the nation's security institutions. In the case of the appointment of a minister of public security, the forum issued a number of public statements against the post being given to an active or retired military official or to someone actively involved in national partisan politics.

At present, the Citizens' Forum is focused on efforts to establish the parameters for a comprehensive, balanced policy on citizen security, to be presented to the National Council for Domestic Security. The discussion on a comprehensive policy will also include an analysis of criminal procedure reforms proposed in Congress, as well as a number of initiatives dealing with young offenders. In this area, especially, the experiment provides a constructive example for the other Central American countries. The concept of having a national representative body capable of seeking consensus on issues of citizen security is an alternative to the situation that prevails in the other countries, where (as has been discussed) crime prevention efforts are scattered, sporadic, and even mutually contradictory.

Conclusions

Crime in Central America has become a large-scale problem. Its growth in recent years serves as a warning sign to Central American societies. Of particular concern is the fact that the greatest increase can be seen in the most violent crimes, with a corresponding impact on the life and physical integrity of individuals. Although the people experience great anxiety over the crime situation, they do not encourage constructive attitudes toward dealing with the problem, leading to an erosion in social capital and in the commitment to building open, pluralistic, and democratic societies.

Faced with such a delicate situation, the entities responsible for preventing and controlling crime have barely begun the process of consolidation in the new context of peace and democracy, a process that has involved radical reforms in basic doctrine, legal frameworks, and institutional practices. The great question in the current debate on citizen security and institutional reform in Central America is whether there will be sufficient time to complete the reform process, or whether the process will be aborted, due to strong social pressures and the authorities' inability to deal effectively with these pressures.

Although the problem is highly complex, hope should not be abandoned. By a process of induction, a number of experiments in the region can be identified that, though few and, as yet, poorly articulated, indicate the potential for successful intervention, not only in combating crime, but in providing a conduit for the expectations of the citizenry. The cases presented here, though dissimilar in their immediate objectives, all deal with the need to address crime through preventive action, relying on providing stronger means of citizen participation and fostering democratic reform of the institutions responsible for social control.

Beyond the measures that each of these experiments must adopt to strengthen its individual efforts, new initiatives must be fostered to find ways to adapt these experiments to new needs. Thus, at a minimum four actions are necessary.

First, the identification and study of other initiatives that could currently be implemented must be encouraged, to enrich the analysis of local crime prevention experiences. Although this chapter has attempted to identify such initiatives, differentiating between spontaneous actions and those with a certain degree of articulation, other valuable experiences may have been overlooked, due to the inherent limitations of this type of study.

Second, on the basis of an exhaustive identification and evaluation of experiments in progress, parameters for success and general guidelines for formulating public crime prevention and control policy must be established.

Third, extensive dissemination of successful experiences should be promoted, to encourage a favorable climate for the adoption of guidelines based on such successes.

Fourth, though the three experiments described here relied on local efforts and involved little (in El Salvador and Honduras) or no (in Costa Rica) outside cooperation, active participation by international cooperation organizations should be encouraged, to provide support for programs currently in progress and ensure their sustainability, as well as to promote and sustain future programs dealing with these issues.

The countries of Central America face an enormous challenge: to realize a historic opportunity for democratic coexistence. Above all, they must address what, in the author's opinion, constitutes the greatest threat to their social cohesion by reclaiming the right of their citizens to a peaceful and secure existence.

Notes

1. Such is the case of El Salvador; see IUDOP 1997.

2. In El Salvador, it is estimated that during the 12 years of civil war that ended in 1990, the average annual death toll was 6,330, whereas, according to data from

El Salvador's National Prosecutor's Office, there were 8,019 homicides in 1996 and 8,281 in 1997 (Diálogo Centroamericano 1998, 16).

3. On the difficulties of an historical analysis of crime, it should be pointed out that though statistical series in some countries have been in place for 20 years (Costa Rica and Nicaragua), they are in their infancy in other countries (Guatemala, El Salvador, and Honduras).

4. Violent crime refers, here, to violations of criminal law, classified as crimes against individuals or against the life or integrity of individuals, e.g., injuries inflicted with knives or firearms, assault, and homicide; for Costa Rica and Panama, this also includes robbery involving violence to an individual.

5. On the possible impact of social variables such as school dropouts, also see the studies on Argentina discussed in chapter 6 of this volume.

6. The Central American situation, in terms of the impact of drug-related activity on organized crime and violence, shows some similarities with the Caribbean countries (see chapter 10 of this volume).

7. For an analysis of criminal reform in Latin America, see Rico (1997) and chapter 4 of this volume.

8. The doctrine of integral protection replaces the so-called irregular situation doctrine that inspired protective legislation covering minors in most Latin American countries. The new doctrine focuses on the social and legal protection of minors, and is reflected in the 1989 Convention on the Rights of the Child. In Central America, Costa Rica and El Salvador have undertaken a thorough reform of their legislation related to juvenile delinquency, following the integral protection and criminal responsibility model contained in the convention. Costa Rica passed the Juvenile Criminal Justice Law (1996) and Childhood and Adolescence Code (1998), whereas El Salvador enacted a number of legal instruments containing standards relevant to children's rights, such as the Family Code (1993), the Law of the Salvadoran Institute for the Protection of Minors (1993), the Minor Offenders Law (1995), and the Law on the Supervision and Control of the Implementation of Measures on Minor Offenders (1995). In this connection, see *La niñez y la adolescencia en conflicto con la ley penal* (1995) and *Ley de Justicia Penal Juvenil de Costa Rica: Un año de vigencia* (1998).

9. Between the time it entered into effect in 1995 and July 1998, twenty-five persons were sentenced to death.

10. The Temporary Emergency Law against Criminal Activity and Organized Crime involved providing more rigorous conditions for investigation, e.g., reducing the period for preliminary procedures, increasing sentences for certain crimes, cumulative sentencing, and limiting nonprosecutorial, alternative procedures for various crimes that had been established in the Minor Offenders Law. The Social Defense Law, which ultimately failed to garner the votes required for passage, involved sanctions such as imprisonment for 30 days for individuals with criminal records and "suspicious" attitudes. Both laws were initially supported by the heads of the legislative, executive, and judicial branches of government.

11. For an analysis of Salvadoran police reform, see Call 1998 and Costa 1999.

12. For an analysis of police reform in Honduras, see Salomon and Castellanos 1996.

13. For an analysis of mechanisms for monitoring the police in Latin America, see Frühling 1998a and chapter 3 of this volume.

14. Such is the case of regional organizations, such as the Commission for the Defense of Human Rights in Central America (CODEHUCA), and national organizations

such as the Human Rights Office of the Archdiocese in Guatemala, the Human Rights Institute of the Universidad Centroamericana (IDHUCA), and the Citizens' Forum in Honduras.

15. These reforms relate to the May 1994 passage of the General Police Law, the first legal regulatory framework applying principles governing police activity in the country, and establishing police employment as a civil service career, though this was limited to the lower hierarchical levels of the force. Until the law was passed, there was no civil service employment for police in Costa Rica, and the members of the security force were appointed through political favoritism.

16. The Guardian Plan was initially designed for military patrols in rural areas, while coverage of the recently created National Civilian Police was being expanded. Later, however, it was extended to urban areas, and today such actions are common practice. The Cordillera Plan was designed to cover certain streets by joint army-police patrols (see Siglo XXI 1997, 5).

17. Despite the fact that such practices were declared unconstitutional, the local press has reported a number of raids since June 1998.

18. In September 1998, the Tegucigalpa mayor's office issued an ordinance preventing people under 18 years of age from remaining in public places after 11 p.m., under penalty of arrest and fine.

19. Extensive information on this is provided in Amnesty International 1997.

20. For a detailed analysis of criminal behavior and the sense of insecurity in Costa Rica from 1981 to 1990, see Chinchilla 1992.

21. Guatemala is the most alarming case. There were approximately ninety executions by private citizens between January 1997 and February 1998. The most extreme case occurred in March 1998 in San Marcos, where an excited neighborhood crowd set fire to a group of six "alleged" robbers. It was later shown that three of the individuals were innocent.

22. Defined in that broad sense, prevention is considered to comprise measures aimed to prevent or limit the commission of crimes. Though some authors consider that prevention should exclude penal or quasi-penal measures—patrols, neutralization, or the rehabilitation of offenders; the use of nonprosecutorial, alternative procedures for dealing with offenders; etc. (Gassin 1990, 713; Cusson et al. 1994, 5), the author believes that these cannot be ruled out, since they have dissuasive effects that, a priori, could lead to intervention by the institutions involved; on this particular issue, see Chinchilla and Rico 1997.

23. This project involved, most notably, a review of police activity, based on the community policing model. An extensive bibliography on this subject can be found in Chinchilla and Rico 1997, 58 n. 57. Some cautionary notes concerning its applicability to Latin America may be found in Frühling 1998b.

24. The results given below are from Ministry of Public Security 1997.

25. Because immunity from dismissal is only guaranteed for lower echelons of the police, those at the higher and middle levels who have been a part of this experiment may be removed at any time. In fact, after the change in government in May 1998, there was a dismissal of police chiefs assigned to this project.

26. The author is referring to the IIDH project "Citizen Security in Central America," which is being carried out with public opinion surveys in Villa Nueva, Guatemala; Ilobasco, El Salvador; Choluteca, Honduras; Masaya, Nicaragua; and Pavas, Costa Rica.

27. These initiatives are being promoted by the Central American Dialogue project of the Fundación Arias para la Paz y el Progreso Humano.

28. Reform began in Honduras in 1993, with the decision to dissolve the investigatory police, which was subordinate to the armed forces and was accused of abuse and corruption, and to create the Criminal Investigation Division under the supervision of the Attorney General's Office. Subsequently, in 1995, the Congress passed the corresponding constitutional amendments, mandating the separation of the Public Security Force from the armed forces; the two had been linked since 1963. In 1998, the law establishing the new National Police was finally passed.

29. According to the legislation passed, the National Police is part of the Ministry of Public Security and has an Office of Criminal Investigations and a Police Crime Prevention Division.

30. Created by Executive Order in 1997, the National Board of Intervention was responsible for creating the organizational foundation for the new police, pursuant to the provisions of the law establishing the police. One of its principal functions has been to select the personnel who are to constitute the new entity, on the basis of a detailed background analysis of each case.

References

Alarcón, Magin Iván. 1997. La perspectiva policial. In *Delito y seguridad de los habitantes*, ed. Elías Carranza et al. Mexico City: Siglo Veintiuno Editores.

Amnesty International. 1997. *Report 1997*. Madrid: Amnesty International.

Caldera, Hilda. 1998. *El crimen en Honduras*. Tegucigalpa: Central American Institute for Advanced Police Studies, National Police.

Call, Chuck. 1998. Police Reform, Human Rights and Democratization in Post-Conflict Settings: Lessons from El Salvador. Address to the Forum on Democratic Coexistence and Citizen Security on the Central American Isthmus, Haiti, and the Dominican Republic, sponsored by Inter-American Development Bank, San Salvador, June.

Carranza, Elías, et al. 1997. *Delito y seguridad de los habitantes*. Mexico City: Siglo Veintiuno Editores.

Chinchilla, Laura. 1992. La seguridad ciudadana: El caso costarricense. *Revista de Ciencias Jurídicas* (San José) 73 (September–December): 10–39.

Chinchilla, Laura, and José Ma. Rico. 1997. *La prevención comunitaria del delito. Perspectivas para América Latina*. Miami: Center for the Administration of Justice, Florida International University.

CICAD (Executive Secretariat of the Inter-American Drug Abuse Control Commission). 1998. *System of Uniform Statistics on the Monitoring of Supply: Preliminary Statistical Summary, 1998*. Washington: Organization of American States.

Costa, Gino. 1999. *La Policía Nacional Civil de El Salvador (1990–1997)*. San Salvador: UCA Editores.

Cruz, José Miguel. 1997. "Los factores posibilitadores y las expresiones de la violencia en los noventa. Universidad Centroamericana José Simeón Cañas, *Estudios Centroamericanos* (San Salvador) 588 (October): 977–92.

Cusson, Maurice, et al. 1994. *La planification et l'evaluation des projets en prévention du crime*. Quebec City: Government of Quebec.

Diálogo Centroamericano. 1998. El Salvador–Violencia. *Diálogo Centroamericano por la Seguridad y la Desmilitarización* (San José) 30 (May): 16.
Frühling, Hugo, ed. 1998a. *Control democrático en el mantenimiento de la seguridad interior.* Santiago: Centro de Estudios del Desarrollo.
———. 1998b. Modernización de la Policía. Address to the Forum on Democratic Co-existence and Citizen Security on the Central American Isthmus, Haiti, and the Dominican Republic, sponsored by Inter-American Development Bank, San Salvador, June.
Gassin, Raymond. 1990. *Criminologie.* Paris: Dalloz.
IDEC (International Drug Enforcement Conference). 1998. *Informe del Grupo de Trabajo de México y América Central.* San José: IDEC.
IDHUCA (Human Rights Institute of the Universidad Centroamericana). 1998. *Los derechos humanos en El Salvador 1997.* San Salvador: IDHUCA, July.
IIDH (Inter-American Institute of Human Rights). 1998. Citizen Security in Central America project; public opinion surveys conducted in five Central American cities Villa Nueva, Guatemala; Ilobasco, El Salvador; Choluteca, Honduras; Masaya, Nicaragua; and Pavas, Costa Rica.
International Peace Bureau. 1998. Arms Trade. Focus on the Trade of Small Arms. *IPB News*, March.
IUDOP (Instituto Universitario de Opinión Pública de la Universidad Centroamericana). 1996. *Encuesta sobre la ley de emergencia y opiniones sobre la delincuencia. Consulta de opinión pública de mayo de 1996.* San Salvador: IUDOP.
———. 1997. La violencia en el Gran San Salvador. *Boletín de Prensa* 12(5): 1–5.
Joint Interagency Task Force East. 1997. Command Briefing. Unpublished.
Judicial Branch. 1991–97. *Statistical Yearbook of the Judicial Research Agency.* San José: Judicial Branch, Planning Department.
La niñez y la adolescencia en conflicto con la ley penal. 1995. San Salvador: Editorial Hombres de Maiz.
Ley de Justicia Penal Juvenil de Costa Rica: Un Año de Vigencia. 1998. San José: UNICEF/ILANUD.
Marroquín, Roberto. 1997. La perspectiva policial. In *Delito y seguridad de los habitantes*, ed. Elías Carranza et al. Mexico City: Siglo Veintiuno Editores.
Ministry of the Interior. 1991–95. *Statistical Compendium 1991–1995.* National Police. Managua: Ministry of the Interior.
———. 1997. *Statistical Yearbook 1997.* National Police. Managua: Ministry of the Interior.
Ministry of Public Security. 1997. *Proyecto Piloto de Seguridad Comunitaria de Hatillo, Evaluación de resultados del primer año de operación.* San José: Ministry of Public Security.
National Police. 1991–95. *Statistics 1991–1995.* Panama City: National Police, Office of Planning.
Observatoire Géopolitique des Drogues. 1997. *Géopolitique des drogues 1995/1996: Le report annuel.* Paris: Le Découvert.
PAHO (Pan American Health Organization). 1999. Programa de análisis de la situación de la salud. In *La violencia en América Latina y el Caribe. Un marco de referencia para la acción*, ed. Mayra Bunivic, Andrew Morrison, and Michael Shifter. Washington D.C.: Inter-American Development Bank.

Portillo, Nelson. 1998. Armas de fuego: ¿Una respuesta a la inseguridad ciudadana? Su impacto y prevalencia en la morbilidad del AMSS. *Realidad* 4 (July–August): 357–80.

Rico, José Ma. 1997. *Justicia penal y transición democrática en América Latina*. Mexico City: Siglo Veintiuno Editores.

Salomon, Leticia, and Julieta Castellanos. 1996. *La inseguridad ciudadana y la reforma policial*. Tegucigalpa: Ebert Foundation.

Siglo XXI. 1997. *La seguridad llega por cordillera*. Guatemala City: Siglo XXI.

State of the Nation Project. 1998. *Estado de la Nación en desarrollo humano sostenible*. San José: State of the Nation Project.

State of the Region Project. 1999. *Informe Estado de la Región en desarrollo humano sostenible*. San José, Costa Rica.

UNDP (United Nations Development Program). Democratic Governance Project for Central America. 1996. *Barómetro centroamericano*. Public Opinion Survey. San José: UNDP.

———. 1997. Democratic Governance Project for Central America. 1997. *Barómetro centroamericano*. Public Opinion Survey. San José: UNDP.

Universidad Centroamericana José Simeón Cañas. 1997. La cultura de la violencia en El Salvador. *Estudios Centroamericanos* (San Salvador), 588 (October): 937–1064.

10

Internationalized Crime and the Vulnerability of Small States in the Caribbean

Anthony P. Maingot

The small islands of the Caribbean are vulnerable in many ways. They can be, and have often been, devastated by natural disasters such as hurricanes, earthquakes, droughts, floods, and destructive pests. Each island's ecological system is fragile, a fragility increased by the interconnected nature of that inner sea whose waters flow like a river from south to north. Their economic vulnerability has long been a matter of record. Their extraordinary dependence on foreign markets, capital, tourists, and overseas destinations for their many migrants make these islands highly susceptible to external factors.

All Caribbean societies are vulnerable, irrespective of their economic and political status (Girvan 1997, 11). Whether the reduced nature of their geography and the small size of their population are the key factors of this vulnerability has long been a matter of debate (Lewis 1976). Although the differential performance among states of similar size tends to indicate that size per se is not the major determinant of state weakness and vulnerability, "a state with few resources and/or a very small population is clearly a weak power but at the same time, because of widely shared values among its people, firmly based institutions, and long recognised borders, it can be a strong state" (Commonwealth Secretariat 1985, 14). But that same study noted with alarm that it was precisely the critical factors of internal social cohesion and institutional strength that were being threatened everywhere in the region, putting these small states at risk.

To be sure, the threats to these states came from many directions. Most challenging, however, precisely because they threatened those parts of the society that were most vulnerable, were those coming from "smuggling, the drug trade and piracy" (Commonwealth Secretariat 1985, 27). These findings were echoed in a highly regarded review of the region, whose sovereignty was said to be under siege (Griffith 1997). The report did not mention the threat from crime that stemmed directly from those illegal activities, a major oversight because there already was—both there and in the rest of the hemisphere—a "crime pandemic" (Dominguez and Lowenthal 1994, 5).

This chapter looks at the nature of this crime pandemic in the Caribbean and asks just how vulnerable these small nations are. Are their internal social cohesion and institutional strength at risk, and are these states doing anything to address the issue?

A "New Type" of Criminal

The prime minister of Saint Lucia was adamant that the island was facing a "new type" of criminal and would have to adjust its institutions accordingly.[1] By February 1999, the island's minister of home affairs was preparing new legislation to counter this crime wave. The specifics were not revealed, but the minister's rhetoric left no doubt as to the new draconian mood, in Saint Lucia and elsewhere in the Caribbean: "The people [criminals] we are dealing with have no scruples, no souls. . . . They are veritable animals, and animals must be hunted down and tamed."[2]

In Jamaica, the mood was equally dark. The Office of the Prime Minister noted that criminal actions were affecting the whole economy, especially tourism, its lifeblood, and asked that criminals be given neither "refuge nor comfort" by the community. The actions recommended were all of a police nature and in keeping with what was occurring in the rest of the region; there were calls for harsher punishments, including hanging and lashing. Meanwhile, specific changes in the enforcement of law in tourist areas were to involve increased communications between tour operators and the police, improved intelligence-gathering capacity of security forces, and new capacity for the Resort Patrols, newly organized police units.[3]

That the region as a whole appeared to be in the grip of a crime wave and eager to strike back, rather than debate the causes, was also evident in Cuba. After a spate of armed robberies and murders of tourists, Fidel Castro announced on January 5, 1999, that Cuba was launching a "war on crime." New penalties included the death penalty for murder and certain types of drug trafficking and 30 years mandatory imprisonment for armed robbery.[4]

This sudden chorus of alarm and call for retribution might leave the uninformed with the impression that the Caribbean had jumped overnight from the days when predial larceny was the most common crime and civil protection was provided by unarmed police on the beat to what is today virtually open combat between heavily armed opponents. The reality is otherwise. Crime, and specifically drug-related crime, has been on the increase for a very long time, but it has only now started to be directly confronted. Dole Chadee, one of the island's most notorious drug lords, had built himself an opulent housing compound over many years, evidence of the virtual impunity with which he operated. He flaunted his wealth as he corrupted members of the island's police and judiciary. This was the reality that Prime Minister Basdeo Panday of Trinidad and Tobago addressed when he noted the great irony that Chadee's luxurious compound was being converted into a drug rehabilitation center (see Maingot 1998b, 197–200).

As pleased as Prime Minister Panday was with his anticrime measures, he had to admit that all was still not well with his forces of law and order. In 1999 another convicted drug lord, Deochan Ramdhanie, had simply "walked out" of a high security prison and fled. "I am yet to know," said Panday, "why someone has not been charged in that disgraceful conduct of some of our police and prison officers."[5] Ramdhanie was captured through a joint U.S. Drug Enforcement Agency and Venezuelan operation and returned to Trinidad. All of which points to one of the most significant aspects of law enforcement in the region: In the face of the inability of the local agencies to control major drug crime, U.S. agencies are being welcomed as close allies into what is generally referred to as "the war."

But the very fact that it has taken the elites of these societies so long to openly address the problem is testimony to the reticence of "modern-conservative" societies (see Maingot 1998a) to own up to collective shortcomings.

The tendency in such societies has always been to interpret departures from accepted norms in moral rather than sociological terms and, consequently, to mete out chastisement and execute punishments on an individual basis. It is a vision of social deviance as the sum of individual, even sinful, actions, not as the behavioral expressions of sociostructural maladjustment. One consequence of this conservatism is a deep hesitation to seek significant reforms in the relevant institutions of law and order. The tendency is, rather, to continue to seek relief through an ever-harsher enforcement of the policies of those same institutions even after they have given evidence of structural failure.

In no area of deviance has this quasi-Victorian reticence to seek sociostructural causes been more evident than in the area of drug use, a major factor in the crime epidemic. The chant of denial in the Caribbean has existed for easily two decades. The cant everywhere has been the same: the North Americans and Europeans use drugs; Caribbean people neither produce nor consume, they merely provide the market function of transporting the goods. Even a cursory overview of the contemporary drug scene in the Caribbean, however, reveals a problem of such enormous dimensions that it defies logic to believe that it is a new phenomenon; rather, there has simply been revealed a "modern" aspect of these societies, which have always been integrally a part of the industrial world.

In fact, the threat of drugs and its extension into raging crime raises anew the question of viability in the Caribbean, not as before in purely economic terms but in terms of sustainably democratic, law-abiding entities. Drugs, and the international cartels that handle them, are now seen as a threat to the very foundation of civil society, to sovereignty, and have turned the concept of a war into less of an analogy and more of a literal description of Caribbean reality. What is more, intelligence experts fear that the war is at best at a stalemate; a worst-case scenario is that it is being lost.

The Internationalization of Crime

The crackdown in South Florida and the Bahamas in the 1980s led to a shift in drug routes from the Caribbean to Mexico and Guatemala and the rest of Central America. Except for Puerto Rico, which continues to be targeted both for transshipment and as a market in its own right, the Caribbean share of the trade was said to have dropped to about 30 percent of the total.

By the mid-1990s, however, an upsurge in movements through the Caribbean became evident. It is now estimated that the Caribbean handles close to 40 percent of the cocaine moving to the United States and Europe. Additionally, shipments appear to be getting larger, as are the cases of corruption. Suriname officials captured a shipment of 1,226 kilograms of cocaine in a remote jungle village. The government of the Netherlands issued a warrant for the arrest of Desi Bouterse, ex-dictator and present leader of the majority party in Suriname, on the charge of drug running. Three shipments of more than a ton of cocaine were captured in the vicinity of Trinidad; given the level of corruption in its own police ranks, the island had to call in New Scotland Yard. In February 1999, British police captured five yachts that had sailed from Trinidad with more than 1 billion Trinidad dollars worth of cocaine on board.[6]

Whatever is not flown out from the labs in Colombia tends more and more to be delivered to Trinidad and the Guianas. U.S. sources offer many reasons for the strong attractiveness of these islands for major international drug cartels that puts the islands at great risk. First is their proximity to both Brazil and Venezuela, each of which borders at least one of the major drug-producing countries of Bolivia, Colombia, and Peru. Second, there is widespread corruption in their police and judiciaries. Third, major opportunities have long existed for money laundering as a result of lax banking laws in most of the islands, an extensive array of nonbanking financial institutions (*cambios*, or currency-exchange houses), and virtually unregulated networks of casinos, bingo halls, Internet betting, and multiple other games of chance. Fourth, in this era of globalization, the "open" nature of the economies provides ever-increasing opportunities for fraudulent invoicing of both imports and exports, participation in privatization programs, and entry into the extensive and historically unregulated expansion of real estate holdings (U.S. Department of State 1998, 67, 68, 102, 103, 114, 178, 179, 250).

One can conclude, therefore, that there has been nothing occurring in mainland cities that has not also been writ large in the islands. That said, it still begs the question of whether size is the key variable in the viability question. A brief review of other aspects of organized crime in the insular Caribbean will explain why size is indeed a key factor and why the polity and civility of these small states are indeed threatened.

In July 1998, the *Miami Herald* began to probe the Miami dimension of the Russian mafia–Cali cartel network.[7] The Russians could offer the Colombians several things: sophisticated weapons; contacts in New York, Miami, Puerto Rico, and several Caribbean off-shore banking centers (Antigua, Aruba, and Saint Vincent); and a cocaine-for-heroine exchange arrangement in Europe. What elevated Miami to the top of the list for Russian organized crime in the United States, said the head of the Federal Bureau of Investigation's organized crime branch in Miami, is its access to banks in the Caribbean and drugs in Latin America. A dozen Russian gangs are believed to be operating in Miami.[8] "There is no need for Russian criminals to come [to Colombia]," said the Russian ambassador in Bogotá, "they make all their contacts with Colombia gangs in Miami."[9]

It is calculated that between $150 billion and $350 billion in Russia's assets now lie overseas. Beyond the Russian case, the International Monetary Fund suspects that up to 8 percent of the world's economy now consists of money from the drug trade, capital flight, and tax evasion.[10] It should come as no surprise, therefore, that an increasing number of Caribbean islands are vying to be havens for this money. They can offer the same as Miami and more: bank secrecy, and also something called "economic citizenship." For $25,000 to $50,000, Antigua, Belize, Grenada, and Saint Kitts offer the Russians new passports with which to travel; Dominica even allows them to adopt new names on the passports. Indeed, Larry Rohter of the *New York Times* quotes a U.S. official who described Saint Kitts as the English-speaking Caribbean state that came "closest to devolution into a narcostate."[11] Aruba had already been described by Sterling (1994, 21) as "the world's first independent mafia state." Sterling also quotes a major Sicilian Mafia boss as boasting: "We own the Dominican Republic" (1990, 241).

It is this sense of local frustration with native capabilities in the face of obvious transnational criminal links, combined with the evidence of increasing U.S. involvement, that has led some observers to question whether these Caribbean islands are indeed viable. Some suggest that, given the enormity of the challenges from organized crime, they are not, and that the United States should consider officially taking on outright police duties (Abrams 1996). The problem with such an approach, however, is that it focuses too narrowly on the islands' small size and fails to understand that the "vulnerability" issue applies to the larger countries, which are also exposed to threats from organized crime. The fact that no reasonable person would suggest a direct policing role for the United States in any of those larger countries indicates that, at least for policymakers, the operative variable in the vulnerability question is size.[12]

The Caribbean has cases that can be used on both sides of the vulnerability–viability debate: cases that show great resilience, great social cohesion and institutional strength, but cases in which these qualities are clearly at risk. The latter demonstrates the greatest need for and dependence on the assistance of outside forces, be they police, intelligence, or even military. The case of Dominica in the 1970s illustrates just how long and how insistently some international criminal forces have been knocking at the door of Caribbean states and how the local institutions of law and order can be transformed under such pressure. Dominica also illustrates how societal and state responses to these threats have reflected on their intrinsically conservative tendency to reinforce the existing institutions inherited from the British colonial past, specifically the Westminster form of government, and apply the existing legal system to its maximum. They rely, in other words, on what has worked in the past.

Dominica and Other Early Cases

For the two and a half decades after World War II, the sole peacekeepers on the island of Dominica were the British-trained police. Unarmed, they walked the beat and had direct contact with civil society; the chief of police during that period was British. Upon being granted internal self-rule by the United Kingdom in 1975 (the usual step before full independence), Patrick John, who was then the premier, established a Defense Force. This change in the structure of the island's forces of order coincided with Premier John's entry into the world of international skullduggery.

John opened negotiations with one Sydney Burnett-Alleyne, a Barbadian international wheeler-dealer and arms merchant. Premier John announced that the government had signed an agreement with Burnett-Alleyne's Dominica Development Corporation to build an international airport, an oil refinery, a petrochemical plant, and a 1,000-room hotel with marina. Funds were to be provided by the Alleyne Mercantile Bank, one of twenty-four companies personally registered by Dominica's attorney general. Virtually every member of the John government was a shareholder in the Dominica Development Corporation. In order to ensure secrecy, the government passed legislation barring the disclosure of any details of the registration of foreign corporations. Thus, the Dominicans did not know that the "headquarters" of the Dominica Development Corporation was a one-room office above a boutique in the English market town of Broadshaw, Cheshire.

In Barbados, Burnett-Alleyne had secured a government license for the Alleyne Mercantile Bank. Opposition Leader (and future prime minister) Tom Adams charged in Parliament that Alleyne had been "subverting" important members of the Barbados government with guns and money (from $600 to $20,000) for months before the license was granted. Whatever the truth of these allegations in Barbados, the grandiose scheme in Dominica came crashing down when French intelligence on Martinique informed Interpol and the British authorities of one of Burnett-Alleyne's other activities: attempting to overthrow the newly elected government of Tom Adams in Barbados. Their evidence was a yacht, captained by Burnett-Alleyne, loaded with weapons and heading toward Barbados (Hoyos 1988, 75, 83, 85).

Three years later, and one month after independence, Burnett-Alleyne and the same John, now prime minister, were at it again. This time Burnett-Alleyne promised John an incredible $11 billion development scheme in exchange for the right to use Dominica as a South African-embargo-breaking transshipment depot. John also was once again to participate in a new plot to overthrow the Barbadian government. Because the Caribbean conspirators had involved a British mercenary recruiter, John Banks, the British authorities intervened and the scheme collapsed.

Patrick John was nothing if not persistent. In February 1979, he signed a 99-year lease for a 45-square-mile tract of prime land on the island with Texan supermarket magnate Don Pierson. Pierson's Dominica Caribbean Freeport Authority would be virtually sovereign in that free zone, including having control over immigration and security.[13]

Threatened with massive demonstrations and public protests over the deal, John canceled the contract. Again—although defeated and imprisoned—John understood why certain international groups were seeking to have their own island. In early 1980, he contracted the New Orleans firm of Nortic Enterprises for a daring job: overthrow of the government of Dominica. The firm—which was headed by white supremacists Michael Perdue and David Duke, former imperial wizard of the Ku Klux Klan (and later member of the Louisiana House of Representatives and candidate for the U.S. Senate)—also had connections with neo-Nazi and underworld figures. The two Americans established links with members of the Dominica Defense Force, with the idea to set up a "revolutionary" government headed by John. In exchange, Perdue would control a 200-man army and have a free hand in any and all business deals: tourism, banking, gambling, and a new airport.

U.S. federal agents arrested the mercenaries and their arms-laden yacht just as they were to leave for Dominica. In Dominica, John's fellow conspirators in the Defense Force assaulted the prison in an attempt to free him, killing three guards in the process. At the trial, only one received the death penalty and was hanged; John and the others got extended jail sentences, which were commuted 4 years later.[14] Prime Minister Eugenia Charles of Dominica later abolished the Defense Force and strengthened the police (Higbie 1993).

Other forces were on the move in the Caribbean by this time, as became evident in the 1979 coup that overthrew the government in Grenada. The new regime immediately aligned itself with Cuba and the Soviet bloc, and Cold War concerns overwhelmed all others. In Dominica, the Marxist menace combined with the experiences of the 1970s to generate significant changes in the structure of law and order. Two steps in particular should be noted. The first was the enactment in 1984 of the Treason Act and the State Security Act—the former mandates the death penalty for acts of armed rebellion against the state, and the latter stipulates stiff prison sentences for acts of treason against the state. The second was the creation of an 80-member Special Service Unit (SSU) within the 350-odd Dominica police force. This SSU was part of the newly created, United States–trained Regional Security System to confront the threat made evident in the case of Grenada (see Meditz and Hanratty 1989, 282–90, 623–24). It was the Cold War atmosphere that led to the SSU, and the "growing concern among island leaders about the Grenadian regime's intentions" (Meditz and Hanratty 1989, 623; see also Maingot 1985).

Unfortunately, the forces that threatened Dominica in the 1970s were a lethal mix for the entire region: small islands with dire economic needs, political leaders eager to attract investments at whatever cost, a network of offshore banks and "corporations" with seemingly inexhaustible amounts of money, and, critically, virtually unhindered freedom to operate. The Cold War had so preoccupied the United States that the forces of international crime had what came close to an open field.

Geopolitics and Transnational Crime

The origins of the type of internationalized crime that became evident in the Caribbean in the 1980s can be found in Havana in the decades from the 1930s through the 1950s. The 1950s especially were the days, as Thomas notes (1971, 972), when "professional gangsters were abundant in the new hotels of La Habana." According to Thomas, the assassination in Chicago of Mafia boss Albert Anastasia was linked to his attempts take over the casinos run by Meyer Lansky, the "brains" of the U.S. Mafia in Cuba. Santos

Traficante Jr.—a member of both the Sicilian and the American Mafias—was the intermediary between the Cubans and drug-running gangs.

Although the Miami–Havana axis was the main center of Mafia activity, even in those early days the syndicate was in constant search for "soft spots" elsewhere in the region. "While Havana remained the centerpiece of mob activity south of the border," write two authorities on the subject, "it also became a model that some of the more ambitious of the American gangsters sought to recreate in other republics around the Caribbean" (Rappleye and Becker 1995, 144). The various mobs had secured footholds in the Dominican Republic, Guatemala, Nicaragua, Panama, and Puerto Rico. "In a world of veiled alliances and raw power plays, the gangsters fit right in" (p. 144).

The history of the Cuban Revolution's eradication of casino gambling and its Mafia managers is well-known; less well known are the consequences this had in two neighboring areas: Miami and the Bahamas. One U.S. response to the Cuban Revolution was the creation in Miami of a veritable "fleet" of speedboats to infiltrate saboteurs into Cuba (Reppleye and Becker 1995, 192). A large number of missions were indeed carried out until the Kennedy–Khruschev treaty following the Cuban missile crisis. After that point, the large flotilla and its well-trained commandos had no official missions or functions. According to Tom Tripodi, then chief of these Central Intelligence Agency (CIA) operations in Miami, the Cuban exiles turned to other operations and businesses: trafficking drugs and also arms throughout the region, especially to Colombia; "Now that we had trained them in the fine art of contraband, some of them put their new skills at the service of trafficking drugs" (Tripodi and DiSario 1993, 132; see also Henman 1981, 132). According to Tripodi, the Cubans were the first to utilize sophisticated electronic equipment to monitor the activities of U.S. law enforcement agencies. The U.S. law enforcement job was made more difficult because the Cubans utilized many of the intelligence-gathering and security techniques used by the military and the CIA. It was the latter, of course, who had been their teachers (Tripodi and DiSario 1993, 169).

There is now evidence that it was these CIA-trained Cubans who first processed cocaine into powder form destined for the U.S. market. According to Bequai (1979, 136), the Colombians learned the ropes of the U.S. market from these Cubans. Eventually, says Bequai, the Cubans and Colombians developed trafficking networks so independent and powerful that they could dispose of any contacts with the U.S. Mafia. Soon even exiled Cuban lobster fishermen were joining the trafficking with their ideally equipped boats.

None of this caused great concern in Washington, which was totally engrossed with the Cold War. Nor was there evident concern about the early signs that the Bahamas was quickly replacing Havana as the center of mob activities—first in gambling and money laundering through the new casinos, but soon thereafter as a major transshipper of marijuana and cocaine. The links the Cubans had established with the Medellín cartel were now incorporating the Bahamas as an integral part of the operation.

According to Gugliotta and Leen (1989, 61), in 1979 the Bahamas was "a country for sale." They claim that there were fourteen marijuana and cocaine "entrepreneurs" operating there with the full connivance of the highest officials of the country. The fact is, however, that the Bahamas had sold itself much before 1979, as events in Miami and Havana played into the evolving nationalist and racial politics of the islands. The accusation of the black nationalist Progressive Liberal Party (PLP) was that law and order had collapsed under the previous white-dominated regimes. There was much truth to the claim that those whom locals called the "Bay Street Boys" had enriched themselves through smuggling during the days of U.S. prohibition and later with the tourism and casino boom following the Cuban Revolution. The PLP promised to lead by moral example, and a newly recruited black-led police force would be part of the change.

In fact, the Bahamas (and before it, Cuba) was an early example of how pluralist, democratic political campaigns could open the door to corrupt influences; paradoxically, thus, "law and order" can suffer under the permissiveness of more "open" political systems. The leader of the PLP, Lynden O. Pindling, understood very well that the party could make no electoral inroads without funds. He found his godfather in Meyer Lansky, a man with ample experience in dealing with politicians in the United States and the Caribbean. The quid pro quo in the Bahamas was the same as it had been in Havana: financial support for the politicians and their campaigns in exchange for future casino concessions (Eddy, Sabogal, and Walden 1988, 135–37).

In 1973 the PLP won a decisive electoral victory and moved the Bahamas toward independence; but, rather than the promised moral "cleansing," the floodgates were opened to internationalized crime. First came an expansion of the casinos; then came Robert Vesco, who would serve as host to an army of criminal elements including Carlos Lehder, associate of the Medellín cartel. When the Bahamas formally declared its independence, there were two other virtually independent islands within its territorial sea: Vesco's Cistern Cay and Carlos Lehder's Norman Cay. The latter island had its own airstrip and private army (recruited in Germany).

Soon the Bahamas would become one of the most complete offshore centers in the Caribbean: a society characterized by close-knit ties among legitimate banks, shady banks, organized crime, and a totally corrupt government. The function of the forces of law and order was to keep the situation stable and quiet.

The crucial lesson from all this is that organized crime maneuvered skillfully to survive, and even prosper, through several major political transitions: from British colony to autonomous semi-colony to full independence. With the United States preoccupied with Cuba and eager to keep its major missile-tracking station on Bahamian territory, there were few barriers to the spread of international crime. As long as the governing elites pursued the "open society" development model and professed anti-communism and an allegiance to U.S. goals in the Cold War, organized crime had clear sailing.

But even on those islands that were larger and more populous, whose economies were not totally open, and that had not adopted the offshore financial development model, there was no escaping the challenges presented by the drug trade and its international criminal connections. Jamaica further illustrates how the modern-conservative societies of the region have dealt, or not dealt, with the internationalization of crime.

Jamaica: A Case of Action Delayed

When the Jamaican murder rate in 1996 reached 889, the same level as 1980, a year of terrible political violence, the minister of national security and justice announced an emergency "twenty-point" plan geared to drastically reducing the murder rate in 1997. Aside from a zero tolerance policy for minor offenses, there was to be a new high-technology center to investigate organized crime. In fact, it was promised that "the full glare of the police searchlight" would from then on be focused on organized crime and criminal gangs.[15] Part of the center's activities would be a database linked to a number of international agencies in countries in which Jamaican criminals were known to have contacts, even networks: the United States, Canada, the United Kingdom, and Colombia.

Just 2 months into 1997, however, Jamaicans were seeing only an increase in crime and were fearful for their nation. Carl Windt, editor of the major newspaper, wrote: "It is idle to debate what is the most pressing problem facing the Jamaican society . . . it is the ogre of crime that stands out. . . . The nation itself is at risk."[16]

Not everyone appeared to share his level of alarm. Geoff Brown, criminologist at the University of the West Indies, noted that despite the threats, many important Jamaicans continued to be "purposefully blind, seeing no evil, hearing no evil and speaking not of the evil." This, he warned, was of concern because Jamaican drug dons now paralleled Mafia bosses in the United States; worse, a Colombia-like situation appeared to be in the making.[17] Brown knew what he was talking about when he described what had already become a familiar pattern in the corporate Kingston area of Jamaica: police shoot an area drug don, then his followers declare war on the security forces and literally control certain "garrison" areas for a period of time, often exacting concessions from the politicians. The police, frustrated with the pandering by the politicians, take the law in their own hands and begin executing gang members.

In April 2000, the killing of the don of Vineyard Town led to the murder of two police officers and the subsequent calling out of the Jamaica Defense Force (army) to protect police stations. The murder rate by then was 260, 170 in the month of April alone. Absolutely no one was doubting anymore that crime was perceived as the gravest threat to Jamaica's society and its future development—economic, social, and even political.[18]

Interestingly enough, as the island's minister of national security and justice told a Miami audience, general crime was down by 20 percent in 1999, but the murder rate was not. Only 30 percent of the murders were attributable to domestic violence; the rest had "substantially" to do with the influx of drugs and the availability of weapons, 99 percent of which were "smuggled in various ways from the United States." The minister then went on to talk about the role of organized criminal activities.[19] That same week of late April, the island witnessed, for the first time in its history, a judge sentenced to prison for a criminal offense. No one seemed surprised that it had to do with a drug case.[20] Basic institutions were clearly being penetrated, a fact being recognized off the island. The U.S. Department of State reported in March 2000 that although Jamaica's counterdrug cooperation was "good and improving," drug trafficking was contributing to one of the island's gravest ills: corruption. In 1999, 6,718 drug offenders were arrested; nevertheless, no major drug traffickers were arrested or convicted during 1999, and they continue to operate with apparent impunity.

How did Jamaica end up being at such risk, vulnerable at virtually all levels to organized international crime? The Jamaica that became independent in 1962 had few of the characteristics that tended to attract organized crime to the Caribbean: no casinos, as in Cuba; no offshore banks, as in the Bahamas; no history of deep corruption on the part of the political elites, as was the case in Dominica. Jamaica's problem was violence between the two political parties organized for electoral and, thus, patronage purposes. Between 1960 and 1970, there were 1,935 violent incidents with 746 deaths; of the latter, 111 were killed by the police (Lacey 1977, 3).

Organized political violence was within, not against, the system, and it began well before there was public consciousness of the drug trade and the violence it spawned. It was this interparty violence that led to the first steps in the transformation of Jamaican institutions of law and order. In 1972, Michael Manley's left-leaning regime introduced the Gun Court and a special stockade for its convicts and ordered a closer collaboration between the police and the army (the Jamaican Defense Force).

As early as 1966, however, the main local newspaper, the *Jamaica Gleaner*, had asked "why it is the police never, ever have sought and brought to justice any of the big wheels in the Western ganja [marijuana] trade; [crime and drugs] are related" (cited in Lacey 1977, 132). It took a major report in the *Financial Times* of London to force home the reality. In a piece entitled "Guns, Ganja and Gangsters," the *Times* estimated that more than a ton of marijuana was exported to the United States from Jamaica every day (September 5, 1974, 5).

Jamaican intellectuals, however, were completely enveloped in the left–right ideological struggles of the 1970s; capitalism and an "unjust international economic order" were to blame for intrasystem violence. This explains why Lacey's major study of violence, written in the 1970s, mostly ignores the drug trade, except to say that the drug trade and elite corruption "can now be openly discussed" (Lacey 1977, 160). "There is little chance of coping with the problems of economic and social development in Jamaica if rackets and gangsters are able to corrupt and undermine Jamaican society" (p. 162).

In the late 1980s, after many years during which the Jamaican electorate had chosen many a new government without any serious debate or discussion of the Jamaican drug problem, a dramatically changed perception of the threat emerged. Drug dealers, wrote Carl Stone, the foremost pollster at the time, were "crippling Jamaica . . . the very future and livelihood of this country and its people are at risk." Such was his sense of threat that he urged steps be taken "in a hurry" to stop this trade, including making "any constitutional changes necessary" (Maingot 1994, 142–62). What explains such a dramatic switch, and what does it say about the nature of the threat to the security of Caribbean countries? The answer is that it was a response to some very real challenges to the Jamaican state's control over its public health and economic activities.

The unique nexus of politics, ganja, arms smuggling, and organized crime in Jamaica began very early, building up steam in the 1960s. Although the word "posse" ("yardie" in the United Kingdom) was not widely used then, the names of the gangs that later became notorious have a familiar ring: the Max, Blue Mafia, Dunkirk, Phoenix, and Vikings. They were first called criminals and hooligans, and they were known to be the "soldiers" of various leaders in both of the dominant political parties, the People's National Party (PNP) and the Jamaican Labor Party (JLP). It is precisely this native origin, their links with political parties, their deep roots in the local culture, and, fundamentally, their tight links with the Jamaican diaspora in the United States and the United Kingdom that explain their independence of action in the growing drug trade and their capacity to shift from ganja to cocaine.

According to Laurie Gunst (1995), a Jamaican researcher, the first known and proven case of Jamaica's involvement in the international cocaine trade occurred in February 1975. Although this involved a prominent businessman, the posses originally recruited in the slums of Kingston soon took control of the business. The sequence, according to Gunst, runs as follows: (1) Party elites make use of gunmen to protect them and their constituencies. (2) With outlaws receiving outside sources of funding from marijuana trade, they begin to act independently from politicians. (3) Politicians, feeling threatened by the crime and generalized violence, unleash the police on these posses (gangs). This transforms the police force from a "British-inspired constabulary into a tribe of killers in uniform" (Gunst 1995, 39). (4) Gang members flee to the United States, Canada, and the United Kingdom just as the crack trade is beginning. "Their timing was superb . . . the Jamaican posses quickly proved themselves indispensable to the Colombians, Cubans and Panamanians who controlled the supply of cocaine and needed street level dealers" (Gunst 1995, xv). (5) The United States begins to deport the Jamaicans, who then unleash a new crime wave on the island.

This sequence certainly holds up to historical scrutiny (see Maingot 1998b, 1999). Less credible, but illustrative of the partisanship that characterizes this field of study, is Gunst's assertion that "whether or not [Edward] Seaga [leader of the Jamaican Labour Party] was feeding cocaine to his paladins, the JLP definitely controlled the trade . . . and several of his government ministers were said to be involved in protecting its movement into and out of Jamaica" (1995, 117).

How to explain the phenomenal growth of this trade and the relative silence about it on the island? Part of the explanation, of course, lies in the delicate issue of the gangs' political ties, present or past. This goes along with a general penchant for sweeping drug-related crimes under the carpet for fear that it might affect tourism and foreign investment. It has taken the writings of courageous journalists to fill the void. In October 1994, the *Jamaica Gleaner* columnist Dawn Ritch began revealing the links among crime, drugs, and politicians. Despite the well-documented reports, in November 1994, the deputy commissioner of police skirted the issue, claiming not to have seen Ritch's columns. His response, when asked why Jamaicans regard crime as the number one national problem, was: "When social conditions exist which do not comfortably accommodate all social classes on an equal level, it is not uncommon for crime to increase."[21]

There is plenty of evidence that the drug-related problems of so much concern in the 1980s have continued to grow. There is also evidence of decline in the integrity of the security forces. In 1994, the narcotics division of Jamaica's police services seized and destroyed 1.3 billion Jamaican dollars worth of crack cocaine, ganja, and cocaine powder. Then, in October 1995, Jamaican narcotics detectives intercepted an aircraft carrying 111 million Jamaican dollars in cocaine. But, in January 1996, it was reported that a significant part of the seized cargo had disappeared from the narcotics department's vault. The distrust and lack of investigatory capabilities was such that three U.S. polygraph experts were brought in to help with the investigation. Officials spoke darkly about a possible "syndicate" operating within the police force.

According to the minister of national security, K. D. Knight, Jamaica is making every effort to contain this trade because it represents a threat to the island's national security. It is not only the container cargo and small aircraft that are involved. In early June 1995, virtually the complete staff of the UPS carrier service in Kingston were caught red-handed loading cases of marijuana onto a UPS courier plane; the plane was seized by Jamaican authorities. One week later, a DHL courier service plane was stopped; ganja-laden honey bottles were on board. When not only the sea shipping lanes, but also the airlines and the courier services are polluted, an export-driven economy faces disaster; if smugglers are successful to any significant degree, there will be no ship willing to transport Jamaican bauxite.

There are also new cocaine contacts with the Colombians. Some of the better known routes appear to be by speedboat from the San Andrés and Providencia archipelago of Colombia, and by air on any of the two airlines with Jamaican connections: SAM, which flies from Medellín, and COPA, which flies from Panama. It is rumored that increasing numbers of Colombians are going to Jamaica on 30- to 60-day visas to organize multikilogram shipments by container and other commercial craft into the United States.

By the mid-1990s, Jamaica appeared to be finally mobilizing to take on what they themselves began calling the "war on drugs." Evidence of this was the temporary transfer of Colonel Trevor MacMillan from the army to the police. The constant attention and honors bestowed on him even after retirement indicate a desperate search for a "savior." No such simple solutions are in the offing. As he collected yet another award, this time in New York, MacMillan related how he had been changing the police force, which he found with low morale, little equipment, and worse—in which criminality, corruption, and power abuse were prominent features.

Whatever Colonel MacMillan's valiant efforts, the fact is that the political elites had let the corrosive forces of drug corruption operate for too long. In 1991, Carl Stone carried out a major survey of public attitudes toward the police and the court system. The results were extremely discouraging; the public trusted neither the police, the court, nor the justice system. The levels of support had dropped to where they had been in the violent 1970s: Fewer than 40 percent believed the police could be trusted. Moreover, the police received a low rating on their fight against hard drugs because many respondents felt the police were deeply involved in the drug trade.

The court system fared even worse in terms of the public perception of their honesty (table 10.1). According to Stone, the strong perception that the courts were blatantly corrupt was a carryover from the strong perceptions that the police and the prison system were corrupt. Indeed, what he

Table 10.1. *The Public's Perceptions of Judges (percent)*

Perception	Those with Court Experiences		Those without Court Exposure	
	Yes	No	Yes	No
Whether judges are fair	88	12	60	40
Whether the poor get justice from judges	52	42	23	68
Whether judges are free of corruption	52	47	25	75
Whether judges understand the situation of ordinary people	82	18	55	44

Note: These perceptions were gleaned from surveys that were part of a U.S. Agency for International Development program to improve the Jamaican criminal justice system.
Source: Stone 1991.

called the alarming rate of deterioration in the justice system stemmed from "a pervasive feeling among the public that all public institutions in the country are corrupt."[22]

The most common interpretation of the high crime rates and the inability of the justice system to deal with it was the "relative deprivation" or social conflict thesis. Social corrections in the economic system and rehabilitation were the preferred remedies. Stone went along with this thesis up to the point that his interpretations matched the views of the island's middle classes:

> In my view, . . . the causes of crime involve more than just social deprivation. A whole set of values and life styles linked to drugs, guns and criminality have infested our inner city urban communities where many youth now feel that work is degrading, hustling is where it's at and that crime pays.[23]

But then came the harsh policy conclusion:

> Many of these youths are not amenable to rehabilitation. These have to be eliminated regardless of whether they read the Bible.[24]

As early as 1986, Stone had explained the rise of vigilante killings as resulting from people's impatience with and distrust of the criminal justice system. Because of these failings in the forces of law and order, citizens took the law into their own hands and sought to establish their own "balance of terror."[25] In such an ambiance, tempers are short and patience scarce. The inclination from all sectors of society toward speedy "justice" is great. Such impatience was immortalized in the 1969 words of then Prime Minister Hugh Shearer: "When it comes to handling crime, in this country I do not expect any policeman, when he handles a criminal, to recite any Beatitudes to him" (quoted in Lacey 1977, 138). The prime minister's words were later repeated by the island's most-read columnist, Morris Cargil, who observed in 1986 that "in the present circumstances" his only complaint was that the police "did not shoot enough criminals."[26]

The circumstances a decade and a half later appear to be worse at all levels. Contributing to this dramatic deterioration is the rise in the number of criminal deportees from the United States, Canada, and the United Kingdom. Between 1993 and 1997, more than 6,000 Jamaican deportees were returned to the island. As the United States and other industrial nations begin to tighten their criminal justice measures, the islands become the recipients of their discards. The Dominican Republic received 6,582 deportees; Trinidad and Tobago received 1,036; the smaller islands received fewer. Griffith (1999, 11) recalls an Eastern Caribbean official noting that many of the deportees were former members of the U.S. Army or Marines. The military skills they bring pose a real challenge to the security forces of these islands.

In 1998, Jamaica's murder rate was 42.53 per 100,000 inhabitants or, as the *Economist* observed in a story on the island's collapsing system of law and order, twenty times that of London.[27] Fifteen policemen had been murdered that year. Flogging was reintroduced, and Jamaica was threatening to stop all appeals to the Judicial Committee of the Privy Council, several of whose British members opposed capital punishment.

It was calculated that on the island there were 20,000 private security guards, three times the size of Jamaican Defense Force.[28] The official threats of draconian responses were interspersed with intimations that the island was descending into "chaos and anarchy." These words were used to describe everything, from the widespread failures in the banking and finance sectors, to the harassment of tourists, the "contamination" of merchandise containers with drugs, and the increasing use of roadblocks to express collective discontent. As an editorial in the *Weekly Gleaner* put it, "The dilemma of this challenge to lawful authority has the seeds of anarchy."[29] Columnist Dawn Ritch wrote an open letter to the prime minister: "If you do nothing else, please restore public order and cut the crime rate instantly. If you have convicted murders to hang, hang them."[30]

It would be an exaggeration to say that Jamaican society is in a state of anarchy or that chaos has overtaken its institutions. The reality is, rather, that it is a case of a modern-conservative society overlooking, or at least being silent in the face of, major problems only to react with energy to seek retribution from the deviants. The purpose is to defend traditional values and institutions at all costs. What to some might appear to be a paradox is nothing of the sort. The concept of a culture of violence, as Chevigny correctly states, finds its counterpart in the generalization that "respectable" Jamaican society "expects discipline in social relations, in the sense of personal self-control as well as public order."[31]

Conclusions

This chapter illustrates the dangerous consequences when countries, indeed, whole regions, ignore significant types of crimes. There are always a variety of reasons: geographical reasons—the United States ignoring the drug-related criminal activities of Cuban exiles and Bahamian leaders; straight political reasons—Jamaicans ignoring the growing marijuana trade and the strengthening of the politically connected posses; reasons of outright corruption—evident in Trinidad and Tobago's overlooking the activities of major drug lords and the spread of drug use in the society; and even reasons of a Victorian type—the Eastern Caribbean's interpretation of drug usage as cases of individuals "falling from grace" rather than as evidence of systemic problems.

This chapter also illustrates the enormous difference that exists between responding to crime and preventing it. The former usually involves a dependence on severe measures by the courts and the forces of law and order; the latter involves a longer-term comprehensive plan of action encompassing all segments of the society, very often being willing to question the utility of traditional structures and values. To a certain extent, this is what has occurred with regard to policing in the United States during the past decade. What has become known as the "broken windows" approach to crime does not express a fundamental departure from past practice but certainly significant change: creating a partnership between the police and the community in such a way as to engender synergies in the fight against crime. As described by Kelling and Colis (1996), the idea is that the police secure community approval and support to attack both big crime and small crime, such as prostitution, public disorder, and nuisances. To ignore certain areas of crime is to create a climate of disorder and licentiousness in which more serious crime can prosper.

The critical question is whether even such conservative societies will begin to doubt the utility of their institutions of law and order as the levels of criminality create a heightened public sense that they are in the midst of a crisis. Specifically, at what point will the military and police elites begin to exercise inordinate pressures and influence on civilian and governmental structures? There is a substantial literature that maintains that this should be a logical consequence of criminal threats operating in the region. What Lasswell (1941) referred to as the "garrison state" hypothesis or the gaining of preponderance of "the specialists on violence" has received renewed attention in the social sciences. Confronted with continual crisis, society is forced into a state of constant readiness. Should this abnormal condition last long, then a process of militarization takes place as distinctions between civilian and military institutions become blurred. Lasswell extended his analysis to internal, domestic situations that affect the police; he would use the terms "garrison-police state" and "garrison-prison" state to explain the theory.[32]

Three fundamental characteristics of the political culture tend to indicate that these societies will resist the onrush of the garrison state. First is the very notable unwillingness on the part of politicians to cede any authority to the military. Evidence of this is the contracting by the Jamaican government, besieged as it is by crime, of consultants to study possible areas of savings in state expenditures. It is too early to assess what the political response will be, but it is a fact that the "AKPMG Management Consulting Strategic Performance Review" submitted to the government calls on the Ministry of National Security and Justice to save 3.4 billion Jamaican dollars, including big cuts in the Jamaican Defense Force and the constabulary.[33]

A second sociocultural characteristic is the penchant for ponderous discussions of any constitutional change. The idea of abolishing appeals to the Privy Council in London has been around since independence, decades ago. No action has been taken despite the fury over the Privy Council's position vis-à-vis the ever-more-popular death penalty. The debates are serious legal and constitutional ones and do not seem to bend to public pressures (see Bryan 1998). Finally, and undergirding all this, is the third characteristic: what is generally called "insular nationalism," invariably a force toward conservatism. Because any significant change among these small islands by definition requires some collective action, there is enormous reticence to cede any island's central authority (see Patchett 1974).

Because there is no evidence of a letup in the crime rate, these societies will certainly not remain still. What this analysis should tell us is that they will use the existing forces and institutions of law and order with even greater determination and harshness on the domestic front. They will also increasingly turn toward the United States for assistance in the more sophisticated and complex areas of combating international crime. This appears to be the kind of tradeoff these civilian democracies can live with.

Notes

1. British Broadcasting Corporation, "Caribbean Report," December 18, 1998.
2. *Miami Herald*, February 22, 1999, 1.
3. *Jamaica Gleaner*, December 24, 1998, 1.
4. *El Nuevo Herald*, January 6, 1999, 1. In Cuba, as elsewhere, one result of the measures taken to combat crime was the serious overcrowding of the jails; from the Bahamas down the chain of islands to Guyana, jails are bursting at the seams (Griffith 1999, 12).

5. *Trinidad Guardian*, March 3, 1999, 1.

6. *Express*, February 24, 1999, 7.

7. See Tim Johnson and Juan Tamayo in the *Miami Herald*, July 3, 4, 5, 1998. In February 1998, the Colombian magazine *Semana* had described some of these very close relationships. In fact the story had already been broken by Douglas Farah of the *Washington Post* (September 27, 1997, 1, 16).

8. *Miami Herald*, July 5, 1998, 18.

9. *Miami Herald*, July 3, 1998, 26.

10. *New York Times*, February 26, 1999, 21.

11. *New York Times*, June 30, 1997, 4.

12. However, no matter how plausible the relationship between state size and vulnerability might appear, it is best left as an empirical question rather than as a given.

13. Taken from the transcript of *State vs. Patrick John, Julian David, Dennis Joseph and Malcolm Reid*, High Court of the Commonwealth of Dominica, November 1982.

14. *New York Times*, June 11, 1981, 3.

15. *Jamaica Gleaner*, December 31, 1996, 1.

16. *Jamaica Gleaner*, February 11, 1997, 8.

17. "Myth Versus Reality," *Jamaica Gleaner*, May 2, 1997, 9–10.

18. *Jamaica Gleaner*, April 20–May 10, 2000.

19. *Weekly Gleaner*, May 4–10, 2000, 18.

20. *Jamaica Gleaner*, April 30, 2000, 1.

21. The redoubtable Ritch was not about to be silenced and, in the face of considerable pressure to keep quiet, she published facts taken from police records. There are constituencies that Jamaicans call "garrison constituencies" because the gangs exercise such control that the police have to be garrisoned in fortified stations. In August 1994, this author toured one of them under the "protection" of the popular local parish priest. The Mercedes-Benzes of the drug dons were everywhere in evidence, signs that the drug trade was flourishing. With the police presence limited to a single highly protected garrison in each neighborhood, the fear of the residents was palpable; *Weekly Gleaner*, November 18–24, 1994, 4.

22. *Jamaica Gleaner*, September 9, 1991.

23. *Jamaica Gleaner*, September 4, 1991.

24. *Jamaica Gleaner*, September 4, 1991.

25. *Jamaica Gleaner*, October 15, 1986, 8.

26. *Jamaica Gleaner*, October 19, 1986, 8.

27. *Weekly Gleaner*, October 10–15 1998, 13.

28. *Weekly Gleaner*, October 15–21 1998, 13.

29. *Weekly Gleaner*, October 22–28 1998, 7.

30. *The Weekly Gleaner*, January 21–27 1999.

31. See Chevigny 1995, 205.

32. Lasswell's thesis was first fully developed in Laswell 1941. For a contemporary review of the hypothesis, see Stanley 1977, 34–35.

33. *Jamaica Gleaner*, March 5, 1997, 1.

References

Abrams, Elliot. 1996. The Shiprider Solution: Policing the Caribbean. *The National Interest* (spring): 86–97.

Bequai, August. 1979. *Organized Crime: The Fifth Estate.* Lexington, Mass.: Lexington Books.

Bryan, Roger V. 1998. Toward the Development of a Caribbean Jurisprudence: The Case for Establishing a Caribbean Court of Appeal. *Journal of Transnational Law and Policy* 7(2): 181–214.

Chevigny, Paul. 1995. *Edge of the Knife.* New York: New Press.

Commonwealth Secretariat. 1985. *Vulnerability: Small States in the Global Society. Report of a Commonwealth Consultative Group.* London: Commonwealth Secretariat.

Dominguez, Jorge I., and Abraham F. Lowenthal. 1994. *The Challenge of Democratic Governance in Latin America and the Caribbean: Sounding the Alarm.* Inter-American Dialogue Policy Brief. Washington, D.C.: Inter-American Dialogue.

Eddy, Paul, Hugo Sabogal, and Sara Walden. 1998. *The Cocaine Wars.* New York: Norton.

Girvan, Norman. 1997. *Societies at Risk? The Caribbean and Global Change.* Paris: United Nations Educational, Scientific, and Cultural Organization.

Griffith, Ivelaw Lloyd. 1997. *Drugs and Security in the Caribbean: Sovereignty Under Siege.* University Park: Pennsylvania State University Press.

———. 1999. The Drama of Deportation. *Caribbean Perspective,* January: 10–14.

Gugliotta, Guy, and Jeff Leen. 1989. *Kings of Cocaine.* New York: Simon & Schuster.

Gunst, Laurie. 1995. *Born fi' Dead: A Journey through the Jamaican Posse Underworld.* New York: Henry Holt.

Henman, Anthony. 1981. *Mama Coca.* Bogotá: Editorial Oveja Negra.

Higbie, Janet. 1993. *Eugenia: The Caribbean's Iron Lady.* London: Macmillan.

Hoyos, F. A. 1988. *Tom Adams: A Biography.* London: Macmillan.

Kelling, George L., and Catherine M. Colis. 1996. *Fixing Broken Windows: Restoring Order and Reducing Crime in Our Communities.* Glencoe, Ill.: Free Press.

Lacey, Terry. 1977. *Violence and Politics in Jamaica 1960–1970.* Totowa, N.J.: Frank Cass.

Lasswell, Harold D. 1941. The Garrison State and Specialists on Violence. *American Journal of Sociology* 46 (January): 455–68.

Lewis, Vaughan A., ed. 1976. *Size, Self-Determination, and International Relations: The Caribbean.* Kingston: Institute of Social and Economic Research.

Maingot, Anthony P. 1985. *Some Perspectives on Security by Governing Elites in the English-Speaking Caribbean.* Keck Center for International Studies Monograph. Claremont, Calif.: Keck Center for International Studies.

———. 1994. *The U.S. and the Caribbean.* London: Macmillan.

———. 1998a. The Caribbean: The Structure of Modern-Conservative Societies. 436–52 in *Latin America: Its Problems and Its Promise,* 3rd ed., ed. Jan Knippers Black. Boulder, Colo: Westview Press.

———. 1998b. The Illicit Drug Trade in the Caribbean. In *International Security and Democracy,* ed. Jorge I. Dominguez. Pittsburgh: University of Pittsburgh Press.

———. 1999. The Decentralization Imperative in Caribbean Criminal Enterprises. In *Transnational Criminal Enterprises in the Americas,* ed. Tom Farer. New York: Routledge.

Meditz, Sandra W., and Dennis M. Hanratty, eds. 1989. *Islands of the Commonwealth Caribbean: A Regional Study.* Washington, D.C.: Federal Research Division, Library of Congress.

Patchett, Keith. 1974. Legal Problems of the Mini-State: The Caribbean Experience. *Cambrian Law Review* 6: 58–64.

Rappleye, Charles, and Ed Becker. 1995. *All American Mafioso*. New York: Barricade Books.

Stanley, Jay, ed. 1977. *Essays on the Garrison State*. New Brunswick, N.J.: Transaction Publishers.

Sterling, Claire. 1990. *Octopus: The Long Reach of the International Sicilian Mafia*. New York: Norton.

————. 1994. *Thieves World*. New York: Simon & Schuster.

Stone, Carl. 1991. Thoughts on the Justice System. *Jamaica Gleaner*, September 2, 4, 9.

Thomas, Hugh. 1971. *Cuba: The Pursuit of Freedom*. New York: Harper & Row.

Tripodi, Tom, and Joseph P. DeSario. 1993. *Crusade*. Washington, D.C.: Brassey's.

U.S. Department of State. Bureau of International Narcotics and Law Enforcement Affairs. 1998. *International Narcotics Control Strategy Report. Executive Summary*. Washington, D.C.: Department of State Publications.

Part III

Conclusions and Recommendations

11

Looking Ahead: Steps to Reduce Crime and Violence in the Americas

Joseph S. Tulchin and Heather A. Golding

The issue of citizen security is at the center of debates over human rights, democratization, institutional reform, resurgent authoritarianism, and the rule of law. Throughout Latin America and the Caribbean, perceived and actual levels of public security have serious implications for transitions from authoritarian rule to democratic regimes, as well as for the peace processes in many nations emerging from periods of civil war. As is evident throughout this book, residual distrust of the state and police forces remains as significant an obstacle to reducing the space and increasing trust between police forces and the communities for which they are responsible as do the capacity of the state or the professionalism of such forces of law and order.

As the chapters in this volume indicate, growing crime rates plague the region, but perceptions of insecurity exaggerate them, indicating that people feel less secure than they really are. Both Catalina Smulovitz in chapter 6 and Carlos Basombrío in chapter 7 emphasize the importance of understanding the difference between the actual and perceived levels of violence in society. Smulovitz warns that differing views over the levels and root causes of violence represent two of the greatest obstacles to reform, because inaccurate perceptions drive citizens and policymakers alike to pursue avenues to reform that do not address the root causes of crime and violence.

In an effort to curb both growing crime rates and perceptions of insecurity, various efforts to reform judicial and police systems have been implemented, ranging from efforts led by police forces themselves to state-led efforts to those designed and implemented by international financial institutions, such as the Inter-American Development Bank and the World Bank. These efforts—the successes and shortcomings of which are analyzed in the preceding chapters—include police–community partnerships, the professionalization of police forces, attempts to modernize the police and judiciary through the use of more technology, more oversight mechanisms to provide accountability, and steps to provide the police with rapid access to systems of justice.

The inability of the state to provide citizens with adequate protection, be it perceived or real, has changed the security landscape of the region. People with economic resources, rather than turning to public institutions to solve their problems, instead choose to hire private security forces or to construct fences to protect themselves. As Smulovitz describes the situation in chapter 6, this privatization of security corrodes a community by highlighting social inequalities and increasing the distance between those who can afford to protect themselves and those who cannot, in turn causing social isolation among different sectors in society.

Another consequence of privatizing security is that it creates a "parallel security system," thus taking away the state's role as the only body empowered to use force. At the very least, it is imperative that these private security forces be made accountable and subject to state regulation and certification. Proposed legislation in Argentina to regulate the private security industry could serve as a model for other countries.

An additional concern in the region is the growing presence of organized criminal networks, notably in the Caribbean and in Central America. Though such networks are primarily linked to drug trafficking, this, in turn, has led to other illicit cross-border activities, such as money laundering and arms trafficking. In chapters 9 and 10, respectively, Laura Chinchilla and Anthony Maingot both explain that transnational criminal organizations are remarkably complex, well financed, and violent—national forces of law are simply no match for such alliances.

Links between these criminal networks and other subversive forces, such as guerrilla groups in Colombia, terrorist cells in Paraguay, and gangs in Haiti and Jamaica threaten democratic governance throughout Latin America and the Caribbean. In this case, the cooperation of the international community is essential. International criminal action requires organized international justice, in the form of intelligence sharing, financial sector oversight, and judicial collaboration. Although collaboration on many different levels (including local, nongovernmental or civil society, state, and international) is ideal, in this instance the absence of multilateral cooperation will render futile all efforts to combat international organized crime networks.

Reform efforts have achieved modest success. That more has not been achieved thus far may be blamed on limited resources, the absence of an appropriate institutional framework, and differing concepts within the polity regarding the role of security and judicial forces in a representative democracy. In addition, as many of the authors in this volume emphasize, one of the most frustrating aspects of the reform process is its failure to yield immediate, tangible results. Therefore, it is vital that all parties involved—citizens, governments, and the international community—exercise a certain amount of patience. Furthermore, as Hugo Frühling underscores in chapter 2, it is difficult to evaluate the success of reform efforts. With limited access to the goals and the methodologies used to evaluate the programs, and only sparse or inaccurate data on crime trends before reform, it is not easy to determine precisely the effects of reforms. As Mauricio Duce and Rogelio Peréz Perdomo conclude in chapter 4, "the criminal justice reform movement is a complex, relatively recent social and political development that is still evolving and whose results cannot yet be assessed."

Recommendations

Citizens will begin to feel secure in a society ruled by law, where due process is available to all, where the forces of law and order are relatively honest and accountable, and where those administering these forces share the common goal of security with the citizenry. To work toward this type of society, we must move ahead to propose policy responses that are appropriate to the objective conditions we observe, are responsive to the subjective feelings we encounter, and are politically feasible in the context for which they are intended.

Seven recommendations emerge from the preceeding chapters. Though they are not comprehensive, they reflect thoughtful approaches to the issues of crime and violence in Latin America and the Caribbean.

First, implement policing strategies that decrease the space between forces of law and order and the citizens they serve and protect. In chapter 2, Frühling points to the São Paulo case as a clear example of how the image of the police can improve through efforts to bring the police closer to the community. In chapter 4, Duce and Pérez Perdomo emphasize that prosecutors must consider community-based prevention a priority in investing human and economic resources. One of the most effective crime-fighting strategies is identifying where and when crimes take place, so actions can be taken to prevent them. The police should work closely with community members to address conditions that lead to citizen insecurity in their communities.

One promising strategy that is discussed at length in this volume is community policing. As Paulo de Mesquita Neto and Adriana Loche note in chapter 8, community policing projects have various origins; they can be the result of governmental, international, or police initiatives. Their common thread is that they all aim to make the police more effective in controlling and decreasing crime, while also making them more accountable and responsive to the citizens they serve. As almost all the authors in the book who discuss community policing agree, though it is difficult to quantitatively evaluate the success of these programs, they certainly have succeeded in strengthening ties between the community and the police. More resources should be invested in these programs, particularly in measuring the effects they have had on actual crime rates.

Second, establish clear indicators to define objectives and measure police effectiveness. This demands more studies in which the definition of crime is consistent. In the short term, modest and realistic goals for reform should be proposed to prevent disillusionment. Andrew Morrison, Mayra Buvinic, and Michael Shifter contend in chapter 5 that policy responses "should respond to the risk factors that are responsible for violence in a given location, and the impact of policy interventions should be carefully monitored." They urge policymakers to consider the "epidemiological focus" when establishing the objectives and measures of police effectiveness. The focus requires four steps: define the type of violence to be addressed and collect data on the magnitude of the problem, identify the risk factors for this type of violence, develop and test intervention(s), and analyze the effectiveness of intervention(s).

Third, demand better internal and external oversight of police activity.
Paul Chevigny emphasizes in chapter 3 that the greatest lesson learned from
the Seabury Investigation in New York City was that controlling police abuse
will be extremely difficult as long as the criminal justice system allows, or is
perceived to allow, such abuses to take place. A transparent system of internal
oversight must be implemented to ensure that penalties are imposed if rules
are broken. Also, an external oversight body must exist to guarantee that police forces implement the necessary reforms. São Paulo's creation of an ombudsman to look into police abuses is an excellent model, and one whose em-
ulation demands serious consideration in neighboring cities and countries.

*Fourth, address crime through preventive action and by strengthening
democratic institutions.* Although punishment can be a forceful crime deterrent, according to a RAND study cited in chapter 5 by Morrison, Buvinic, and Shifter, treatment strategies are less cost-effective than the preventive approach. The authors contend that prevention measures can
"reduce risk factors for violence, increase protective factors, and address
either situational or social determinants of crime and violence." They also
urge governments to invest in early childhood development and in economic opportunities for poor people, which contribute to violence prevention by aiming to reduce inequality and spur economic growth in low-income areas. Each of the cases that Chinchilla examines in chapter 9—in
Costa Rica, El Salvador, and Honduras—addresses crime by relying on
preventive action, particularly by encouraging citizen participation and ad-
vancing the democratization of institutions.

*Fifth, enable the forces of law and order to become professional and
well paid and to have access to the latest technology.* Many countries—
specifically Argentina, Chile, El Salvador, Nicaragua, and Peru—have
embarked on reforms that emphasize the need to professionalize the police. In chapter 2, Frühling describes the importance that countries are putting on training and recruiting practices emphasizing such personal characteristics as discipline, obedience, strong character, interpersonal skills, and
imagination. Mental stability and a past history free of violence are also
very important. Many countries are also raising the levels of education
needed by a person who aspires to serve as a police officer. As Frühling
mentions, in Nicaragua entry-level personnel are required to have a secondary school degree, and for executive positions police must be under 30
years of age and hold a bachelor's degree.

To attract and retain qualified candidates, it is imperative that police be
paid competitive salaries and receive adequate benefits, including health

benefits, paid vacation time, and access to continuing education. Also, the police should be supplied with modern equipment, in the form of weapons and information technology. In chapter 10, Maingot discusses the difficulties that small Caribbean islands face in their efforts to combat drugs and weapons trafficking. The only solution is for the countries to work together in intelligence gathering and information sharing; a mission that will require a more sophisticated level of technology than these countries currently possess.

Sixth, when designing public policies, be sensitive to scars left over from periods of military rule. Duce and Pérez Perdomo state in chapter 4 that "in those countries that most recently have had military dictatorships, illegal conduct by the police is less accepted than in countries with a stronger democratic tradition . . . the memory of excessive repression counterbalances the desire for order at any cost." In chapter 6, Smulovitz emphasizes that, especially in Argentina, the population is distrustful of government institutions, including the police and judiciary. Efforts must be made to repair the damaged relationship if democracy is to be strengthened.

Seventh, encourage partnerships among international organizations, the state, and civil society groups. In chapter 10, Maingot calls for coordination between national forces of law and order and international organizations, particularly in the Caribbean, which he predicts will continue to look to the international community for support and assistance as the countries struggle to combat the "sophisticated and complex" threats associated with fighting international crime.

Conclusions

If governments do not effectively address the issue of citizen insecurity, or if the citizenry perceives such efforts as insufficient, it is possible that citizens will call for more repressive means of protection. Or, as Basombrío warns us in his discussion of Peru in chapter 7, citizen insecurity may be exploited by governments seeking to apply oppressive or militaristic policing techniques. In analytical terms, we must seek out and test more ways in which civil society groups and citizens can become part of the system of law and order; we must learn how to involve the community in security, to make people feel part of the solution. And, perhaps most important, we must disseminate successful experiences in crime control and police reform so that officials can learn from the experiences of other countries.

As Smulovitz reminds us in chapter 6, "Machiavelli, Hobbes, and Montesquieu warned long ago that subjects who are in fear tend to consider restrictions on their liberty preferable to threats of insecurity." Whatever the institutional framework, democratic governance will be enhanced by decreasing the distance between the people and the forces of public security. Citizens in a democratic society must feel themselves to be participants in establishing law and order—to be accountable and to hold their elected representatives and the agents of the state accountable.

Contributors

Carlos Basombrío is vice minister of the interior of Peru. Until September 2001, he was president of the Board of Directors of the Institute of Legal Defense, where he had worked since 1986 and had been codirector of the monthly magazine *Ideele*. He was a member of the National Executive Committee of the National Coordinator of Human Rights and is a founding member of the Press and Society Institute (IPYS). He is a member of the International Council on Human Rights Policy (ICHRP) headquartered in Geneva, Switzerland. He has written several books and numerous essays.

Mayra Buvinic is chief of the Social Development Division of the Sustainable Development Department and special adviser on violence at the Inter-American Development Bank. Before joining the Inter-American Development Bank in 1996, she was a founding member and president of the International Center for Research on Women. She has published in the areas of poverty and gender, employment promotion, small enterprise development, reproductive health and, more recently, violence reduction.

Paul Chevigny is a professor at New York University Law School. His research interests center on the relation between the citizen and the state, especially in the fields of human rights and criminal law. He is the author of *Edge of the Knife: Police Violence in the Americas* (1995).

Laura Chinchilla is an international consultant on security and justice reform, congresswomen, and former minister of public security in Costa Rica. Her research interests include citizen security policies, police reform, and criminal justice. Her most recent book is *Seguridad ciudadana en América Latina: Hacia una política integral* (2002), which she coauthored with José María Rico. She was also editor of *Seguridad ciudadana y justicia penal: Perspectiva de la sociedad civil* (1999).

Mauricio Duce is director of the Center for Juridical Research, Diego Portales University, School of Law, Santiago, Chile. His research interests include criminal justice, criminal procedure, criminal justice reform, human rights, and legal education. His most recent publications include *Nuevo sistema procesal penal* (2002), written with Cristián Riego, and *Tortura, derechos humanos y justicia criminal en Chile* (2002), coauthored with Francisco Cox, Cristián Riego, Alejandra Mera, Andrea Repetto, Martín Bernales, and Francisco Estrada.

Hugo Frühling is a professor in the Institute of Public Affairs and director of the Center for Citizen Security Studies, both at the University of Chile. He has written extensively on human rights, policies confronting crime, and police reform in Latin America. His most recent work includes *Police, Society, and State: Modernization and Police Reform in South America* (2001), which he coedited with Azun Candina.

Heather A. Golding is a student at the University of Connecticut School of Law and former program associate of the Latin American Program at the Woodrow Wilson Center.

Adriana Loche is finishing a master's degree in the Latin America Integration Program at the University of São Paulo. Her research focuses on the human rights movements in Brazil and Argentina in a comparative perspective.

Anthony P. Maingot is a professor of sociology at Florida International University. His ongoing research addresses the risks of the offshore financial services sector as a development strategy. His most recent book is *The U.S. and the Caribbean in the Post–Cold War Period* (2003), written with Wilfredo Lozano.

Paulo de Mesquita Neto is a senior researcher at the Center for the Study of Violence at the University of São Paulo and executive secretary of the São Paulo Institute against Violence. His research interests include democratic transition and consolidation, human rights, armed forces, police institutions, police reform, police accountability, community policing, public security policies, crime control, and crime prevention.

Andrew Morrison is a senior social development specialist in the Social Development Division of the Inter-American Development Bank, where he works on issues of violence prevention and the labor market participation of disadvantaged groups. In the area of violence prevention, he has recently published several articles and books, including estimates of the social costs of violence in Mexico City, a *Foreign Policy* article on trends in violence in the world, technical notes to guide the design of project interventions, and a book on the socioeconomic costs associated with domestic violence against women.

Rogelio Pérez Perdomo is a professor at the Instituto de Estudios Superiores de Administración in Caracas. His research interests include the legal profession, judicial systems, corruption, and violence. He is the author of *Los abogados de America Latina, una introducción histórica*.

Michael Shifter is vice president for policy at the Inter-American Dialogue, a Washington-based forum on Western Hemisphere affairs, and adjunct professor at Georgetown University's School of Foreign Service, where he teaches Latin American politics. His recent articles on United States–Latin America relations and hemispheric affairs have appeared in *Foreign Affairs*, *Foreign Policy*, *Current History*, the *Washington Post*, the *Los Angeles Times*, the *Miami Herald*, and the *Journal of Democracy*. His writings on democracy and human rights, multilateralism, drug policy, security issues, and Colombian and Peruvian politics have also been published in many Latin American and Caribbean countries.

Catalina Smulovitz is a professor of political science at the Universidad Torcuato Di Tella University and adjunct researcher at the Consejo Nacional de Investigaciones Científicas y Tecnológicas (CONICET) in Buenos Aires. Her current research examines the judicialization of politics in Argentina. Her recent publications include "¿Cómo consigue el imperio de la ley imperar? Imposición de costos a través de mecanismos descentralizados" in *Política y Gobierno* (2002) and "The Discovery of the Law: Political Consequences in the Argentine Experience" in *Global Prescriptions: The Production, Exportation, and Importation of a New Legal Orthodoxy*, edited by Brian Barth and Yves Dezalay (2002). Her most recent book, *Controlando a la política: Ciudadanos y medios en las nuevas democracas latinoamericanas* (2002), was cowritten with Enrique Peruzzotti.

Joseph S. Tulchin is director of the Latin American Program at the Woodrow Wilson Center. Before moving to Washington, he was a professor of history and director of international programs at the University of

North Carolina at Chapel Hill, where he taught for 20 years. Before that, he taught at Yale University for 7 years. His areas of expertise, in which he has published widely, are U.S. foreign policy, inter-American relations, contemporary Latin America, strategic planning, and social science research methodology. His most recent book is *Latin America in the New International System* (2001) edited with Ralph Espach.

Index

Note: Page numbers followed by *t*, *fig.* or n indicate the presence of tables, figures or notes.

criticism of police, summarized, 16
Cuba, 241
Cuban Revolution, 242
culture of violence, 251

DALYS. *See* disability-adjusted life
    years
damage claims, 57, 65
death penalty, 83, 213, 228n9, 253
death squads, 80–81
decentralization: planning process, 26;
    police reform, 17, 39; São Paulo, 34
defendants: in detention, 76; inquisito-
    rial process, 71, 72
defense lawyers, inquisitorial process,
    71
demilitarization of police, 27; Central
    America, 215; Panama, 215
democratization, 78
demonstrations, 142, 143
Denmark, 24
deportees, criminal, 250–51
dictatorships, 6, 80, 83, 126
DINCOTE. *See* National Anti-Terror-
    ism Division
Dinkins, David, 60
direct costs of violence, 108*t*, 109–10,
    118–19n17
disability-adjusted life years
    (DALYs), 97, 97*t*; rape and domes-
    tic violence, 110; social violence,
    110
discipline of police: Brazil, 58; civil
    service rules, 60; oversight, 59–60;
    province of Buenos Aires, 63; sys-
    tem, 58; transparent, 64; United
    States, 58–59; well-defined, 64
discretion of police: Argentina, 53,
    148n7; Brazil, 53; courts, 65; prose-
    cution, 55–56; United States, 52–53
discrimination, social, 136, 147
distrust of police, 16; disciplinary pro-
    cedures, 23
doctrine, 70
Domestic Security Council (Hon-
    duras), 225

domestic violence: authoritarian
    household norms, 106; Canada,
    109; defining, 118n10; direct costs,
    109; economic development,
    107–8; economic multiplier effects,
    111; Jamaica, 245; police and judi-
    cial services, 118n16; poverty, 106;
    prevalence of violence against, 98*t*;
    nonmonetary costs, 110; social ef-
    fects, 100; social multiplier effects,
    112–13; statistics, 118n8; types of,
    100, 101; United States, 118n15,
    119n22; women affected, 98. *See
    also* children; women
Dominica, 238, 239–41
Dominican Republic, 238; juries, 73
drug trafficking: Bahamas, 243–44;
    Brazil, 183, 190; carabineros, 38;
    Caribbean, 234, 235, 236–37,
    243–44; Central America, 211–12,
    211*fig.*, 216, 217, 228n6; criminal
    networks, 260–61; Cuban exiles
    and CIA, 242; Guatemala, 211; in-
    ternational aid, 28; Jamaica,
    245–51; military operations, 217;
    Peru, 169, 177n43; recommenda-
    tions, 264; resources, 32
Duhalde, Eduardo, 28–29, 30, 138

early warning system, 61, 62, 63
economic development, domestic vio-
    lence, 107–8, 111
edictos policiales, 53
efficiency, survey, 40n1
elites: Caribbean, 235–36; rights of
    suspects, 75
El Salvador: arms collection program,
    223–24; citizen security, 217–18;
    crime rates, 163, 164; criminal jus-
    tice reform, 212, 213–14; criminal
    procedure, 77; demilitarization,
    163; discipline, 23; economic mul-
    tiplier effects, 111–12, 112*t*; homi-
    cide rates, 80, 96, 163, 164,
    208–209, 209*t*, 227–28n2; human
    rights, 23, 215–16; military links,